You Have a Point There

By the same author

A DICTIONARY OF CATCH PHRASES
2nd edn

A DICTIONARY OF CLICHÉS
5th edn

A DICTIONARY OF SLANG AND UNCONVENTIONAL
ENGLISH
8th edn

THE ROUTLEDGE DICTIONARY OF HISTORICAL SLANG

ORIGINS
An Etymological Dictionary of Modern English
4th edn

SHAKESPEARE'S BAWDY
3rd edn

A SMALLER SLANG DICTIONARY
2nd edn

You Have a Point There

A Guide to Punctuation and its Allies

Eric Partridge

With a Chapter on American Practice by
John W. Clark

London & New York

First published in Great Britain 1953 by
Hamish Hamilton Ltd
Reprinted 1977, 1978, 1983 by
Routledge & Kegan Paul Ltd

Reprinted 1990, 1998
by Routledge
11 New Fetter Lane, London EC4P 4EE
29 West 35th Street, New York, NY 10001

© 1953 Eric Partridge

Printed and bound in Great Britain by
T.J. International Ltd, Padstow, Cornwall

ISBN 0–415–05075–8

For
HAMISH HAMILTON
who doesn't need it

CONTENTS

PAGE

FOREWORD   ix

BOOK I:
PUNCTUATION

CHAPTER

1. INTRODUCTORY   3
2. PERIOD OR FULL STOP OR FULL POINT   9
3. COMMA   14
4. PERIOD AND COMMA IN ABBREVIATION   42
5. SEMICOLON   44
6. COLON   52
7. PARENTHESES; DEGREES AND VARIETIES OF PARENTHESIS   63
8. DASH; VARIOUS MEANS OF INDICATING DISRUPTIVE MATTER   68
9. QUESTION MARK AND EXCLAMATION MARK   79
10. 'TWOPENCE COLOURED': COMPOUND POINTS; MULTIPLE DOTS   82
11. PUNCTUATION AT ALL POINTS; RELATIVE VALUES OF THE POINTS   90
12. 'NOT TOO LITTLE, NOT TOO MUCH': PUNCTUATION, CLOSE AND OPEN; OVER-PUNCTUATION AND UNDER-PUNCTUATION   94

BOOK II:
ALLIES AND ACCESSORIES

13. CAPITALS   107
14. ITALICS: EMPHASIS; DIFFERENTIATION AND DISTINCTION; QUOTATION   118
15. QUOTATION MARKS OR INVERTED COMMAS, ABSOLUTE AND RELATIVE   122
16. MODES OF EMPHASIS   127
17. HYPHEN, ABSOLUTE AND RELATIVE; DIVISION AND SYLLABIFICATION – THE VIRGIL OR VIRGULE OR OBLIQUE – THE BRACE OR VINCULUM   134
18. APOSTROPHE   155
19. CAPITALS AND ITALICS, QUOTATION AND EXCLAMATION MARKS, HYPHENS: IN TITLES OF BOOKS, PERIODICALS, CHAPTERS OR ARTICLES   162

vii

CHAPTER   PAGE
20. INDENTION AND PARAGRAPHING   165
21. VARIOUS MODES OF QUOTATION IN PROSE AND
    VERSE; RELATIONSHIP OF QUOTATION TO
    PARAGRAPHING AND INDENTION   170

BOOK III:

ORCHESTRATION

22. ALLIANCE OF PUNCTUATION AND QUOTATION:
    PUNCTUATION AN ART, NOT A HAPHAZARDRY
    NOR YET A PERFUNCTORINESS   179
23. FULL ORCHESTRA:
    (i) SINGLE SENTENCES AND PARAGRAPHS   185
    (ii) CONSECUTIVE PASSAGES   190

BOOK IV:

AMERICAN

24. A CHAPTER ON AMERICAN PRACTICE: *by* JOHN W.
    CLARK, *University of Minnesota*   211

APPENDIX I: A FEW NOTES ON OTHER WORKS   223
    ,,   II: A BRIEF LIST OF ACCENTS   225
SUBJECT INDEX   227

FOREWORD

SOME DAY a doctorate will justly be awarded to a scholar brave enough to write a history of the theory and practice of British and American punctuation, from the time when there certainly was none until the time when there will perhaps be none.

I have aimed at something much less ambitious. Eschewing all but the most recent history – except, here and there, for the sake of an example – I deal only with the theory and especially the practice of punctuation as we know it today and knew it yesterday; and with such allies or accessories as capitals, italics, quotation marks, hyphens, paragraphs.

Acquainted with 'the literature of the subject', I recognize the merits, both of such books as that of T. F. and M. F. A. Husband, that of Mr G. V. Carey and that of Mr Reginald Skelton, and of the chapters or entries in such works as the Fowler brothers' *The King's English*, H. W. Fowler's *Modern English Usage* and G. H. Vallins's *Good English*. This recognition and that knowledge strongly confirm me in a determination (publicly stated in the article on punctuation in *Usage and Abusage*, 1942 in U.S.A., 1947 in Britain) to write a comprehensive guide to punctuation and its concomitants. Such a guide is very badly needed, especially in what I have called 'orchestration': and orchestration forms the subject of the quite painfully practical Book III.

Except for those persons who already know something useful about punctuation, all the works I have examined (nor are they few) exhibit at least one very grave fault. Whether they start with the full stop, as logically they should, or, as most of them do, despite the inescapable presence of a full stop, with the comma, they adduce examples containing either one or more stops of which the learner presumably knows nothing at this stage. There is only one logical, only one sensible, only one practical, only one easy way in which a beginner can learn punctuation: and that is, progressively. The examples in the opening chapter, The Full Stop, will contain only the full stop. The ensuing chapter, The Comma, has examples in which only full stops and commas are used. If the next chapter is The Semicolon, the examples will or may contain also the full stop and the comma. The next would then be The Colon, and here the examples can exhibit all the four main stops: full stop, comma, semicolon, colon. The two minor stops (dash and parentheses) can then be treated; but if we begin with the dash, the relevant chapter or section should, in its examples, contain no parentheses, although they will, or may, contain the four main stops. Having disposed of all six true stops (full stop, comma, semicolon, colon, dash, parentheses), we can pass to the two signs, ? and !, which, so far from being stops, are mere indications of tone: or, as we say, 'marks' – the question mark and the exclamation mark. Such subtleties as the relationship of stops and marks to either parentheses or quotation marks, or indeed both, cannot safely be treated until the ground has been entirely cleared.

Book IV deals with some differences in American practice, a chapter generously contributed, with some valuable comments, by a former collaborator, John W. Clark of the University of Minnesota. The emphasis rests upon 'differences', for, in general, American practice is identical with British. It would be absurd for either Professor Clark or myself to catalogue the identities, which outnumber the differences by at least ten to one, British and American opinion being in entire accord on literally all major, and on very nearly all minor, topics.

E. P.

Book I
PUNCTUATION

Book I

PUNCTUATION

Chapter I

INTRODUCTORY

§ 1: A Few Opinions

ALL THE parts of Syntaxe have already beene declared. There resteth one generall affection of the whole, disposed thorow every member thereof, as the bloud is thorow the body; and consisteth in the breathing, when we pronounce any *Sentence*; For, whereas our breath is by nature so short, that we cannot continue without a stay to speake long together; it was thought necessarie, as well for the speakers ease, as for the plainer deliverance of the things spoken, to invent this meanes, whereby men, pausing a pretty while, the whole speech might never the worse be understood.

The English Grammar made by Ben Jonson, written
ca. 1617, published in 1640

POINTS, serving for the better Understanding of Words, are either *Primary*, or *Secundary*.

Primary Points, which shew their Tone, Sound and Pauses, are eight: four simple and more common; Period, [.] Colon, [:] Semicolon, [;] Comma, [,] and four mixt and less frequent..........

The mixt Points, are *Erotesis* [?] *Ecphonesis*; [!] *Parenthesis*, ( ) *Parathesis*: [ ] which have always some simple Point, exprest or understood, in them...............................

Secundary Points, now shewing Tone, Sound, or Pause, are *four*: Apostrophus, ['] Eclipsis, [—] or [- —] Dieresis, [..] and Hyphen, [-] or ["].

CHARLES BUTLER, *The English Grammar*, 1633

Great care ought to be had. in writing, for the due observing of points: for, the neglect thereof will pervert the sence.

RICHARD HODGES, *The English Primrose*, 1644

3

Pointing is the disposal of speech into certain members for more articulate and distinct reading and circumstantiating of writs and papers. It rests wholly and solely on concordance, and necessitates a knowledge of grammar.

ROBERT MONTEITH, *The True and Genuine Art of Pointing*, 1704

I know, there are some *Persons* who affect to *despise* it, and treat this whole Subject with the utmost *Contempt*, as a Trifle far below their Notice, and a Formality unworthy of *their* Regard: They do not hold it difficult, but *despicable*; and neglect it, as being *above* it.

Yet many learned Men have been highly sensible of its Use; and some ingenious and elegant Writers have condescended to point their Works with Care; and very eminent Scholars have not disdained to teach the Method of doing it with Propriety.

JAMES BURROW, *An Essay on the Use of Pointing*, 1771

The pauses which mark the sense, and for this reason are denominated *sentential*, are the same in verse as in prose. They are marked by the usual stops, a comma, a semicolon, a colon, or a period, as the sense requires.

NOAH WEBSTER, *Dissertations on the English Language*, 1789

Punctuation is the art of dividing a written composition into sentences, or parts of sentences, by points or stops, for the purpose of marking the different pauses which the sense, and an accurate pronunciation require.

LINDLEY MURRAY, *English Grammar*, 1794

The sense, or meaning, of the words is very much dependent upon the points which are used along with the words.

WILLIAM COBBETT, *A Grammar of the English Language*, 1819

It has already been frequently shown by writers on the subject that our punctuation-marks do not indicate the most suitable places for pauses in reading aloud; the voice of an intelligent reader ignores some of the textual pointing and introduces breaks at places other than those where there are points. The pointing of matter 'to be sung or said' is, in fact, a subject apart. With regard to constructional pointing it may be urged that in reality it rests on sense and meaning, since grammar is the analysis of the forms in which rational expression is made. We think, however, that all the complexities and divergences and confusions of grammatical pointing arose just because it was not in constant and direct touch with meaning.

A PRACTICAL PRINTER, *A Manual of Punctuation*, 1859

Of all the subjects which engage the attention of the compositor, none proves a greater stumbling-block, or is so much a matter of uncertainty and doubt, especially to the mere tyro, as the Art of Punctuation. This arises partly from the necessarily somewhat inexact nature of the art itself, but far more from ignorance of the principles on which its rules ought to be founded, and the illogical construction of the sentences with which the printer has sometimes to deal.

HENRY BEADNELL (some forty years a Printer's Reader), *Spelling and Punctuation*, 1880

Modern printers make an effort to be guided by logic or grammar alone; it is impossible for them to succeed entirely; but any one who will look at an Elizabethan book with the original stopping will see how far they have moved: the old stopping was frankly to guide the voice in reading aloud, while the modern is mainly to guide the mind in seeing through the grammatical construction.

A perfect system of punctuation, then, that would be exact and uniform, would require separate rhetorical and logical notations . . . Such a system is not to be desired.

H. W. & F. G. FOWLER, *The King's English*, 1906

When punctuation was first employed, it was in the role of the handmaid of prose; later the handmaid was transformed by the pedants into a harsh-faced chaperone, pervertedly ingenious in the contriving of stiff regulations and starched rules of decorum; now, happily, she is content to act as an auxiliary to the writer and as a guide to the reader.

HAROLD HERD, *Everybody's Guide to Punctuation*, 1925

Intellectually, stops matter a great deal. If you are getting your commas, semi-colons, and full stops wrong, it means that you are not getting your thoughts right, and your mind is muddled.

WILLIAM TEMPLE, Archbishop of York, as reported in *The Observer*, 23 October 1938

We ought to deplore the growing tendency to use only full stops and commas. Punctuation is an invaluable aid to clear writing, and I suggest that far too little importance is attached to it by many journalists.

FRANK WHITAKER, in an address to the Institute of
Journalists: reproduced in *The J.I.J*, January 1939

Mr Partridge's account of punctuation shows by its wealth of possible effects that punctuation can be made a part of the art of writing – instead of the simple, almost mechanical routine that American schools recommend.

W. CABELL GREET, in his gloss at 'Punctuation' in
Usage and Abusage, American edition, 1942

We indicate time by means of stops known as punctuation marks. These marks also help to make the sense clear, to show the expression, and to avoid confusion in reading.

L. A. G. STRONG, *An Informal English Grammar*, 1943

§ 2: Clearing the Deck

A thoughtful reading of § 1 will have shown that already in the 17th Century the principal points were being used. It will not have shown that they arose late in the 16th Century and that we owe them to the ingenuity of Aldus Manutius, the distinguished Italian printer (Aldo Manuzio: 1450–1515) whose 'Aldine' Press operated at Venice.

Before him, punctuation had been virtually confined to the period or full stop and, in several countries, to the question mark. Before that, punctuation was unknown. But, as we are not concerned with the history of the subject, I refer the curious to T. F. and M. F. A. Husband's *Punctuation*, 1905, or to the briefer, yet adequate, treatment in Reginald Skelton's *Modern English Punctuation*, revised edition, 1949.

As § 1 shows, there have been two systems of punctuation: the rhetorical or dramatic or elocutionary, seen at its height in Elizabethan and Jacobean plays, but after the 17th Century very rarely used; and the grammatical or constructional or logical, which has always predominated in prose and has predominated in verse since ca. 1660. On the subject of dramatic punctuation, the standard work is Percy Simpson's *Shakespearean Punctuation*, 1911.

But to insist upon the dichotomy *dramatic-grammatical* would be both pedantic and inept. For much of the time, as is inevitable, the two coincide: a speaker tends to pause wherever either logic or grammar makes a pause; and even the most 'logical' or 'grammatical' of punctuators tends, when he is writing dialogue, to point what is clearly an elocutionary or dramatic pause, as in 'He speaks often of freedom. But, he takes good care to avoid going to prison for the cause of freedom', where the comma represents a dramatic pause. (In dialogue, however, the sensible way to indicate that pause would be to italicize 'But', not to punctuate it with a comma.)

The elocutionary element occurs again in the second of these two sentences: 'He intended to finish the task, but then he fell ill' and 'He fell ill; but then, he was always falling ill' and 'He fell ill, but *then* he was always falling ill'. In the first sentence, *then* means 'at that point of time'; in the third, *then* means 'at, or during, that period'; in the second, however, *then* has no temporal meaning. 'He fell ill; but then, he was always falling ill' could have been written '. . .; but he was *always* falling ill'. With *then*, the sentence is much more colloquial and idiomatic; here, *then* is hardly less interjectional than *alas* is in 'He fell ill; but *alas!* he was always falling ill'. However elocutionary *then* may be, the comma is demanded by logic: the omission of this comma would not only create ambiguity, it would positively falsify the intended meaning.

In short, English – or, if you prefer, British and American – punctuation is predominantly constructional or grammatical or logical, yet it has what is in some ways a non-logical, non-grammatical element, necessitated by the part played in speech by intonation and pause and in writing (or printing) by emphasis.

Even that modification slightly exaggerates the importance of logic and the power of grammar. In punctuation, grammar represents parliament, or whatever the elected body happens to be called: logic represents King or President: but the greatest power of all is vested in the people or, rather, in the more intelligent people – in good sense rather than in mere commonsense. Commonsense can and often does produce a humdrum, barely adequate, wholly unimaginative punctuation: good sense (another name for wisdom) can and sometimes does produce a punctuation that is much superior to the barely adequate.

One could write a monograph upon the psychological principles of punctuation. That monograph would form an exercise in psychology and occupy an honourable place on the shelves of a psychologist's library; it would hardly benefit the writer, the journalist, the student;

and to the pupil, as to the ordinary person who rarely writes anything other than a frequent cheque or an infrequent letter, it would, so far from being a help, be a hindrance.

The most abysmal low-brow, like the dizziest high-brow, needs punctuation in order to make his meaning clear. The good journalist and the conscientious writer (whether of essays at school or of larger works elsewhere) will find, if he has not already found, that punctuation forms an integral part of composition and an invaluable assistance to both the public expression and perhaps even the private formulation of lucid thinking.

Punctuation too often ranks as an adjunct. In the fact, it should rank as a component. It is not something that one applies as an ornament, for it is part of the structure; so much a part that, without it, the structure would be meaningless – except after an exhausting examination.

Chapter 2

PERIOD OR FULL STOP

THE STOP that comes at the end of a sentence or of any other complete statement has been called *point*, elliptical for *full* (or *perfect*) *point*; *full* (or *complete*) *pause*; *full stop*; *period*. The second is obsolete; the first, obsolescent. Of the other two, *period* and *full stop*, the former is preferred by most scholars and printers, the latter by most other people. Nobody will go to heaven for using *period*, nor to hell for using *full stop*.

A *period* is so named because it comes at the end of a period, strictly of a periodic sentence, but now loosely apprehended as any sentence, even if it consists of only one word, e.g. 'Yes', elliptical for 'Yes, that is so', 'Yes, I will', etc. Compare the modern catchword 'Period': indicating the end, not only of a statement, a telegram, a letter, but also of a holiday, an indulgence, a permission, and so forth. Compare also Chaucer's 'And there a point, for ended is my tale'.

Full stop virtually explains itself: a full stop, like a full or perfect point, is obviously not an imperfect point or stop, whether as brief as a comma or as clear-cut as a semicolon or as disruptive as a dash or as smooth as a pair of parentheses or as culturedly poised as a colon: here ends the statement, here ends the sentence. The etymology of *period* is helpful, as etymology so often is. *Period*, French *période*, Latin *periodus*, Greek *periodos* (*peri*, around + *hodos*, a way, a road), means literally a going round, hence a rounding off, especially as applied to time, more especially still the time represented by a breathing. At the end of a breathing, a sentence, a statement, one pauses to take breath, either because one must or because it is convenient to do so. This explains why the elocutionary term *pause* and, for the full stop, *full pause* were formerly used as synonymous with (*full*) *point* or (*full*) *stop*.

The one indispensable stop is the full stop. In most simple sentences – those containing one verb – this stop suffices. In the following examples, only an over-punctuator would increase the punctuation:

He went home early that day.
He could hardly have done anything else.

9

He knew all about it.
Quite unconcernedly she continued her knitting.
She said No.

Many compound and some complex sentences require nothing but a full stop. A consideration of the following examples will show the kind of compound sentence where this is permissible and, indeed, correct:

He went home early that day and got the chores finished by seven o'clock.
He went home early that day in order to do a number of small things that could not very well be left until the next morning.
He went home early that day and finished his chores before he went to bed.
He did not get home early that day because he had been delayed in town.
He did not get home early that day because he had been delayed in town by a friend he had not met for quite twenty years.
When I saw him I departed as soon as ever I could.

The factor common to all these sentences is continuity of subject. Take that last sentence:

When I saw him I departed as soon as I could.

If we changed it to

When I saw him he ran away,

we should not be wrong; some elegant writers, however, would put a comma after 'him'. An abrupt change of subject usually demands a comma, especially if the conjunction happens to be 'but' or 'however' or 'for' or 'since'. For instance,

I looked hard at him but he took no notice of me

would be improved thus:

I looked hard at him, but he took no notice of me.

That, however, is to anticipate.

Beginners, especially children, overdo the period, inasmuch as they seem to think that no other stop exists. This is what the Fowler brothers call 'the spot-plague'. Few practised writers would commit themselves to such simplicity as this:

My father drove to the town yesterday. He had to go there because he needed flour and salt and sugar for the house and equipment for the farm and some special food for some hens that seemed to be off their food for some reason or other. When he reached town he went straight to the store and got what he needed before he went to arrange with the agent for agricultural machinery for the delivery of a new tractor and certain repairs to be done to the harvester. But he did find the time for a cup of I don't know whether it was tea or coffee. The poor man felt so thirsty that he thought that his throat had been cut or so he told my mother when he finally got back home after dusk. She said that he ought to have had a square meal because it didn't do him any good to go for so long on such a tiring day without food. But he said he had been so busy and so anxious not to overlook anything that he wasn't even aware that time was passing so rapidly and that if he wasn't careful he would be caught in the dark.

Nevertheless, the lack of all punctuation other than that of the full stops is much less tedious in such a passage, where, in fact, the unrelieved full stop is shown at full stretch and almost at its best, than in the following: –

He was a good man. He was a brave man. He was also a very kind man. He had a very kind wife. She was not brave but she was certainly very good. He and she formed an almost ideal couple. At least I think so. You may think differently. I shouldn't blame you if you did. They were very popular with everyone in the district. It was a large district. And so their popularity meant a good deal both to themselves and to the district. There exist few people like them. Perhaps I should say 'live' instead of 'exist'. But I must return to my subject. This couple lived in that district for eighty years. They lived there from birth to death. That is a long time. I mean eighty years is a long time. But perhaps I am boring you. I must stop. You won't speak to me again if I don't stop now. So I do at last stop.

The educated will say, But nobody writes like that. The trouble is that a vast number of people write exactly like that: and some of them, if not well-educated and cultured, are certainly not illiterate; a few pass for (and, in the sobering fact, are) averagely educated persons. If anyone objects, But that is a matter of style, not a matter of education, some such reply as the following could be made:

Punctuation is not something apart from style, which, after all, means no more than the way in which a person writes, whether badly or well; punctuation does form part of English in its practical aspects, a part far more important than most of us realize. The ability to write at least a letter is extremely important; and if you think that you can write an even passable letter without knowing how to use one and preferably two other stops (comma and semicolon), you are making a grave mistake. To go further: if you think you can write a good business report or an essay or an article, without knowing also how to employ at least two of the remaining stops – the colon, the dash, and parentheses – then you are probably over-estimating your own abilities as a writer and the intelligence of your readers.

Punctuation is not something that, like a best suit of clothes, you put on for special occasions. Punctuation is not something you add to writing, even the humblest: it forms an inescapable part of writing. To change the metaphor, punctuation might be compared to the railway line along which the train (composition, style, writing) must travel if it isn't to run away with its driver (the writer of even a note to the butcher).

To revert to the period or full stop. It ends a sentence, i.e. a statement, i.e. the expression of a self-contained or complete thought. So, of course, does a question mark or an exclamation mark. To avoid illogical anticipation, however, this implication of a period being somehow contained in either of those two supplementary marks will be treated in Chapter 9.

Then there is the non-constructional, non-syntactical use of the period in, for instance, 'i.e.' and 'e.g.' and 'Prof.': that is, in abbreviation. This aspect of the period will be considered in Chapter 4.

But there remain several uses relevant to the present chapter. Examine the following sentences:

She did not dislike him. Far from it.
He acted as though he were an all-powerful dictator. Not that he ever would be one.
You could hardly have been there. Of course not.

'Far from it' and 'Of course not' are neither complete thoughts nor even sentences. They form a kind of shorthand for 'She liked him very much' and 'Of course you could not have been there'. 'Not that he ever would be one' may be a complete sentence, although some grammarians contend that sentences of this sort are imperfect; it certainly is not a complete, self-contained thought, for strictly it belongs to 'He acted as though he were an all-powerful dictator'. Many writers would prefer the single sentence, 'He acted as though he were an all-powerful dictator – not that he would ever be one'. That sentence introduces a dash and therefore rather unhelpfully forestalls Chapter 8. Perhaps a better example is this:

He said that he intended to commit suicide. As if he would.

There, 'As if he would' represents 'Yet he intended to do nothing of the sort'.*

Of this kind of imperfect sentence there is a variation, equivalent to an intermediate stage, for in addition to

The angry man protested. Vehemently.

we have

The angry man protested. Protested vehemently.

'Protested vehemently' merely omits the subject, presumably 'He'.

A secondary aspect of the clipped sentence will be examined in Chapter 14, Italics.

Much more importantly: the relation of full stop to comma appears, by indirection, in Chapter 3; its relation to all other stops whatsoever appears, in its simpler forms, in Chapter 11, Punctuation at All Points, and, in its complex forms, in Chapter 22, Alliance of Punctuation and Quotation, and Chapter 23, Full Orchestra.

An Anomaly

There is one conclusion that is left unconcluded. After one's signature at the end of a letter (or note) one omits the period; even in

Your loving
Ann Smith
(not much longer to be Smith)

—for a period is felt to be pedantic.

---

* A more forceful writer would probably have punctuated 'As if he would' thus: 'As if he would!' The dot-obsessed would have written: 'As if he would . . .' But these are anticipations.

Chapter 3

THE COMMA

Introductory

NEXT IN importance to the longest pause of all, the period or full stop, comes the shortest, the comma. The practice does not seriously differ from the theory implied by the etymology: *comma*, the Latin transliteration of Greek *komma*, related to *koptein*, to cut, means literally 'a cutting', hence 'a cutting-off', hence 'a part cut off', hence a clause, which, after all, is nothing but a part, especially a (comparatively) short part, cut off from the rest of the sentence; hence the sign that indicates the division. In modern practice, the comma serves to separate not only clauses but phrases and words; more precisely, certain kinds of clauses and certain kinds of phrase and certain groupings of words.

In modern usage, the comma subserves predominantly the grammar, the construction or syntax, of a sentence; formerly the comma indicated primarily the rhetorical pauses, as, quite often, it still does. To attempt a rigid dichotomy of rhetorical and grammatical uses of the comma would be crassly stupid: and this condemnation, as we have already seen, applies to punctuation in general.

Although the separation, whether of single words or phrases from other single words or phrases, or of single words or phrases from clauses, is, on the whole, more modern than the separation of clause from clause, it is easier to treat the comma in the following apparently arbitrary, yet practical and convenient, order:

I: (1) commas between single words:
      (*a*) nouns or pronouns
      (*b*) adjectives
      (*c*) verbs
      (*d*) adverbs
      (*e*) prepositions
      (*f*) conjunctions
  (2) commas between word-groups (other than phrases) apprehended as units
  (3) commas between single words and word-groups

(4) commas between single words (or word-groups) and phrases, and between phrases and phrases
(5) commas between place-names and in dates
(6) commas in addresses, letter-headings and letter-ends
(7) commas in figures and symbols
(8) commas between single words, word-groups, phrases – and clauses

II: commas between clauses:
(9) principal and principal
(10) principal and subordinate
(11) subordinate and subordinate
(12) principal(s) and subordinate(s) linked complexly
(13) restrictive (or defining) clauses and non-restrictive (or non-defining) clauses
(14) the stating and the stated.

Since, obviously, these various functions of the comma are relevant only within the framework of a single sentence, the functional distinctions are slight. But if one failed to establish and then adhere to some such arrangement of material that is much more complex than all pupils, most students, and many scholars, writers, journalists realize, one could easily fail to do justice to the subject. Both the learner of punctuation and the reviser of his own punctuation will rightly ignore the schema and assimilate the lessons implied by the examples.

§ 1: The Comma between Noun (or Pronoun) and Noun (or Pronoun)

Two nouns or pronouns, or a noun and a pronoun, do not, when joined by *and*, need a comma:

Jack and Jill
Jack and Jill went up the hill
He and she climbed the hill
Jack and she climbed the hill
He and Jill climbed the hill.

That rule is perhaps so childishly obvious that it should not even be formulated. Yet there is an exception, as in:

Jack, and Jill, went up the hill:

where the meaning is 'Jack went up the hill. But, remarkable though it may seem, so did Jill'. This rather fine point forms one of those which will be treated in Chapter 16, at the section on the various manners in which emphasis may be conveyed. The same exception could be applied to such sentences as

> Jack and Jill and Tom went up the hill
> He and she and I are cousins,

for a different nuance is perceptible in 'Jack and Jill, and Tom, went up the hill', Tom being an unwanted addition.

The usual sentence-form, however, is:

> Jack, Jill and Tom went up the hill
> He, she and I are cousins:

rather more usual, in the 20th Century, than:

> Jack, Jill, and Tom . . .
> He, she, and I . . .

To say that the latter form is incorrect would be wrong. But the commas after 'Jill' and 'she' are excessive, for they perform no useful work. The second comma should be inserted only when the writer wishes to emphasize the third element by disjoining it from the first two elements. The same rule applies where there are more than three elements of the subject or, naturally, of the object or the complement of a sentence, as in:

> Their names are Tom, Dick, Harry and Jim.
> He named his sons Tom, Dick, Harry and Jim.
> I saw you, your wife, your son and your daughter enjoying yourselves
at the circus last night.

Slightly more tricky, though still far from difficult, is the punctuation of word-groups, such as:

> Jack and Jill, like Tom, Dick and Harry, and John Doe and Richard
Roe, form units in the popular mind.

That example presents no difficulty. Less easy is:

> Jack and Jill, Tom, Dick and Harry, John Doe and Richard Roe form
units in the popular mind:

for one might well, as many of us do, put a comma after 'Roe'; but that comma fails to dispel a certain ambiguity. The ambiguity does not exist for those who already know, nor for those who immediately perceive, that *Jack and Jill – Tom, Dick and Harry –* and *John Doe and Richard Roe* are units. To a foreigner, completely ignorant of English idiom, the division might appear to be:

Jack – and *Jill, Tom, Dick and Harry – John Doe and Richard Roe*; or *Jack –* and *Jill, Tom, Dick –* and *Harry, John Doe and Richard Roe*; and one or two others. Clarity demands the simple:

Jack and Jill, like Tom, Dick and Harry, and John Doe and Richard Roe, form units in the popular mind:

which could be further simplified by the insertion of 'like' or, better still, 'also like' before 'John Doe', thus:

Jack and Jill, like Tom, Dick and Harry, and (also) like John Doe and Richard Roe, form units.

A careful writer might mention that these groups form 'three units'. But whatever else a careful writer does, he will certainly put a comma after 'Harry'.

It is better to avoid difficulties syntactically than to have to resolve them by subtle punctuation; if they are syntactically unavoidable, punctuation has to be especially good. Even such variations as I have shown above will, to the inquiring mind, suggest that punctuation does truly form an integral part of style.

§ 2: The Comma between Adjectives

The rule here is, in essentials, the same as for nouns and pronouns.

(*a*) A good and great king
(*b*) George VI, good and great, died in 1952
(*c*) An odd, strange, curious, queer creature
(*d*) An odd, strange, curious and queer creature
(*e*) Dim and hazy, vague and nebulous, the inchoate mass baffled all but the keenest eyes.

Of these examples, (*a*) and (*b*) are straightforward; in (*e*) there are two pairs of adjectives, which must be separated not only from each other but from the subject, 'the inchoate mass'; (*c*) and (*d*) exemplify the rule that the adjective immediately preceding its noun has no separative comma; (*d*) exemplifies also the rule that, as for a set of nouns, the word preceding 'and' has no comma: compare 'Jack, Jill and Tom went up the hill'.

Now, (*b*) could have been written:

George VI, a great and good king, died in 1952;

it could be varied thus:

George VI, great king and good man, died in 1952

or:

Great king and good man, George VI died in 1952.

'George VI' – 'a great and good king', and 'George VI' – 'great king and good man', like 'Great king and good man' – 'George VI', are in apposition; they stand side by side; the one part of the subject balances the other. Compare, in (*e*), 'Dim and hazy' – 'vague and nebulous', which, though standing side by side, are not described as being in apposition.

One kind of apposition causes trouble. Whereas the type indicated by

George VI, King of England, died in 1952
The King of England, George VI, died in 1952

is easy, the following type, which used to be punctuated:

King of England, George VI, had no reason to doubt his subjects' loyalty
George VI, after being a prince, became a king

is now, more logically, more sensibly, much more fluently punctuated:

King of England, George VI had no reason to doubt his subjects' loyalty
George VI, after being a prince became a king.

Compare the awkwardness of

The invader of England, William the Conqueror, in 1066, had to fight a pitched battle

with the naturalness and grammatical good sense of

William the Conqueror, invader of England, in 1066 had to fight a pitched battle.

Another sort of sentence is this:

(*a*) He was a very able and dishonest man
(*b*) He was a very able and thoroughly dishonest man
(*c*) He was a very able but dishonest man

(*d*) He was a very able but thoroughly dishonest man

(*e*) He was a very able but also a thoroughly dishonest man.

All five sentences are punctuated in the modern fashion. The objection to (*a*) is that the sentence is slightly ambiguous: does it mean 'He was a very able and very dishonest man' (or 'He was a very able and a very dishonest man') – or 'He was a very able dishonest man' (where 'dishonest man' is a unit and equivalent to 'a cheat', 'a thief', etc.)?

If the emphasis lies rather upon 'dishonest' than upon 'able', the punctuation should be

(*a*) He was a very able, and dishonest, man

(*b*) He was a very able, and thoroughly dishonest, man

(*c*) He was a very able, but dishonest, man

(*d*) He was a very able, but thoroughly dishonest, man

(*e*) He was a very able, but also a thoroughly dishonest, man.

When the emphasis upon 'able' and 'dishonest' is equal, or nearly equal, some writers would, in every sentence, omit the second comma; to do this, however, is to create a very odd effect in (*a*) and (*b*), and in (*c*) a rather odd one. But in (*d*) and (*e*) the second comma could well be omitted.

§ 3: The Comma between Verbs

As with nouns, pronouns and adjectives, so with verbs. The following examples should clearly indicate the rules – although 'rules' is almost too definite a word to apply to practical punctuation:

(*a*) He danced and sang with more energy than elegance

(*b*) He danced well, but sang badly

(*c*) He danced well but he sang badly

(*d*) She turned, saw, shuddered

(*e*) She turned, saw and shuddered

(*f*) Dancing, he was graceful

(*g*) Dancing, he was graceful, but walking, clumsy

(*h*) Dancing, he was graceful and, singing, he was superb.

Of these examples, several call for a cursory remark: as (*b*), if written without a comma, would be more fluent but less emphatic, so (*c*) would be more emphatic with a comma after 'well'; in (*e*) there is no need for a comma after 'saw', although a few old-fashioned people would put one there; many would, in (*g*), inset a comma after 'but', thus creating an over-punctuated effect; the same effect, though less noticeably, would mar (*h*) if one were to insert a comma after 'graceful'.

But commas are obviously needed in such sentence-types as these:

(*a*) He thought quickly, acted promptly, escaped immediately

(*b*) He thought quickly, promptly acted, escaped immediately

(*c*) He had been, was being, feared that he would go on being, persecuted

(*d*) He had been, was being, and feared that he would go on being, persecuted.

Of these examples (*a*) and (*b*) could not be punctuated less; (*c*) could dispense with the comma after the second 'being'; and (*d*) could, without loss to the sense, dispense with the comma after the first, as well as that after the second 'being', those two commas being purely rhetorical. Sentences (*c*) and (*d*) verge upon obscurity: they are over-brief and over-compact. That, however, is a stylistic objection.

§ 4: The Comma between Adverbs

As for nouns, pronouns, adjectives, verbs, so – in the main – for adverbs, which manifestly are comparable especially with adjectives. Let us look at a few sentences:

(*a*) He rode fast and furiously down the hill

(*b*) He rode fast, furiously and hazardously down the hill

(*c*) Suddenly and noisily, hideously and eerily, the bell clanged on the night air

(*d*) Suddenly, yet not unexpectedly, he yelled

(*e*) Abruptly she rose and suddenly turned

(*f*) Disastrously in 1852, off the Naze in foul weather, with all hands lost, the *Gloria* sank quite without warning, without reason and without trace

(*g*) Lovelily, graciously, tenderly, on that September morning in the year 1939 and over a Europe so soon, so dreadfully and so fatefully to be plunged into war, the sun rose unconscious of the onset of a colossus about to darken, sinisterly and savagely, a world no sun, however brightly shining, however beneficently, could quite succeed in lighting.

Sentences (*a*) and (*c*) and (*e*) hardly call for remark. In (*b*) it would be excessive to have a comma after 'furiously'; in (d) a more fluent, less emphatic and also less arresting effect could be obtained by omitting both of the commas, as also in 'He yelled suddenly yet not unexpectedly', the midway stage being 'He yelled suddenly, yet not unexpectedly'.

Sentence (f) is clumsy, yet this sort of thing is constantly happening in the best-regulated newspapers; the punctuation is tolerable. The sentence would be improved by the deletion of 'Disastrously' and of the comma after 'lost'. Sentence (g) is intolerably 'poetic' and superannuatedly rhetorical. But unless we rewrite the entire sentence, we could not safely alter the punctuation.

Much trouble can be avoided by observing the 'natural' order of adverbs. But that is a stylistic matter.*

§ 5: The Comma between Prepositions

The practice for punctuating prepositions is so nearly the same as that for adverbs and adjectives, and indeed for verbs and nouns, that the following examples will very clearly exemplify and most compulsively imply the rules or, rather, the precautions applicable to ninety-nine per cent. of the potentialities:

(a) For him, as for her, the ceremony is binding

(b) Whether it is in, on or beyond the house makes a difference merely academic

(c) In but not of the throng, he went silently about his business of spying

(d) Whether one says at or in a city depends upon the size of the city.

To omit the commas in (a) would produce an odd effect; in (b) no comma is needed after 'on'; if particular emphasis is required, (c) could be punctuated: 'In, but not of, the throng, he went . . .'; the same applies to (d).

§ 6: The Comma between Conjunctions

Two conjunctions can, in good English, occur together only in

---

* Both *Modern English Usage* and *Usage and Abusage* contain information upon this vital subject.

complex sentences; when they do, they are usually separated by a comma, thus:

(*a*) He asked whether, if it were convenient, he might look over the house.

(*b*) He hastened to the station, but, when he arrived, he found that the train had already gone.

(*c*) When, however, he arrived, he found that the train had gone.

(*d*) I don't like suggesting this, but, if it's at all possible, I should be grateful for your help.

(*e*) Now, as you see, I can obtain all the supplies I need, whereas, when you were here, it was difficult to obtain even flour.

(*f*) Whenever, since I began to work, this has happened, I've told myself that, because I couldn't do anything useful about it, I should not worry.

In (*b*) many writers would omit the comma after 'but', a few would daringly omit the one after 'station', and a comma-shy person might have only a single stop in the entire sentence: the full stop at the end. In (*d*) the sparse-punctuators would have only one comma – the comma following 'this'; I myself tend to write

I don't like suggesting this, but if it's at all possible, I should be grateful for your help;

but only 'tend', for the resulting sentence is ambiguous. In (*e*) the fourth and fifth commas could be omitted with advantage to fluency and a slight disadvantage to clarity; the better comma to discard is that after 'whereas'. Sentence (*f*) is clumsy, despite a clarifying punctuation; it might be rewritten thus:

Since I began to work, I have, whenever this happened, told myself that I should not worry, for I could not do anything useful about it.

The only single conjunctions necessitating a comma after them are *however*, *all the same*, and, if coming in the second or third or later place, *therefore*.

He felt ill. However, he went to work the next day.
He felt ill. All the same, he made seven jokes.
He felt ill. Therefore he felt that he had to make jokes.
He felt ill. His wife, therefore, kept him in bed.

Strictly, however, there is syntactically no need for a comma ever to be put after *therefore*; therefore do not put one there – except for elocution or stylistic * reasons.

* Of the stylistic reasons, several are bound up with the differentiation between *therefore* and *therefor*.

§ 7: Commas between Word-Groups (other than Phrases) apprehended as Units

A few word-groups have been insinuated into the preceding sections. Word-groups, whether of nouns, adjectives, verbs, etc., or of mixed parts of speech, follow the same punctuational course as do single words, as the following examples will show:

Simple sentences, compound sentences, complex sentences, like adjectives of quality and adjectives of quantity, and also like adverbs of manner, adverbs of degree and adverbs of negation, are refinements of grammar, useful in description, classification, reference, but, in essence as in character, so simple and indeed so obvious that they cause no averagely intelligent child or foreigner any more trouble than would be caused by eating an orange, learning a new word or walking across the street.

A flock of sheep, a herd of cattle, a gaggle of geese, a flight of birds, a fortuitous heap of stones, would, by many Australians, especially in country districts, be called a *mob*.

The English language exhibits many pairs of words that have become not only units but idioms, such as far and wide, well and truly, true and faithful, by fits and starts, for good and all, hue and cry, safe and sound, high and dry and, not to make a catalogue of it, hard and fast.

A free-for-all, a getting-together, a brush-off and similar hyphened nouns could all be written without hyphens, yet with exactly the same punctuation.*

English topography abounds in picturesque place-names consisting of two elements, e.g. Much Hadham, Market Harborough and Market Rasen, Chipping Camden and Chipping Norton, Stoke Poges, Nether Stowey, Upper This and Lower That, Bognor Regis and Lyme Regis, King's Lynn, Bishop Auckland and Bishop's Stortford, sometimes of three elements, as Weston-super-Mare or Bradwell-juxta-Mare, and even of four, as Stow-on-the-Wold, or, believe it or not, five, as in the world-famous Much Binding in the Marsh.*

§ 8: Commas between Single Words and Word-Groups

If one uses a little sense and avoids laughable collocations and time-losing ambiguities, one should have no difficulty: a word-group, like a word, is a unit: and when have units caused trouble? Trouble comes

* In these two sentences, a few hyphens have purposely been admitted.

only when one passes from either singles or word-groups to pairs and triplets. The ensuing examples are tolerably representative:

A great tern, a seagull, a solan goose, a common gannet, a crow, a thrush, a sea duck and a duck may not rival in beauty the swan, the golden eagle, the pheasant, the bird of paradise or the humming bird.

King, Emperor of the Gorgeous East, Ruler, the Just and the Wielder of Justice, these formed a few of his claims to remembrance, a place in the sun and a seat in Valhalla.

§ 9: Commas between Single Words and Phrases; between Word-Groups and Phrases; and between Phrases and Phrases

Several phrases have already been shown at work, especially in § 6: for instance, *far and wide, by fits and starts, hard and fast*. Since phrases are functionally identical with word-groups and since word-groups are functionally identical with single words, whether those single words be nouns or pronouns, adjectives or adverbs, verbs or prepositions or conjunctions, it follows that the punctuation for phrases is the same as for single words, as these examples will indicate:

(*a*) By fits and starts, sometimes unexpectedly and sometimes expectedly, yet never for any apparently good reason, he would get up, sit down, then fidget like a cat on hot bricks or stare like a madman.

(*b*) In these circumstances he felt that he must, now or never, act daringly, without excessive compunction and with the utmost decisiveness.

There is no need to insert a comma after 'circumstances'; 'now or never' has been fenced off in order to emphasize the urgency.

§ 10: Commas between Place-Names and in Dates

To formulate a rule would be excessive. The following examples should suffice:

At the corner of Oxford Street and Regent Street, London, the traffic tends to become congested.

Abilene, Taylor County, Texas, must be distinguished from Abilene, Dickinson County, Kansas.

Newcastle, N.S.W., Australia, was named after Newcastle, England.

On June 4, 1878, the human race was run, as usual.

On the fourth [or, 4th] of June, 1878, something remarkable happened.

August 4, 1914, witnessed the outbreak of World War One.

Sunday, September 3, 1939 [or, Sunday, the 3rd of September, 1939] witnessed the true beginning of World War Two.

§ 11: Commas in Addresses, Letter-Headings, Letter-Endings

Addresses should normally contain no commas, except before 'Esq.' or 'Esqre' and before 'letters after the name'. The following is both natural and so usual as to constitute usage:

> John Smith, Esqre, M.A.
> (or, Mrs Alice Smith, M.A.)
> 16 Parker Street
> London
> S. W. 33.

If, however, the district number is written in the same line as the name of the city, the punctuation

> London, S. W. 33

is customary. Yet if the district number consists of only a figure, the customary form is

> Liverpool 3.

Above all, avoid this sort of thing, formerly seen rather frequently on envelopes, packets, parcels:

> Master James Jameson,
> 773, St Michael's Square,
> Daffington,
> Berkshire,
> England.

with even a full stop to show that the address ends there.

Many over-conscientious people insert a comma after a street number, as in

> 16, Parker Street
> 4, The Close.

It is hardly necessary to do so. Nor is it necessary, in the names of

American streets or squares, to set off S.E., S.W., N.W., etc., from the preceding part of the street or square. Thus:

287 Cherry Street S. E.

is usual; not:

287 Cherry Street, S. E.

Letter-headings follow the same general principle. Whereas

98 Thomlinson Road
Putney, S. W. 15
12 June 1952 (or June 12, 1952)

exemplifies the modern practice,

98, Thomlinson Road,
Putney, S. W. 15.
12 June, 1952.

shows an old one, wasteful of time and serving no useful purpose.

It is, however, customary to punctuate the beginning of a letter, thus:

DEAR (*or*, MY DEAR) JAMES,

It is a long time since

I wrote to you.

The same applies both when, in dialogue, one addresses somebody:

James, come here a moment, please
Oh, James, be careful, please

and when one poetically indulges oneself, or one's reader, with that figure of speech which we call Apostrophe:

O eloquent, just and mighty Death.
Grant, O Lord, my prayer.

Letter-endings follow this general pattern:

Believe me
yours truly,
JOHN SMITH

I am,
Sir,
yours truly,
JOHN SMITH

Yours sincerely,
JOHN SMITH
As ever,
JOHN.

In the first, some correspondents punctuate illogically:

Believe me,
yours truly,
JOHN SMITH.

§ 12: Comma and Full Stop in Figures and Symbols

The usual division of figures runs in groups of three:

1,000;   27,000;   270,000;   2,700,000;
12,700,000;   112,700,000.

An exception occurs when the commas would set up a confusion with the matter before or after the set of figures. Thus we write

On September 3, 1939, 5 000 000 men were under arms;

not:

On September 3, 1939, 5,000,000 men were under arms.

Ambiguity or delay caused by matter coming after a set of figures occurs less often, simply because good or even common sense forbids such foolish risks. Such an example as

Men, 3,789, 683 horses

would suggest that the asylums for the insane are less populated than they might be.

Men, 3,789. 683 horses

is better, yet still foolish. Either

Men, 3,789, and horses, 683

or

Men 3,789 and horses 683

or

3,789 men and 683 horses

is clear, the third being the best.

Symbols are of so many kinds that it is difficult to generalize. Modern usage tends to punctuate symbols as little as possible. To take an obvious example, the stops and marks of punctuation. We write

. , ; : – ( ) ? !

not:

.., ,, ;, :, –, ( ), ?, !

which would be absurd. The same stricture would apply to the mathematical, chemical and other scientific and technical symbols; and, of course, no less to the full stop than to the comma. The simplest method of separation is to provide adequate spacing between the symbols. For abbreviations, see Chapter 4.

There remain, however, several interallied uses of the nonpunctuational period. These can perhaps be more clearly exemplified than explained:

For style, read the books by X. and Y. and Z. and, for composition in the school sense, consult Mr A. and Miss B. and Mrs Z.

Chapter I, § i. Opinions of famous poets.
　　　　§ ii. Criticisms by infamous critics
　　　　　　1. Foreign.
　　　　　　2. Native.

The book is catalogued as A.f.8.

Those three examples should suffice to convey the fundamental idea: wherever classifications need, as usually they do need, the utmost lucidity of arrangement and exposition, the period – or the comma or, in complexities, both – will often prevent confusion.

§ 13: Commas between Single Words (including Participles), Word-Groups, Phrases (including the Participial), on the one hand and Clauses on the other

We need not theorize. A few examples will supply all the additional impressions required to complete the general impression that must already have been formed, largely by the painless process of assimilation, in the course of reading §§ 1–12. Thus:

A hero, fearing neither man nor devil, he regarded his fellow men as his equals, as heroes, and therefore assumed that they too feared neither man nor devil, neither cunning nor devilry, neither this life nor the next.

Evil, he thought all others evil
Evil himself, he thought all others evil
Being evil, he thought all others evil.

Fearing, he fled and, fleeing, ran into a trap.

Courage, like fortitude, can be cultivated
Like fortitude, courage can be cultivated.

When, a child, he went there, he knew only his parents, but when, in advanced middle age, he left, he had too many friends and, a misfortune this, no parents.

Too few words, an insurmountable obstacle, and too many, a deplorable weakness, these are the Scylla and Charybdis, but also the tornado and doldrums alike, of a writer's career, uncharted for the most part, yet, where charted, requiring no chart other than that provided by horse sense, mother wit, native wit, natural intelligence, ordinary sense, sound sense.

§ 14: Commas between Clauses – Principal and Principal

The relationship of commas to the structure of a sentence has inevitably been implied in many examples given in §§ 1–13. The time has arrived for us to be methodical. Being methodical, we shall begin with sentences consisting of two or more principal clauses.

The simplest type of sentence is this:

John felt ill and went early to bed
They did not wish to make themselves conspicuous and so behaved most circumspectly:

where no comma is needed. Compare:

John felt ill but continued to work
They wished to remain inconspicuous but did not behave very circumspectly:

there, too, no comma is needed.

In none of those four examples is the subject ('John' – 'They') repeated. The following sentences have a repeated subject:

John felt ill and he went early to bed
They did not wish to make themselves conspicuous and so they behaved most circumspectly

John felt ill but he continued to work
They wished to remain inconspicuous but they did not behave very
circumspectly.

Whereas in the first pair, only an over-punctuator would insert a
comma after 'ill' and 'conspicuous', in the second pair (adversative
type of sentence) one could insert commas after 'ill' and 'inconspicuous' if one wished to emphasize the contrast. If, however, one wished
to emphasize that contrast, it could be done better by using a
semicolon.

In all the preceding examples, we have seen only an identical
subject. What happens when the subject of the sentence is changed?
Consider:

John felt ill and so did his father
They did not wish to make themselves conspicuous and we could only
approve their attitude.

There again the only reason for inserting a comma after 'ill' and
'conspicuous' would be to emphasize the second statement: but why
emphasize it?

Now look at

John felt ill, but nobody seemed to care
They did not wish to make themselves conspicuous, but we rather
wished to be precisely that.

The two commas represent my own practice, for I feel that the
second statements – 'nobody seemed to care' and 'we rather wished
to be precisely that' – stand in such sharp opposition that to fail to
set one statement off against the other would be to fail in clarity;
that a very marked pause occurs, or should occur, at 'ill' and 'conspicuous'; and that, the demands of speech coinciding with the
demands of sense, the omission of the comma at these points would
be rather silly. The half-and-halfers would punctuate the second, not
the first sentence. The whole-hoggers for the least punctuation
possible would punctuate neither sentence.

Where there are three or more principal clauses joined by 'and',
thus:

John felt ill and so he returned home and went to bed:

there is no need to punctuate. If, however, we introduce 'but', we
find that a comma, if not absolutely necessary, is at the least advisable:

John felt ill and so he returned home, but he did not go to bed

They wished to remain inconspicuous, but they acted foolishly and they even spoke very indiscreetly.

There again the whole-hoggers would probably omit the comma after 'home' and 'inconspicuous'; if they did, they would certainly jar a sensitive reader.

'And' and 'but' are not the only conjunctions employed to join two principal clauses. In

He was a very able young man, yet he was poor
He meant well, nevertheless he acted stupidly:

to omit the commas would be suicidal. The addition of a third or even a third and a fourth principal clause does not alter the conditions. Thus:

He was a very able young man, yet he was poor and seemed to be also unlucky
He meant well, nevertheless he acted stupidly and did much harm and caused much trouble.

Where the conjunction is omitted in these compound sentences – two or more principals either congruent or adversative – a comma is obligatory. Thus:

He was a very able young man, he also seemed to be unlucky
He meant well, acted stupidly, did much harm.

§ 15: Commas between Principal and Subordinate or between Subordinate and Principal

To avoid confusion, we shall in this section confine ourselves to the simplest type of complex sentence: that in which there exist only one principal and only one subordinate clause; those sentences in which the principal precedes the subordinate and those in which the subordinate precedes the principal. With the subordinate following:

A: He went to bed soon after he arrived home
He went to bed immediately he arrived home
He went to bed because he felt ill
He went away because I was ill
He refused to leave the house before we did
He has not had a day's illness since he returned to New York thirty-one years ago.

B: He doesn't like me, for I very closely resemble him
He doesn't like me, because he thinks me a rival
He hasn't liked me, ever since I too became a doctor.

With the subordinate preceding:

C: Soon after he arrived home, he went to bed
Immediately he arrived home, he went to bed
Because he felt ill, he went to bed
Because I was ill, he went away
Until we left the house, he refused to go
Since he returned to New York thirty-one years ago, he has not
   had a day's illness.
D: Because I resemble him very closely, he doesn't like me
Because he thinks me a rival, he doesn't like me.

If we examine those four sets of examples, we notice the following salient facts:

In group *A*, a comma at the end of the principal clause – that is, immediately after 'bed', 'bed', 'bed', 'away', 'house', 'illness' – would not only serve no useful purpose but also check the easy flow of the sense;

in group *B*, the omission of the comma would cause ambiguity;

in group *C*, the insertion or the omission of the comma is a matte of taste, and I have inserted them because I believe it advisable to help a speaker no less than a silent reader;

to group *D*, the same remark applies, for, after all, *D* differs from *C* only in the change of subject; that slight difference, however, does rather strengthen the case of the full punctuators.

When either the principal or the subordinate clause is long (as in the last example in the *C* group) and especially when both principal and subordinate are long, the comma becomes, if not obligatory, at the least advisable, as in the following sentences:

If ever he finally decides to stop acting like the silliest of silly asses, he will probably become an excellent citizen
When, thoroughly exhausted and not a little afraid, he reached home at some unascertained hour in the early morning, he locked every door in the house
He always spoke his mind with the promptness, decision, courage and clarity so characteristic of him, because he thought it the only thing to do.

It is easy to perceive the vagueness that would result from the omission of those commas.

§ 16: Commas between Subordinate and Subordinate

Normally, a sentence contains a principal clause, the relevant exception being afforded by such an example as

That is, if life permitted –

where the preceding sentence would perhaps have been

He did not doubt that success would come his way.

But let us, for a moment, consider subordinate clauses within an ordinary sentence without taking into account the principal clause that must exist. We are justified in this arbitrary consideration on only one ground: that of practicality: the practicality of our being thus enabled to deal more satisfactorily with the next section, wherein we shall examine complex sentences containing either one principal and at least two subordinates or two principals and at least one subordinate. This apparently theoretical treatment of the comma can be exemplified by the following partial sentences:

When he comes to town, if ever he does come, . . .
If ever he comes to town, and we don't know that he will, . . .
Since he came to live in town, as he has done ever since 1940, . . .

Those arbitrary parts of sentences do at least imply, indeed they almost prove, the necessity of separating the subordinating clauses either by using a comma, as here, or by using some other stop; as we shall see later, that other punctuation will consist of a pair of dashes or semicolons or of parentheses – themselves obviously a pair.

§ 17: Commas in Fully Developed Complex Sentences

By 'fully developed', I mean 'consisting either of one principal and at least two subordinate clauses or of two principals and at least one subordinate'.

It is difficult – it is also unnecessary – to formulate a rigid set of rules; much more difficult, even more unnecessary, to state a generalized rule that is in the least rigid. My aim is to be helpful, not dogmatic. The following examples will, if examined and pondered, supply the data from which any person of average intelligence can, without strain, assimilate an unformulated set of working rules and

from which the person of more than average intelligence can easily
deduce the general principles by which he may deploy his commas
and thus clarify his statements and questions. The sentences are so
graduated that the student may, without exhaustion, climb the ascent
from the obvious to the subtle.

(1) He travelled at great speed over most of the United States and,
   whenever he could, slept on the train or the aircraft or in his car.

(2) He came, he saw and, when he had seen enough, he conquered.

(3) He who can does, and he who can't talks.

(4) They eat what they can, and what they can't they can.

(5) Whenever it was safe or whenever he judged it to be salutary, he
   delegated authority to the senior members of his staff.

(6) If you recommend him so strongly, he will be appointed as soon
   as I can summon a meeting of the other selectors.

(7) Because he could not arrive in time, he telegraphed to say that he
   would postpone his visit until the next morning and, very
   charmingly, he hoped that the delay would cause only minor
   trouble.

(8) If, when you read the book, you find that a certain character resembles yourself, do not take offence and do, please, remember that,
   so far as there is portrayal at all, it constitutes a portrayal of your
   good qualities, as indeed it must, for you have no others.

(9) I do not know whether, if the position falls vacant, you would care
   to consider applying for it, but, when you make up your mind,
   you will, I hope, tell me of your decision, be it Yes or be it No.

(10) Anyone who feels about it the way you evidently feel must exercise
   especial care to avoid giving offence to those who happen to feel
   differently, and you should, moreover, prevent them from dis-
   covering your attitude towards a matter that concerns them so
   intimately.

The majority of literates, although they might not agree on every
point, would probably agree that, in the main, those ten sentences
have been correctly punctuated. The devotees of abstention might
omit the following commas:

in (1) – both;
in (2) – the second and the third;
in (3), (4), (5), (6) – the single comma;
in (7) – either all three or, at the least, the first and the second;
in (8) – that after 'If', that after 'book' and that after 'yourself',
       as well as those introducing and dismissing 'so far as
       there is portrayal at all';

in (9) – that after 'but' and that after 'mind';
in (10) – that after 'differently'.

On the other hand, the upholders of a lavish punctuation might insert commas at the following places:

(1) – after 'speed';
(2) – after 'saw';
(4) – before and after 'what they can't';
(5) – after 'safe', as I should myself do if I wished to emphasize 'or whenever he judged it to be salutary';
(7) – after 'morning';
(8) – after 'offence' and probably before and after 'indeed';
(9) – perhaps after 'Yes', although I hope that even the over-punctuators would refrain from that excess;
(10) – after 'evidently feel'; I suspect that, in some moods (for instance, in a dialectical mood), I might well do so.

§ 18: Restrictive (or Defining) Clauses and Non-Restrictive (or Non-Defining) Clauses

With the syntax of these adjectival clauses we are hardly concerned.* The rule is very simple. Non-defining or non-restrictive clauses are supplementary or incidental; defining or restrictive clauses are essential to the meaning. The former are punctuated, with a comma before and after; the latter are not. Thus:

Non-Restrictive: The headmaster, who was present, agreed to the project. The Castle, which was built in the time of William the Conqueror, is well worth seeing.

Restrictive: The castle that was built in the 11th Century is up for sale, but the castle that was built in the 18th Century is still fit to use. The horse that runs furthest is the sort we need in this sort of country.

* See any dependable work on usage, e.g. H. W. Fowler, *Modern English Usage*; or P. G. Perrin, *An Index to English*; or my own *Usage and Abusage*, where the subject is treated at some length.

§ 19: The Stating and the Stated

Modern writers tend to discard the comma that was formerly regarded as obligatory after 'He said that' – 'I asked why or whether or what, etc.' – 'It appeared that' – 'Can you doubt that' – and so forth. Modern practice is exemplified in:

> He said that he wouldn't wait any longer
> I asked whether I could help him
> It appears that you have learnt no Latin
> He stated that, to gain his ends, he would go almost as far as to turn honest
> I do not doubt that she is kind and generous.

Where direct speech is involved, the usual practice has long been to insert a comma after the stating, as in

> I said, I should like to help you.
> He stated, To gain my ends, I'm almost prepared to turn honest.

Certain advanced writers, however, omit this comma. But this is a matter that cannot be satisfactorily examined until we treat of the quotation mark.

When the statement precedes the stating, the comma is, as it always has been, obligatory. Thus:

> There remains nothing to do, he said.

When the stating interrupts the statement, it is customary to separate the stating by inserting a comma both before and after, as in:

> There remains, he said, nothing to do.

Certain very modern writers omit the commas when quotation marks are used, thus:

> 'There remains' he said 'nothing to do'.

But we cannot go fully into this question until we deal with the quotation mark.

§ 20: Recapitulatory

The use of the comma in its simplest aspects – that is, in relation only to itself and the period—may be summarized thus:

In apostrophe and appeal: You, sir, will help.
O Caesar, hearken to my plea.
  In dates: Sunday, June 30, 1952, was a very hot day.
Sunday, 30 June 1952, was . . .
   Avoid: Sunday, 30 June, 1952, was . . .

for the comma after 'June' is unnecessary.

  In figures: 1,357,999
1,690
£6. 17. 6, £9. 16. 9, £10. 10. 5
$9.50, $17.75, $19.39
In run-on addresses: He has lived at 17 Christmas Street, Ealing, London, for some fifty years.

A stating that either concludes or interrupts a statement:

He couldn't see why it shouldn't be done, he said
He couldn't, he said, see why it shouldn't be done
I don't, he said, see why it shouldn't be done
I don't see why it shouldn't be done, he said.

Apposition:

George VI, King of England, died far too young
She, their favourite author, has just written another romance, entitled A Horrible Dilemma, or How She Came to Marry Him, lush and sentimental, cloying and maudlin
John, who was ugly, married Jane, who was beautiful.

Parenthetical:

Her latest novel, A Horrible Dilemma, has sold in thousands
He knew that he could get home, for it wasn't far, in less than three hours
On New Year's Day, it was a Sunday, he died in the pulpit from which he had so often preached, quite a thousand times, I should think.

Participial:

Being ill, he had to cancel his speech
He couldn't go, it being a wet day and he suffering from a heavy cold
He couldn't go, it being a wet day, to watch cricket.

Adversative:

Although ill, he insisted on going
However enthusiastic, he still had some sense
Although he was ill, he insisted on going

However enthusiastic he might be and indeed was, he retained a little sense
He was enthusiastic. He did, however, act sensibly
Of course you may, but I don't understand why you should.

Assent, dissent:

Yes, I'll be there
No, I sha'n't be there.

Adverbial phrases of opposition:

On the other hand, it was generous of you
On the contrary, I think it very generous of you.

Other long adverbial clauses:

In order to do this, he had to go the long way round (But: He had to go the long way round in order to do this)
So as to ensure independence, he took out an annuity
As a logical consequence, the plan failed utterly (Some writers would omit the comma)
By and large and in the main, it was a good programme.

Conditional:

If you continue to behave like that, I shall leave you
If it rains, I shall not go
I shall not go, if it rains.

(Where the conditional clause is short, the comma is occasionally omitted, especially if the writer feels that a comma interrupts the even flow, the onward movement, the train of thought. Usually, however, the comma should be retained.)

Temporal:

When you have finished playing the fool, you might help your mother to clear the mess you've made
He looked weary, after he had played that long match
Since you came to town, the town has changed.

Causal:

Because it was his duty, he enlisted
He enlisted, because it was his duty to enlist
It isn't certain, for nothing human is certain.

(In the second example, as in all short explanations, some writers would omit the comma; *for*, however, demands a comma.)

Separative:

Faith, hope and charity

Here we have a peach, an orange, an apple, a pear and thirty, perhaps thirty-one, grapes
΄   The house was compact, modern, extremely easy to run, but small, ugly, far from town and far from friends.

One could classify still further, but there would be little point in doing so. Most of the simple uses of the comma fall under one or other of the above heads; the remainder are analogous to one or other of them.

§ 21: Distinction with a Difference

Whereas §§ 1–19 and the recapitulatory 20 concern everyone who aims to punctuate adequately, this section is only for those who have a feeling for style and the wish to acquire one.

Let us examine the following variations of a central theme:

A 1: My cousin John Smith went to town
  2: My cousin, John Smith, went to town
  3: A town-lover, John Smith went to town
B 1: My cousin John Smith is a good fellow
  2: My cousin, John Smith, is a good fellow
  3: A town-lover, John Smith is nearly always in town
C 1: That is my cousin John Smith
  2: That is my cousin, John Smith
D 1: I saw my cousin John Smith in town
  2: I saw my cousin, John Smith, in town
(But not 3: I saw my cousin, John Smith in town)
E 1: My cousin John Smith, a good fellow, went to town
  2: My cousin, John Smith, a good fellow, went to town
(But not 3: My cousin John Smith, a good fellow went to town
  nor 4: My cousin, John Smith, a good fellow went to town)
F 1: My cousin John Smith, a good fellow, is ill
  2: My cousin, John Smith, a good fellow, is ill
(But not 3: My cousin John Smith, a good fellow is ill
  nor 4: My cousin, John Smith, a good fellow is ill)
G 1: That is my cousin John Smith, a good fellow
  2: That is my cousin, John Smith, a good fellow.

First, we note that D 3, E 3 and E 4, F 3 and F 4, are impossible: they just don't make sense.

Secondly, that the first sentence of each group exemplifies the fluid, uninterrupted, continuative impression one gains from contemplating an indivisible unity, an entity: my cousin John Smith.

Thirdly, that in the second sentence of each group we have no longer an entity but two ideas in apposition: my cousin; John Smith.

Fourthly, in –

A 3: A town-lover, John Smith went to town
B 3: A town-lover, John Smith is nearly always in town –

we have a feature that occurs only in the subject of a sentence. The purpose of this subtle sentence-type is revealed by a recasting –

A 3: John Smith, because he is a town-lover, went to town
B 3: John Smith, because he is (or, who happens to be) a town-lover, is nearly always in town.

A second refinement occurs when one wishes to be neatly causal or neatly concessive:

A lax Catholic, John Smith seldom heard Mass (= Because he was a lax Catholic, . . .)

A convinced Protestant, Bill Smith often heard Mass (= Although he was a convinced Protestant, . . .)

A third refinement is embodied in the following sentences, good sense dictating the punctuation:

My father, Thomas Smith, died in 1952
My boss, William Black, died in 1952

but:

My cousin John Smith died in 1952
My friend Bill Able died in 1952

If I write –

My cousin, John Smith, died in 1952
My friend, Bill Able, died in 1952 –

I am implying that I have only one cousin and only one friend; the former is unlikely, the latter would be disastrous.

§ 22: Comma-less Apposition

This section concerns only those interested in, or who are, either futurist writers or scientists and other scholars.

One occasionally sees this sort of thing:

(1) Tall dark handsome melancholy, James caused 'bobbysoxers' to swoon

(2) James the tall dark handsome and melancholy caused, etc.

(3) He thought it silly fatuous futile even disgusting to regret the past.

Clearly the reason for the omissions is dislike of full punctuation. Sometimes the dislike is moderated thus:

(2) James, the tall dark handsome and melancholy, caused, etc.

(3) He thought it silly fatuous futile, even disgusting, to regret the past.

The compromise in (2) has something, that in (3) nothing, to commend it.

Scholarly omission of commas occurs, for instance, in philology and especially in lexicography. At *seam*, a pack-horse load, *The Oxford English Dictionary* has:

Med. L. *sauma, salma, sagma* load . . . , whence It. *salma, soma* burden, Pr. *sauma* beast of burden, F. *somme* burden, Sp. *salma, jalma* tonnage (of a ship).

Webster's New International Dictionary follows the same practice. Some European philologists go further. In Boisacq there are many such passages as this – translated, with accents omitted, abbreviations written out, Greek words transliterated:

Ionic *masso*, Attic *matto* to mould; Attic *maktra* tin, kneading-trough, mortar: Old Slavic *mekuku* soft *meknati* to become soft *meca meciti* to soften *maka* flour *maka* torment Lithuanian *minkyti* to knead *minksgtas* soft, Old High German *mengen* Anglo-Saxon *mengan* to mix

Boisacq, you will have noticed, does at least, with the aid of a comma, separate the Slavic from the Germanic cognates.

That there are stylistic and also punctuational devices whereby one can avoid this erudite telegraphese is doubtless obvious to every thinking person.

Chapter 4

PERIOD AND COMMA IN ABBREVIATION AND CONTRACTION

STRICTLY, ABBREVIATION covers both initials, as in *A.D.*, *B.C.*, *a.m.*, *p.m.*, and contractions, as in *Gen.* (Genesis), *sha'n't*, and *bldg.* Whereas *M.L.* is initials, *Med. Lat.* is a contraction; and *Med. L.* is a mixture.

Contractions fall into three groups: *Med.*, Medieval; *schol.*, scholarship; *Gen.*, Genesis; *abbr.*, abbreviation; and other such formations, where the point usually falls at the end of the first syllable of a word;

don't and *sha'n't* (often written *shan't*) form, like *isn't*, contractions that are words in their own right; *c'd*, *sh'd*, *b'l'd'g*, *rec'd*, for *could*, *should*, *building*, *received*, are preferable to the more usual *cd.*, *shd.*, *bldg.*, *recd.*, but, in practice, they are inferior to *cd*, *shd*, *bldg*, *recd*.

Dr., *Ld.*, *Mr.*, *Mrs.*, *St.*, are much inferior to *Dr*, *Ld*, *Mr*, *Mrs*, *St*, because the respective *r*, *d*, *r*, *s*, *t*, form the final letter of *Doctor*, *Lord*, *Mister*, *Mistress*, *Saint* – why, in the name of sense, insert a period where none is needed? Compare, in addresses, the conventional *Rd.* for *R'd* (never used): the sensible contraction is *Rd*, without a period. The same good sense might well be applied to contracted given-names: why write *Wm.* for *Wm*, *Jas.* for *Jas* (James)?

In chemistry, physics, electricity and several other sciences, it is customary, whether in contractions or in initials, to omit points: thus: *na* or *Na*, natrium, and *amp-hr* or *Ah*, ampere hour, and *cm*, not *c.m.*, centimetre, *H*, hydrogen, and *O*, oxygen.

For non-scientific and non-technological terms, it is usual to point the initials, as in *P.M.*, Prime Minister—*p.m.*, post meridiem (after 12 noon) – *A.D.*, anno domini – *C.W.S.*, Co-operative Wholesale Society – *W. E.* Gladstone, William Ewart Gladstone. Personal initials are always pointed, as in *J.* and *J. B.*: and it seems advisable that they should continue to be so.

But from the United States of America has come a practice that is rapidly growing and that could advantageously become universal. If it did, it would merely fall in line with the very general abandonment of points in chemistry, physics, electricity, etc.

During the New Deal, introduced at the beginning of the 1930's, a number of new designations arose, such as the National Industrial Recovery Act and the Tennessee Valley Authority (or Administration), abbreviated not *N.I.R.A.* and *T.V.A.*, but *NIRA* and *TVA*. The War of 1939–1945 greatly strengthened this new, sensible, time-saving practice. Whereas many Britons wrote A.M.G.O.T., Americans wrote AMGOT, later AMG, for Allied Military Government of Occupied Territory, precisely as for British *U.N.O.*, later *U.N.*, Americans have preferred UNO, later UN.

For the initials of all organizations, the omission of points would be – for Americans it already is – an excellent thing. Indeed, I should, except for initials before surnames, retain points only where their omission would cause ambiguity. Nor am I being madly pro-American (I'm an Americanophile, not an Americanomane) in this recommendation.

What, then, of geographical abbreviations? Even there, I think, points will disappear. If *NYPL* is already at least as common as, and likely soon to displace, *N.Y.P.L.* (New York Public Library); if *NYC* is seen almost as often as *N.Y.C.* (New York City), then why not *NY*, instead of *N.Y.*, for New York (State)?

If ever there was – who doubts that there is? – a strong case for mankind *v.* useless conventions, the discarding of all but clarificatory points constitutes such a case.

There remains one aspect: what punctuation is there after contracted or otherwise abbreviated words? The answer is, The same as after any other sort of word. Thus:

W.J., not W.L., are his initials
We write Med., instead of Mediev., for Medieval, but M.L. is commoner than Med. L.

There is, however, one exception: a point after a contraction or an initial or set of initials precludes the use of a period. We do not write

Last week I saw J. L..

but:

Last week I saw J. L.

In other words, a point that serves to indicate a contraction or an initial serves also as the full stop.

Chapter 5

THE SEMICOLON

§ 1: Introductory

As the name *semicolon*, half a colon, indicates, the semicolon comes historically after the colon; but in practice it is more important – at least, in the sense of being more popular. If anybody uses one more than the two simple points, period and comma, that additional point is usually the semicolon. By its very form (;) it betrays its dual nature: it is both period and comma. As it is half a colon, so is it also a modified period and a strengthened comma.

Stronger, more decisive than the comma, the semicolon is slightly weaker, slightly less decisive than the colon, and considerably weaker than the period; it is, however, both slightly stronger and notably more elegant than the dash. (For the relative values of the points, see Chapter 11.) The semicolon, in short, sets off one part of a sentence from another more decidedly and more distinctly than does the comma; unlike the period, it does not end a statement. Except in certain rather literary contexts, the semicolon separates clauses, seldom phrases, rarely mere single words; those clauses may be – and often are – principal clauses.

Having left the intricate yet safely navigable Mediterranean of the various uses of the comma, one comes out into the Atlantic, where, for a safe crossing, one needs more than the utilitarian comma and the unavoidable period. Except in literary or aesthetic or philosophic writing, by far the most important additional requisite is the semi-colon; and even there it outweighs the colon and those two super-numeraries, parentheses and the dash. Suddenly, perhaps a shade apprehensively, one realizes that the use of the semicolon is not so simple as one had thought.

Semicolons may occur between clauses; between phrases or other word-groups; and even between single words or between single words and short word-groups.

§ 2: Semicolons between important Syntactical Elements, especially between Principal Clauses

Semicolons can separate clauses, whether principal and principal, subordinate and subordinate, or principal and subordinate. It is easier to exemplify than to generalize these uses; and probably impossible to be adequately comprehensive even in generalization. The uses or, otherwise regarded, the purposes of the semicolon as it affects clauses include the following:

(1) accumulation – cumulative development of narrative or exposition; progression from one principal to another; the adding of one principal to another; the continuation of the main theme by the use of two or more principal clauses separated by semicolons. These shaded aspects of what is essentially one process appear in the following sentences:

Like most other human beings, she was born; she married; she had children; she died.

He worked hard; he played hard; indeed, he lived hard.

The Indians roamed the plains for centuries before the white man came; for centuries since, they have roamed or tried to roam them.

The day dawned grey and cold; the snow continued to fall relentlessly; escape from that cabin in the remote mountains grew more and more improbable; hope slunk away like an optimist from a group of ferocious pessimists.

In 1890 he wrote *The Fleas That Bit Them*; in 1892, he continued the theme in *Fleas ad Infinitum*; in 1899, when his friends had begun to think that fleas no longer bit him, he published *The Fleas Have Ceased to Bite*.

In his novels, John Bartley described life as he dreamed it; in his plays, he pictured life as he wished others to picture it; in his autobiography he tore sham to shreds and hypocrisy to tatters.

(The slight elaborations added to the last three sentences constitute not an oversight but intelligent anticipation.)

(2) to convey antithesis, whether explicit or implicit, and whether an *and*, *but*, *yet*, etc., occurs or not, as in:

He was a brave man; but he quailed at the prospect of entering that inferno of flame and falling timber.

He quailed at the prospect; yet he was a brave man.

Mary liked him; she disliked the uniform.

As a poet he commanded admiration; as a novelist he excited puzzlement, pity and derision.

The sun shone brightly; in the ravine the air was chill, the scene forbidding.

Hate me, you may; despise me, you cannot.

(3) linked with (1) and (2) is the use of a semicolon merely to compensate the theme – and the reader – for the omission of a connective, whether, as usually, a conjunction, or, as occasionally in narrative and argument, an adverb. Thus:

The tiger lay on the ground; it had fallen from sheer exhaustion; it had fought and striven for six unending hours. (*where* or *because* it had fallen . . . ; *because* or *for* it had fought . . .)

Eclipse was not merely a fast horse; he liked to race. .

We cannot perform the impossible, gentlemen; we can perform the incredibly difficult; we have been known to fail with the apparently easy, simple thing; we merely do our best.

He was desperately ill; he spoke less well than usual; the crowd jeered at him.

You do it; Jim cannot; strange though it seem, even John cannot.

(4) Certain connectives demand, at least they usually receive, a semicolon immediately before them; such connectives as *also, moreover, nevertheless, however, hence, thence, therefore, then* (conjunction). Witness:

He was a brave man; moreover, he was intelligent.

You have these three rooms for yourselves; also you may use the bathroom whenever it is free.

Historians believe implicitly in documents; nevertheless they believe, although much less fervently, in mankind.

He is a foreigner; therefore you cannot expect him to speak English as well as an Englishman.

The Pharaohs preferred architecture to be massive and monumental; hence the pyramids. (= hence, they had the pyramids built.)

He's a dangerous fellow; however, you must know that even better than I do.

You are a linguist; then, you're a scholar. (Whether *then* = also or consequently.)

(5) the semicolon that, in an ordinary sentence, is forced to do a comma's work simply because the sentence contains so many commas that, if one or two of them were not promoted, confusion would ensue.

As a man, you are hungry; as a fighter, you are weary; as an idealist, you are disgusted; and, again as a man, you will, your hunger satisfied, need a long sleep.

This ancient city offers some fine examples of pottery and bronze, a little, still rather crude, ironware, and a mound of discarded fish shells; but it exhibits no receptacles for food, water, self-adornment; it does, however, contain what was at one time a crematorium.

(Contrast: This ancient city offers fine examples of pottery and bronze, no receptacles for food and water, but the remains of a crematorium.) Compare the semicolon exemplified in the next subdivision.

(6) In lists – enumerations, inventories, bibliographies, exact and erudite references.

The Fall of Grecized Sardinia, Book II, chapter vii, § 5; *ibid.*, III, viii, § 1; *ib.*, III, ix, § 3; IV, ii, § 2.

Dining room, 1 table, 6 chairs, 1 sideboard; drawing room, 2 tables, 7 chairs, 1 glassware case, 1 grand piano, 1 piano stool; main bedroom, 1 double bed, 2 chairs, one chest-of-drawers, one wardrobe, 1 dressing table; guest room, 2 single beds, 3 chairs, 1 wardrobe, 1 dressing table.

40,000 infantrymen; 5,000 cavalry; 1,000 artillerymen; quartermaster's department, 2,800 men; medical service, 200 men.

(7) Not dissimilar are the semicolons employed to divide appositional clauses; the second of two such clauses may be elliptical. The apposition may run to three or more clauses.

The silly fellow sighed gustily; the silly girl sighed wearily; the pair of simpletons sighed simultaneously in imagined forswearing. (Compare: The silly fellow sighed gustily; simultaneously, the girl wearily.)

Who robs me of money, deprives me of a necessity; who slanders me, robs me of that intangible, a good name; who kills me, relieves me of a burden.

The King, who was well; the Queen, who was stricken with fever; the Princess, who looked to be sickening for that fever; such were the passengers in that ill-fated coach-and-four.

(8) A particular modification of group (7) occurs in sentences introduced, usually and sensibly with a semicolon but occasionally with an inadequate comma, by *that is* (or *i.e.*), *that is to say, I mean to say*; by *to wit* (or *viz.*); by *namely* or *specifically*; by *at least*; by *for example* or in full, *as, for example*. This group obviously has something in common also with (6) – lists, enumerations, particularizations.

Here, precepts are confusing; examples, absurdly clear.

He enjoys the company of women; that is – *or*, that is to say – of some women.

You can't do that, old fellow; I mean to say, it just isn't done; at least, not in this country.

The incoming tenant is entitled to take over, free, certain fixtures; to wit, the *x*, the *y* and the *z*. He also has an option on certain other articles, at cost price; namely, the *a*, the *b*, the *c*, the *d* and the *e*.

Several types of noun are of interest even to the person ignorant of the meaning of etymology; for example, those exemplified by nausea, alcohol, gas, burble.

There remain three important uses of the semicolon; they have been left to the end because, although fairly easy to exemplify, they are anything but easy to explain.

(9) has been neatly defined and even more neatly illustrated in *Webster's New International Dictionary*: 'To separate clauses or phrases having common dependence; as, ''There is tears for his love; joy for his fortune; honour for his valor; and death for his ambition'' '.

Let us, however, take several more examples, because a Shakespearean quotation might not convince someone who of Shakespeare knows only the name.

John adores his father; Tom loves him; Mary seems to think he's some kind of god; Brigid regards him as she would some strange object cast up by the sea.

He needs her; she needs him; the child needs both of them.

To describe is one thing; to narrate is another; to characterize is something else; yet even these three divisions of the art of novel-writing form only a portion of even the conscious part of that art.

If you can possibly do so, come; if you cannot come, write; if you haven't the time to write, send a telegram.

(The last example is deliberately anticipatory.)

(10) *So*, when used as a conjunction (= *and so*, hence *therefore*), has caused dissension. Some writers prefer the punctuation 'comma before *so*', as in

'The matter was debated in the House of Lords quite recently, for the alteration cuts at the basis of understanding, so nothing more is to be said', a correspondent in *The Times*, 31 July 1952.

Like Mr V. H. Collins, who has sent me that quotation, I feel that the comma before 'so' is weak – far too weak – and that the stop should be a semicolon; all the more because there has already been a comma after 'understanding'; the sentence is complex. Where the sentence is merely compound, as in –

He is a criminal, so he has to be watched –

the decision between comma and semicolon must be made on grounds of emphasis or, if the compound sentence be long, on grounds of clarity and perhaps of euphony.

Thus we come to:

(11) the literary semicolon: in the late 17th–early 19th Century, a use confined to educated and scrupulous writers; since about 1930, revived by certain writers priding themselves upon variety, subtlety, fine grammatical as well as super-fine elocutionary, or rhetorical, distinctions; occasionally an affectation or, at best, an archaism. Carefully used, this the literary or 18th Century semicolon can be effective; and, now and then, whether effective or not, it is necessary to those who regard punctuation as a delicate instrument, not as a callous imposition.

To define it; even to describe it; is difficult.

And now we are coming to a clearing in the woods; a little glade, bright green with the soft moss-grass; in the centre of which glade a stream ran between deep banks (MICHAEL HARRISON, *When All the Trees Were Green*, 1936).

Shakespeare; Dante, with his complicated cosmos; Milton, with his Classical training and partly Puritan conscience; Blake with his visions; fascinated him.

If the world had; or rather, took; the time to think, the world would be much better off.

The idealist; there are many things to which an idealist cannot stoop; stooped as far as he could possibly go in compromise.

With good fortune on his side; with anybody by his side, to believe in him; he would have succeeded.

The semicolon, we see, can bear a heavy weight. It can also gracefully bear even comparatively light weights.

§ 3: Semicolons between Principal and Subordinate Clauses and therefore also between the Subordinates within a Sentence-Frame

Such uses of the semicolon as fall under consideration are susceptible of analysis, but I doubt whether the result would justify the trouble. As so often, examples are much more useful than analysis.

He fell asleep; when, after a long, exhausting, tedious journey, he had finally reached this one-horse town.

He did what he was told; because he knew better than to disobey.

They helped him to get a new job; that being the least they could do; that being also the most they were prepared to do. (The two elliptical clauses represent 'That was the least' and 'that was the most'.)

When the explorer returned to England, he tried to buy a house; when he left England, he tried to sell it.

The mountaineers immediately climbed the mountain; because, when they departed for Switzerland, they had been told that the weather would soon deteriorate, and also because they wanted to climb as many peaks as they could before the blizzards rendered all climbing impossible.

When the storm descended, the worst of their fears were more than realized; they were augmented, for, in addition to the appalling weather, their stock of food turned out to be very much smaller than had been arranged; and the party itself far worse chosen than even an enemy would have thought to choose it.

When he has eaten; when he has slept; when he has rested, he will take a very different view of things and perhaps he will even become optimistic; if, that is, he is capable of so cheerful an excess.

§ 4: Semicolons between Sentence-Elements other than Clauses

The principal non-clausal uses have already been described in § 2, group (6), lists and enumerations, and in § 2, group (8), *that is, to wit, for example*, etc.

If the importance of the subject warrants a decisive particularization and a weighty consideration of each division of that subject, semicolons should be inserted between divisions, even when single words are concerned. Thus:

Fear; shame; remorse; contrition. Such are the subdivisions of this notable book. (or: Fear; shame; remorse; contrition; such are . . .)

The Earl of – ; Lord – ; Lady – ; Sir – – ; Mrs – – ; Mr – – ; 'all the world and his wife' were there.

The mingling of single words and phrases or other word-groups can lead to ambiguity, as it does in:

Jack and Jill, Tom, Dick and Harry, John Doe and Richard Roe, John-a-Nokes or John-o'-Noakes and John-a-Stiles are generic collocations of personal names with almost nothing personal about them.

Unambiguously:

Jack and Jill; Tom, Dick and Harry; John Doe and Richard Roe; John-a-Nokes, or John-o'-Noakes, and John-a-Stiles; these are generic collocations of personal names with nothing personal about them.

We have already seen that internal commas often render semi-colons not merely optional but advisable and sometimes unavoidable, as in

Speech is silvern, silence golden; Keep your bowels open and your mouth shut; Nothing too much; these and similar proverbs and proverbial sayings imply a widespread belief that usually it is better to say little rather than much.

Richard, afraid of no man; Tom, known to all men hereabouts; Jack, the handyman; these would be my partners.

Chapter 6

THE COLON

§ 1: Introductory

WHEN WE are very young, we tend to regard the ability to use a colon much as a budding pianist regards the ability to play with crossed hands: many of us, when we are older, regard it as a proof of literary skill, maturity, even of sophistication: and many, whether young, not so young, or old, employ it gauchely, haphazardly or, at best, inconsistently.

Etymologically, *colon* (Greek *kōlon*) was originally a person's or an animal's limb; hence, portion of a strophe in choral dancing, hence a division in prosody; hence, also, a clause – notably a principal clause – in a sentence; hence, finally, the sign [:] marking the breathing-space at the end of such a clause.

Historically, the colon not unnaturally preceded the semicolon. In English the colon long predominated over the semicolon, but throughout the 19th Century and indeed until the middle 1920's, except in such writers as the Landors, it fell into disuse for structural purposes and seldom occurred for any purpose other than the annunciatory. Since 1926, when H. W. Fowler's admirable book, *A Dictionary of Modern English Usage*, appeared, the colon has been returning to favour and a much more various employment; twenty years earlier the Fowler brothers (H. W. and F. G.) had, in *The King's English*, sown the seed of this fruitful counter-revolution. To be mulcted of our money and mutilated of our property is serious enough: to be deprived of our colon would be intolerable. Several writers, whom it were invidious to name, have perhaps been somewhat too revolutionary; nevertheless, they are performing a service more than yeoman, for they have re-introduced the colon to a public indifferent to its value and almost ignorant of the name, some good souls associating *colon* with nothing more literary than the large intestine.

The main purposes and chief uses of the colon may be summarized thus:

annunciatory
explanatory
appositive

52

equipoised; equipollent
parallel or parallelistic
antithetic and oppositional
compensatory and second-thoughted
interpolative
substitutive
cumulative or progressive
conclusive or completive
promotional
and non-punctuational.

§ 2: Annunciatory

In the various annunciatory uses, the colon serves as a mark of anti-cipation. (It does the same thing, less obviously, in the next section.)

The colon serves to usher-in a speech, whether literal or cast into the third person, whether in full or in part or in précis; here, speech includes everyday conversation and brief utterance as well as polished conversation and political addresses. As in:

His oration, which lasted eighty minutes and, at the time, sounded most eloquent, amounted to this:

Work, for the night is coming. We do not know when night will fall. We do not know whether our work will be useful. But let us work, for the night is coming.

Almost exactly the same part is played by the colon in introducing a quotation. Thus:

The real quotation, as opposed to the form usually given, is: To-morrow to fresh woods, and pastures new.

To err is human, to forgive divine: that constitutes a noble sermon and an example of terse writing.

The commonest of all ways in which to introduce a list is to announce it with a colon, with or without such a stop-gap as *namely*.

In the injured man's pockets we found an extraordinary assortment of objects: a chequebook and a pawnbroker's ticket; a farthing, a penny, thirteen one-pound notes; a Bible and a ready reckoner; a very dirty hand-kerchief and a very expensive cigarette-case; three rusty nails and an exquisite nail-file.

The books the auctioneer offered for sale were these: an attractive collection of Shakespeare's songs, three 19th and thirty 20th Century novels, two volumes of sermons, a prayer book, a hymnal, a glossary of modern Greek.

Compare the use of the colon to announce a summary or a recapitulation – a use very similar to that for a speech, whether complete or summarized.

If we recapitulate the day's lessons in English, we shall find these constants: everybody believes that practice makes perfect; that war is exciting, but destructive, except for language; and that life is more precious than anything in it.

Here, then, is a summary: [*and summary follows*].

In modern practice, especially in the United States, many people begin a letter –

> DEAR SIR:
> Your request is impossible –

although it is more usual, in Britain at least, to begin –

> DEAR SIR,
> Your request is impossible.

§ 3: Explanatory and Definitional

Very closely related to the annunciatory colon is the explanatory, including the definitional, colon. This use, which hardly requires definition, can be exemplified thus:

Being questioned how he would define man, and finding that his questioner meant mankind, therefore not man, the human male, but a human being of either sex, the lexicographer hummed, ha'd, hesitated and finally said, very rapidly and very glibly, that he would define it thus: man is the only animal that has so little sense as to stay up when he can go to bed. –

I should explain it in this way: first, you catch your hare; then you jug him; then you eat him.

Many writers would dignify the initial word – 'man' and 'first' – with a capital letter, on the analogy of the capital that announces the initial word of a quotation. There exists no hard-and-fast-rule about this; but a sound working-rule could be stated thus:

If you wish to emphasize that the explanation or the definition is, for any reason, important, or to make it stand out more clearly from its context, begin with a capital, but if you do not wish to emphasize it in any way and especially if you wish it to merge with its context, then begin with a small letter. (That is my own practice; more relevantly, it seems to form the practice of the majority of reputable writers and to agree with the opinion of the more trustworthy of the theorists.)

§ 4: Appositive

As

George Washington, first President of the United States

shows the words after the comma to be in apposition to those preceding it, so are the adjectival clauses appositive, the one to the other, in:

George Washington, who was the first President of the United States of America and who was his country's first truly great man, died at the end of the century he adorned.

Translating that sentence into colon form, we obtain:

George Washington, who died in 1799, was the first President of the United States: he was his country's first truly great man.

A slightly different kind of apposition occurs in:

George Washington died in 1799: his country's first President and a truly great man.

§ 5: Equipoised; Equipollent and Equivalent

Equipoise or *balance* is not exactly co-extensive with a pair of terms complementary each to the other: *equipollence* (equality of power) and *equivalence* (equality of value or worth). But for convenience 'the *equipoised*, or *balancing*, colon' is preferable to 'the *equipollent and equivalent* colon': moreover, since *balance* is the usual term for the function performed by the colon that forms the subject of this section, I suggest that this particular colon should be called 'the *balancing* colon'.

Usually the balance between clauses in a compound sentence obtains when they lack a conjunction. Such clauses therefore differ little from the appositive and the parallel (§ 6) and the antithetic (§ 7): an expositor naturally prefers a seemingly pedantic precision to an unpedantic and genial vagueness; he also and no less naturally prefers a helpful comprehensiveness to a baffling inadequacy.

The various shades of the balancing colon can perhaps be discerned from the following examples:

He died poor: he died indigent: he expired in penurious circumstances. Those three statements represent an ascent in pomposity and a descent in dignity.

He can do it: and he will do it. (*Or* He can do it: and he will.)

Balance of power is one thing: equality of worth is quite another. (Here we have an example of a sentence exemplifying both balance and antithesis.)

If you do this, you live, but you live disgraced: if you refuse to do it, you die, but you die at peace with yourself and honoured by your survivors.

In those four sentences, the balance is predominantly a balance of sense. In the next section, the balance is predominantly, though far from overwhelmingly, a balance of sound – of rhetorical form – and especially of rhythm.

§ 6: Parallel

The parallel colon might more learnedly, perhaps more accurately, be called the parallelistic colon. This is the colon that exemplifies rhetorical balance, especially a balance of rhythm, as in *Psalms*, a useful source, for it shows that the colon'd clauses need not all be principal:

> Also my flesh dwelleth securely:
> For thou wilt not leave me to Sheol.

> My sovereign Lord mocks at them:
> Then in His anger He speaks unto them,
> And in His burning anger terrifies them:
> Declaring the decree of Yahweh.

> Yahweh, do not in Thine anger rebuke me,
> Do not in Thy rage chasten me:
> Be gracious unto me, for I am languishing.

Lift up, O gates, your heads;
And exalt yourselves, ye ancient doors:
And the King of glory will enter.*

The parallel may take the form of a modified reiteration; this, indeed, is the commonest form, as in:

At her feet, he bowed, he fell:
Where he bowed, there he fell down dead
(*Judges* v, 27: quoted by WEBSTER).

§ 7: Antithetic and Oppositional

Antithesis can be conveyed either, few-worded, by commas, as in 'measures, not men' – 'mind, not matter' – 'spirit, not spirits'; or, less briefly, by semicolons, as in 'The industrious apprentice enriches his master and himself; the idle apprentice impoverishes both'; or, this being the most literary, but also the most definite and the strongest, by the colon, as in:

Where there's a will, there's a way, they tell us:
where there's a way, there need be no will,

a sentence that would be strengthened rather than weakened by the insertion of 'but', preferably a comma'd 'but', before 'where'.

United we stand, divided we fall: He travels fastest who travels alone. The literature of proverbs abounds in such contradictions.

The colon, however, can separate also phrases and other word-groups:

God in man; man as God: such was Christ on earth.

Allied to the antithetic is the merely oppositional, as in:

A good man, I allow: a fool, I assert.
All humanity is frail: but all humanity is, theoretically at least, potentially divine.

* The text is that of The International Critical Commentary.

§ 8: Compensatory and Second-Thoughted

A few examples will show the use of the compensatory colon and of its close ally, the second-thoughted colon.

He behaved very oddly at times: yet [or, and yet] he was a very good fellow

Although the story sounded impossible and although many accredited critics swore that it could not be true: yet it was a sober account of his own experiences.

(Here the colon is much stronger than a comma would be.)

Second thoughts may produce the effect of antithesis and often, in fact, constitute antithesis:

He turned out to be a thorough scoundrel: and I had told everybody that I'd trust him with my life: clearly, I did not have cause to do so.

He returned the money: in the circumstances he could hardly have omitted to return it.

§ 9: Interpolative

The interpolative colon performs, a shade more definitely and even more literarily, the same purpose as does the interpolative or·'18th Century' semicolon. Yet both of these stops are far from being confined to the literary. Recently I read a popular novel that, published in 1952, contained perhaps ten examples of this sort of interpolation –

He was good: he himself thought he was very good: at extricating himself from difficult situations.

You could not: I repeat, you could not: have done anything else.

He was: as all men knew: a rascal.

In such circumstances: such circumstances are distressingly common: it is usual for the matter to go before a coroner's jury.

§ 10: Substitutive

A substitutive colon is one that is directly and solely caused by the omission of a conjunction.

You like him: nobody else does.

(You like him, but nobody else does.)

If a soldier causes much trouble not only to the officers but also to his N.C.O.s, he soon finds himself in trouble: if he causes none and is good at his work, and is brave as well, he finds that officers and N.C.O.s will help him to keep out of it.

(If a soldier . . . soon finds himself in trouble, but if he causes none . . .)

I called you: you did not answer.

(When I called you, you did not answer.)

§ 11: Cumulative or Progressive

The progression and the accumulation may be established by a series of related acts, by the logical development of an argument or of an exposition, or by the deliberate creation of an increasing effect. Sometimes the writer intends to achieve a linked succession, a chain of events, an inevitable reasoning, an impressive plurality.

The day dawned clear and still: fighting began almost immediately: as the day neared its height, so did the battle: and as the sun sank, golden, to its rest, the battlefield, gory and grim, was vacated by victors and vanquished alike.

Charles rose warily to meet the threat: the intruder rushed at him: attacker and attacked fell heavily.

You are our best Federal agent: this man is Public Enemy Number One: the struggle between law and order merely begins once again. He has the strength of evil on his side: you have the entire Department behind you: we ourselves have the support of every right-minded citizen.

He deploys a rich array of artistic gifts: he possesses a mind that many a philosopher would envy: he is esteemed by those few who, both individually and collectively, matter: he is idolized by those who, individually, matter not at all but who, collectively, matter far more than many of us care to admit.

A master of rhythm: a virtuoso of style: a modernist of the best kind: he has, therefore, succeeded in popularizing even the poetry of the piston and the pylon.

As the twig is bent, so grows the tree: spare the rod and spoil the child: rule by kindness rather than by fear: kindness is greater than law: kindness out of season is the same as enmity: these proverbs and maxims, ancient and modern, Greek and Latin and English, pose a problem.

In the last two examples, a sharper, subtler differentiation would have been made by substituting a semicolon for all but the final colon in each. In the last example but one, the first two colons or semicolons are rather pompous and commas would have been preferable; even the third colon might well be a comma.

§ 12: Conclusive

The conclusive colon has, in one of its aspects, been exemplified in the preceding section. Another aspect occurs in –

Your work has recently been very bad: you must do better than that.

The conclusive colon of logical propositions appears in –

John is a man:
All men are unpredictable:
Therefore John is unpredictable.

(Some writers would, to the former of the two colons, prefer a semicolon.)

If one does such things, one suffers, and you have done such things: therefore you are suffering; or you will.

From these three examples and from those in § 11, we see that, however much we may deplore the colloquialism, there is something to be said for the description of this particular colon as 'the pile-driver' or, alternatively, 'the last straw'.

§ 13: Promotional

We have already seen how a multiplicity of commas in a sentence necessitates the use of a semicolon or two or three. So a multiplicity or even a plurality of semicolons will necessitate the use of a colon or two.

This process of a progressively strong punctuation can best be seen in a carefully graduated series.

That is an inevitable conclusion.

The circumstances being such and such, that is an inevitable conclusion.

Since the man is dead, since his wife cannot be found, we must search for the son.

Since the man is dead, since his wife cannot be found; for we have inquired about her; we must search for the son.

Since the man is dead, as you're aware; since his wife cannot be found, for we have, you know, asked about her; since even the son, or so I have been assured, cannot be found: we must insert an advertisement in the national Press.

(A semicolon instead of the colon would not be condemned as a grave mistake; it would, however, weaken the effect.)

In the springtime, when a young man's fancy turns to love, as also does a young woman's; in the summer, when all men's fancies and some women's, or so I have heard, turn to the open, sunlit fields, the shady, cooler grove, the gay, bracing, sparkling seaside: so, in the autumn, when one snatches, not altogether greedily, at the skirts of the sun, the human fancy assumes a sobriety, a quietness, maybe a very slight discouragement: so too, in the winter, another pandemic will preoccupy mankind, for now, instead of being saddened, as by the autumn one is saddened, men and women set themselves, some grimly, some with a humorous fortitude, some with a laugh of defiance, to endure the discomfort and the inclemency.

§ 14: Non-Punctuational

The non-punctuational colon; that is, the colon employed not nearly so much to indicate punctuation as to serve as a convenience, sometimes as a long-established convention; this colon has at least five well-known functions.

(1) *Addresses*, when they are not written on several levels. For instance,

He lives at 13 The Court: Carter's Terrace: Megalopolis 23.

Admittedly, the comma is more usual, at least in Britain –

He lives at 13 The Court, Carter's Terrace, Megalopolis 23.

My own practice, in letter-headings, follows the pattern:

John Doe, Jr, Esqre, M.A., LL.B.: 27A Academy Street S.E.: Xenopolis: Utopia.

(The comma before 'Jr' is better omitted.) This address shows the advantage of the colon over the comma when units of the address contain internal commas.

(2) *Dates* consisting entirely of figures, as

4: vii (or 7):1952 or, American usage, 7:4:1952 (or 7/4 1952).

Variants: 4.vii.1952 or, American, 7.4.1952.

(3) *Times* in hours, minutes, seconds, as:

He walked from A. to B. in 3: 17′: 6″ (*or* 3: 17: 6) –

the latter being, especially in the United States, the customary notation.

(4) *Ratio*, as in

3:19, i.e. $\frac{3}{19}$.

A compound ratio is written –

3:19::12:76

i.e. 'as 3 is to 19, so is 12 to 76'.

(5) *Bibliographical Reference*, as in

Quarterly xx:96 (Americans prefer '*Quarterly* 20:96')

for 'See *The Quarterly Review*, volume xx (or 20), page 96'. Compare

Fortnightly 1928: vi (or 6): 16

for 'See (or, in) *The Fortnightly Review*, June 1928, p. 16'.

Chapter 7

PARENTHESES; DEGREES AND VARIETIES OF PARENTHESIS

PARENTHESES – INDICATED by ( ) – are primarily punctuational, secondarily a non-punctuational convenience or convention. Parentheses and dashes (Chapter 8) are supernumeraries, the basic stops being the period, the comma, the colon, the semicolon.

Etymologically, *parentheses* is the plural of *parenthesis* (with adjective *parenthetic* or *parenthetical*), adopted, through Medieval Latin, from Greek. The Greek *parenthesis* consists of *para*, beside + *en*, in + *thesis*, a placing, from *tithenai*, to place, put, set: literally, therefore, *parenthesis* signifies 'an insertion beside'; here, beside the basic meaning of the sentence.

I: PUNCTUATIONAL

The essence of all parentheses is that, without them, the sentence is grammatically and logically complete: they explain or modify, but they do not determine the sense.

'The test of a parenthesis is whether the other words make sense without it' (CHARLES C. BOYD, *Grammar for Great and Small*, 1928): if they don't, either the whole or a part of the parenthesis should be removed from within parentheses, as in:

An adjectival clause (which plays essentially the same role as the simplest adjective) may be compared with an adverbial clause, which is nothing but an adverb expressed finitely at some length:

where clearly the parentheses should be displaced by commas.

Thus, 'Mr Jones (a famous surgeon) was hastily summoned to perform an urgent operation' remains, in essence, unchanged by the omission of '(a famous surgeon)'. Compare 'Mr Jones (who was a famous surgeon) was hastily summoned . . .'

The four principal functions of parentheses are:

comment
explanation

63

unimportant afterthought
reference:

and the additional matter, whether insertion or attachment, consists
of a sentence, a phrase or other word-group, or a single word.

§ 1: Parenthesis of Comment

A few examples will establish the nature and uses of commentarial
parentheses:

> He is a scholar (admittedly he doesn't look like one) and (oddly enough)
> a seeker after adventure. (Usually: .... and, oddly enough, a seeker ...)
> The Red Indians have (to some, a disquieting thought) much in com-
> mon with Mongols.
> Rosie, the Cockney flower-girl (a dasher), was unusually bright, even
> for a Cockney, in repartee.

§ 2: Parenthesis of Explanation

Manifestly, this group is closely linked to the preceding, thus:

> This novelist (after all, he *is* a foreigner) has written a book called The
> English and Their Little Ways.
> *Virtue* (Latin *virtus*, courage) has undergone a fascinating series of
> sense-changes.
> Hetty Lakenside (typically a Lakenside, you see) married a second-
> cousin.

§ 3: Parenthesis of Unimportant Afterthought

An important afterthought would require a colon, a semicolon or at
least a dash (see next chapter). An unimportant afterthought:

> He didn't know what to do (poor fellow) and therefore he did nothing.
> (Or: He (poor fellow) didn't know ...)
> You should read *The Welsh Mind*, by Gwyn Caradoc (a Welshman),
> for I'd like to have your opinion.

Each of these three kinds of parentheses may take the form of an aside, whether to oneself (soliloquial) or to one's audience (dramatic) or to one's reader (literary) or to, occasionally at, one's interlocutor (conversational). Thus:

Chief (not that you'll long remain one), grant my request and grant it speedily (or it'll be too late).

If I lived in Alaska (I sometimes wish I did) I'd fish during the brief summer and read and sleep throughout the very long winter (by no means too long for my purposes).

Friends, Romans, countrymen (as if any of you were), lend me your ears (and your purses).

He gazed around him and then (please note the genial cunning of the man) pretended to catch sight of an old friend and slowly and naturally (neither hurriedly, of course, nor slyly) so placed himself that he could leave, quietly and speedily, at any moment.

§ 4: Parenthesis of Reference

A couple of examples will suffice:

In his recent book (*Life among the Atomists*) the intrepid publicist has rendered a great service to his country: and in the last chapter but one (pp. 336–372) he has devised a plan that could save it.

At this point (Book II, p. 97) the excited grammarian becomes humanly and agreeably ungrammatical; in the next chapter he often refers (pp. 103–9) to a certain monograph (for your information, *The Passive Voice among the Martians*) that he omits to particularize; indeed, he fails to mention even the author's name (Julius Augustus Kupfernickel); and in Book III he develops (pp. 17–99) a theory he has not referred to, although apparently he thinks he has done so.

§ 5: Degrees and Varieties of Parentheses

Ordinary parenthesis is shown by ordinary parentheses ( ). These parentheses, the only sort many people know of, are certainly the only sort most people know how to use.

There are two other sorts of parentheses: [ ] and ⟨ ⟩. The 'square parentheses' [ ] are, in the United States of America predominantly and in the British Commonwealth of Nations quite often, called 'brackets' – something of a misnomer.

'Square parentheses' are properly used when they tell the reader that here is matter belonging not to the writer of the letter, the memorandum, the newspaper article, the book, but to an outsider: matter that, in short, forms an interpolation, as in –

SIR: Is it not time that these hooligans [not all of the offenders are hooligans] were taught a lesson? [True; but it is difficult to discover the right sort of lesson.] Life is more precarious now than at any time since the Middle Ages. [He forgets 1940–41.]

Indignantly, Sir,
I am
PRO BONO PUBLICO.

Here the text runs: Iam [perhaps Tam] longa vita [i.e., uita], tam breve [read: breuis] spes.

Square parentheses are employed no less properly, though perhaps less frequently, when a writer, whether of a private letter or of a public exposition, interrupts himself with matter too extraneous or remote, or too violently discrepant, for ordinary parentheses fittingly to contain, yet too fundamentally parenthetical to be allowed outside the double gates of parentheses. Thus:

DEAR TOM:
Would you care to help me in a tricky piece of research [certain historians we know might say: Well, hardly research, perhaps] that I must begin within a month and finish within the year? Old Mundungus is failing in health; no one but Billy Muggins is available. The title is: Bats in the Belfry. A Chronological Study. (You must remember Fergus Mundungus and his chronological studies.) This, you think, is a new line for me [it might be a new line for Professor Never Lost a Date and Never Found One]; fortunately it's nothing of the kind. But I'll tell you more about it when we meet.

Yours continuingly,
JACK THE UPHOLSTERER.

The third sort of parentheses, we have seen, is ⟨ ⟩, the least used; these parentheses are the most external, the most obtrusive of all. Strictly they should be employed only to segregate matter that simply does not belong to the text and therefore would not appear either in a final typescript or in print. In manuscripts, they contain directions to the typist or the typographer; in typescripts, they contain directions to the typographer or the compositors. Thus: –

At the Battle of Hastings, sometimes called the Battle of Senlac, '1066 and All That' ⟨or in italics without quotes⟩, William of Normandy became William the Conqueror.

II: NON-PUNCTUATIONAL

In mathematics, parentheses ( ) serve to enclose two numbers or quantities that are to be assessed and treated as a unit, as in

$$(3a + 9b + 15c) \times (3x + 9y + 15z).$$

Chapter 8

THE DASH

THE DASH – written singly or, as in this interpolation, in pairs – resembles parentheses, in that it is supernumerary to the four true marks of punctuation – period, comma, colon, semicolon. The dash further resembles parentheses, in that, in one important function, it expresses rather more strongly, rather more abruptly, what parentheses express less strongly and much more smoothly.

A *dash* derives from 'to *dash*', to shatter, strike violently, to throw suddenly or violently, hence to throw carelessly in or on, hence to write carelessly or suddenly, to add or insert suddenly or carelessly to or in the page. 'To *dash*' comes from Middle English *daschen*, itself probably from Scandinavian – compare Danish *daske*, to beat, to strike. Ultimately the word is – rather obviously – echoic.

The employment of the dash falls into two main divisions: strictly punctuational; in the main, non-punctuational. There is, by the way, no fundamental difference between a single dash and a pair of dashes: usually position rather than function is the determining factor.

I: PUNCTUATIONAL

§ 1: Parenthetical

A pair of dashes, sometimes a single dash in the final position, can serve the same purpose as a pair of parentheses – but in a slightly different way. The difference consists in degree. The dash or the pair of dashes sets off the parenthetical matter both more clearly and more decisively: when parenthetical, the dash or dashes are stronger. Thus:

John the Hedger – to be accurate, he was a blacksmith – acted so eccentrically that people began to wonder – very naturally wonder – whether he were not, in fact, mad.

(I should have punctuated: John . . . people began to wonder, very naturally wonder, whether . . .)

The country's exports might have gravely – but certainly not disastrously – decreased in that short period.

68

He was a soldier – a very remarkable soldier – whom the politicians disliked.

William Smith – William Jonas Smith, as he always signed his name – hailed from Texas.

§ 2: Appositive

Words or phrases in apposition are usually – where any punctuation exists – separated by commas. If, however, one wishes to emphasize the apposition, to make it emerge prominently and thus to prevent it from being slurred over, one will separate the words or phrases (or other word-groups) by dashes.

Boy – king – genius – he had, by the time he was twelve, more impressed the world than many a king of sixty.

(For the dash after 'genius' I should substitute a comma.)

We must never forget this truth – the truth that human nature is not made up of black and white, but of black and white and all the intermediate shades.

His book, bearing the remarkable – not to say dramatic – title, *Nights without Days*, met with a no less remarkable, not to say dramatic, success.

Hearing this news – quivering as he listened to it – dreading the result, he seized the nearest horse and galloped away into the night – and into oblivion.

In the appositive we may include the repetitive, as in:

The house was beautiful – yes, beautiful.

Compare § 7 (a variety of emphasis).

§ 3: Abrupt Beginning

The abrupt beginning, as distinct from the abruptness of a dash-emphasized subject of a sentence (see next section), can scarcely have a definition more satisfactory than that of its description – 'abrupt beginning'. Here, examples are even more important than usual:

– Well, there it was. He had caused the ruin of a public figure.

– That being so, he concluded, I can do no more to help you.

– Danger. He'll have to be removed. Such were the ominous words he read in a letter he had accidentally found.

Clearly, the dash could be omitted in all three examples. Yet, in all three, it does add something – something worth adding – to the dramatic touch.

§ 4: Heightening of the Preliminary Word or Word-Group

Usually the preliminary word or word-group is the subject of the sentence. But it might be adjectival or adverbial; in an inverted sentence, especially in verse, it could well be the object of the sentence.

The heightening may come either directly as emphasis or indirectly as segregation. The dash effectually and effectively fulfils the purpose of heightening. Thus:

Captain John Smith – Pocahontas and all that – became a notability in the early days of American settlement.

Gradually – yet with a deadly sureness of touch – he opened the safe that contained the secret of the invasion.

Mary – Mary, Queen of Scots, not Mary Tudor – was an attractive person.

Him – not his brothers – the chieftain feared.

Him – how right he was to do so, I shall prove – the chieftain feared.

§ 5: Abrupt Cessation

Apart from the normal devices of style, an abrupt, arresting, dramatic sentence-ending can be achieved – can perhaps best be achieved – by the use of a dash.

A handsome, upstanding man, he was delivering his speech with verve and vigour, when suddenly he fell – and where he fell, he died within five minutes.

Where he fell, he died – from an enemy bullet.

Of course you may do it, I shall be delighted if you do it – but why you should do it, I cannot see.

There he stood – the greatest man America has known.

He arrived quietly, quietly went about his business – and quietly made off with a vast sum of money.

He said nothing – simply stood there and looked.

They'll be very glad to see him – the traitor.

§ 6: To Segregate a Final Member

Segregation of the final member of a sentence obviously forms one of a group of three: abrupt cessation; segregation of the member; emphasis of the member (next section). Occasionally the dividing line is so thin as to be almost invisible.
Segregation is often a rhetorical device, as in:

He seemed to be one who did not seem to be anything in particular – this, the greatest spy ever employed by France.
He was brave, loyal, energetic, ingenious – was Tom Jones, the country's youngest soldier.
After all, there is but one race – humanity.
(GEORGE MOORE, quoted by *Webster's Dictionary*.)
The noblest work of God and a very rare person is – a genuinely good man.

§ 7: To Emphasize, Very Decisively, a Final Member

The final grammatical member of a sentence can be strongly and sharply emphasized in many ways, mostly stylistic. We, however, are concerned only with one of several punctuational ways – the vigorous, or it may be the cunning, use of the dash.

He was afraid of no person and of only one thing – fear.
(A slightly different emphasis would be obtained by: The greatest privilege life has to offer – is life. And a rather less marked emphasis by: The greatest privilege life has to offer is – life itself.)
He had expected to discover a marvel. What, after that long and arduous search, he did finally discover was – a grave.

This section inevitably exhibits something of that epigrammatic effect of a dash which we shall consider later (§ 15).

§ 8: The Interjective Dash

The interjective dash expresses such varieties as interruption of one's speech, either by oneself or by one's interlocutor or by a third person, perhaps some complete outsider; as an author's interpolation into his own writing, occasionally an editor's interpolation into his author's.

This dash, which tends to be – and usually is – abrupt or, at the least, forceful, may be single or double, according to the point at which the interrupter or the interpolator intervenes.

This generous man – Why, Jim interposed, he was the most generous man of his generation – had a spendthrift cousin, who actually called him a skinflint.

Somewhere over there – yes, there he is – you can see the heavyweight champion of Gambogia.

It is impossible, the author sagely quotes, to be in two places at once – but his own thoughts were quite often elsewhere – and, he goes on to say, he was certainly not in Germany – not so certainly as all that, for he could have been dropped from an aircraft – at any time in 1917, because he was serving in the British Army.

§ 9: Resumptive and Annunciatory

After an elaborate beginning – a resumptive word or word-group; before an elaboration, or a list, or a detailed exposition – an annunciatory or collectively anticipatory word or word-group; these two stylistic situations and functions can be met and fulfilled by the use of either one or two dashes. Thus:

A pair of sparkling eyes, a dimpled chin, a pert nose, shell-like ears – in short, a pretty face – will sometimes obtain more than a brilliant mind could hope to obtain.

(Certain writers prefer to substitute a comma for the second dash, especially if they wish to keep their writing fluent and to achieve an effect that is fluid rather than static.)

In this book Mr X. has evidently sought to present a careful picture – the psychological as well as the physical features of the country, its ethnography and its ecology, its politics and its commerce, its art and its literature.

He swiftly gathered his few possessions – gun and guitar, book and best bolero, one spare shirt and two pairs of socks – and crossed the border.

§ 10: 'The End at Last!'

A speaker will occasionally find himself continuing a sentence to infinity – and, in a panic, dashes to a conclusion. A skilful speaker, on the other hand, may set going a sentence that looks as if it might all

too easily grow most impressively or perhaps most hazardously long –
and end it abruptly. Many a tedious list, threatening to disappear
over the horizon and to drag with it the somnolent reader or auditor,
will, either from the narrator's exhaustion or maybe a timely forget-
fulness or by his firm intent, unexpectedly and blessedly, suddenly
and mercifully – end. To paraphrase Swinburne, 'Every tiresome
fellow winds somewhere safe to goal'.

§ 11: The After-Thoughted Dash

An afterthought can be conveyed by many stylistic and several punctuational devices. We are here concerned only with the dash. The
dash serves to set off, to emphasize, and also to set apart, to segregate, the afterthought, more definitely than a comma, more forcibly
though less decisively than a semicolon, would do.

Let us take a few examples:

Yesterday he left for Spain – and yet I wonder whether, in fact, he did
leave England at all.

She was wearing a flowered dress – very odd flowers, I seem to remember.

When you reach the house, you'll find your friends awaiting you – the
bailiff, too.

Certainly you shall have all the money you need – if only I can find
some.

§ 12: Question and Answer; Dialogue

In dialogue, the dash serves both to separate one character's speech
from another's and to separate question from answer. In liberally
spaced, well arranged dialogue, no dash is necessary; but where
the characters themselves are not clearly indicated and where the
dialogue is written consecutively, the dash is always helpful and
often obligatory.

(In the following examples, I have had to introduce the question
mark (?) and thus to break an important rule of all good exposition:
the rule whereby examples contain nothing not already explained.)

Where will you be tomorrow? – At Land's End, I hope. – But can you
get there in time? – Oh, yes, I should think so.

John: So you'll be at Land's End. Isn't that rather like being at life's end? – James: That is a witticism that has even less wit than point. I'm surprised at you. – John: I blush. It was purely verbal and entirely thoughtless. – James: Entirely.

§ 13: In Hesitant or Incoherent Speech

A speaker hesitant or incoherent introduces pauses that belong neither to rhyme nor to reason: the dash forms a very convenient way to represent these pauses.

I don't know – I can't think what to do. I – er – hardly like to – er – say outright – I mean definitely – decisively – how I feel about this – er – about this difficult situation.

§ 14: Deliberate Incompleteness, Intentional Dubiety

When the thought is hinted or a statement is merely begun or at the least incompletely expressed, the unexpressed complement is often indicated by a dash.

If, of course, you cannot see your way clear to do this—.
You are permitted to ruin yourself, but, well—.
He thought that he might find out whether he was still being followed; on the other hand—.
That was an order, and if he doesn't obey it—.

§ 15: The Epigrammatic Dash

A few examples will suffice to show the use of the epigrammatic turn, even the complete epigram, that can be achieved by pointed speech and significant pause – a pause indicated by a dash – or by a pair of dashes.

That fellow will be a thundering success – if he's very lucky.
He always pays his debts – if he thinks of it.

In the distance – now the very near distance – you will see the plane you've been hearing.
At home – a lion; elsewhere – a mouse: that's the sort of man he is.
Those who can, play baseball; those who can't – talk it.

II: NON-PUNCTUATIONAL

The principal non-punctuational uses of the dash are to indicate omission, whether optional or obligatory; to serve as a symbol for 'ditto'; and to link either an author with a quotation or a source to an extract.

The dash of omission can be complete, as in

The famous Mr – – was seen dining last night with the infamous Mme – ;

or incomplete:

He doesn't care a d – n what the h – you think.

The obligatory omission is seen at its best in:

John Carterson (1883- –) is better known for his epigrams than for his essays.

It is, however, more sensible to write:

John Carterson (1883-) is . . .

A dash serving for 'ditto' occurs in lists, especially of prices; in bibliographies; in catalogues. Thus

John Smith, A Summer at the North Pole, 1863,
——— , A Winter in the Sun, 1866,
——— , A Spring on Parnassus, 1870.

Mattress, paper-filled: £2. 5. 0
——— , kapok: 6.12. 0
——— , feather: 7. 7. 0

Opus 1: Fantaisie,
— 13: Tragedy.

In the attachment of author to quotation, or of source to extract, the dash operates thus:

Very like a whale. – SHAKESPEARE.

Where more is meant than meets the ear. – MILTON.
Ye shall be as gods, knowing good and evil. – Genesis, iii, 5.

Incidentally, it is perhaps worth mentioning that the dash is the only point allowed by printers to stand at the beginning of a printed line.

III: THE WAYS OF PRESENTING INTER-RUPTION AND INTERPOLATION

It is doubtless impossible to establish, at all exactly, an affective gradation of interpolation and interruption: it is probably impossible to establish an external gradation of the mechanics of interpolation and interruption – the symbols, the points, the punctuation. For the external gradation, however, one can attempt an approximation.

The ascensive gradation, from the smoothness of parentheses to the abruptness of dashes and to the dignity of colons, would perhaps follow these lines:

parentheses
separative dots
commas
dashes
semicolons
colons.

Some writers might prefer to set commas between parentheses and separative 'dots'; but a little thought will show that the paired 'dots' (. . . interposed matter . . .) are almost as brief and smooth as parentheses. Other writers might set dashes at the crest of the grade, and it is easy to see why: dashes are more abrupt, more violent, than semicolons and even than colons. Nevertheless, dashes require a pause noticeably briefer than that required by semicolons, and notably briefer than that by colons.

To leave the theoretical for the practical, here is a graded ascent of interpolation, interruption, interjection:

> *Parentheses:* He was (strange as it seems) an excellent oarsman
> William Shakespeare (1564–1616) was an almost
> exact contemporary with Cervantes (1547–1616)
> In his book on rats and mice (p. 116) the scientist
> has propounded an entirely new theory.

Separative Dots: The whole place . . . it seemed to me . . . had an
(rarely used)   air of neglect, almost of abandonment

In that far land . . . Arabia Deserta . . . he travelled
slowly and inquisitively, for although he was a
pilgrim he was also a scholar

Mr Josiah Jenkins . . . typical 'little man' of the
British Press . . . slid unobserved through life
and unnoticed into death.

Commas: He was, to me at least, a figure less memorable than
pathetic

It appeared unlikely, perhaps I should rather say
impossible, that he could escape

You could, indeed you should, do something
about it.

Dashes: Mr Josiah Jenkins – here we have a perfect example of the 'little man' of the British Press –
slid unobserved through life and unnoticed into
death

William Shakespeare – both died in 1616 – was an
almost exact contemporary with Cervantes

He was – to me at least, if not to you – a figure less
memorable than pathetic

Semicolons: In the London of ca. 1750–84; a London of sharp
(a literary use)   economic and social contrasts; Dr Johnson was
something of an anomaly

He surveyed the peaceful scene; a gracious forest,
a small brook purling through it, an otherwise
nearly complete silence; with gratitude and
delight, with comfort and hope

Jane Austen's most important works; Emma, Sense
and Sensibility, Pride and Prejudice; have, in the
20th Century, more readers than ever they had
during her lifetime.

Colons: In such surroundings: a desert of palely golden
(even more   sand, desolate mountains on the remote horizon,
literary)   a stillness void of human beings: he felt smaller
than a flea and much less important

At this period: the embryonic England of the first,
uncertain stage of the Industrial Revolution:
William Blake was the greatest revolutionary of
them all.

To say that the ordinary person and even the average writer (as
though there has ever been one) employs, for the purposes of inter-

polation, interruption, interjection, only three means – parentheses, commas, dashes – would be correct. To say that most people use only two – parentheses and dashes – would also be correct. Yet both statements, pragmatically correct, admit of several modifications. Intercalary semicolons are not restricted to serious writers (notably historians and belle-lettrists): I have seen it effectively used by several modern novelists, notably Mr Michael Harrison. Intercalary colons I have seen in at least one popular novelist. The intercalary dots I have seen in a novel published in 1951.

These last are, in this connexion, the rarest of all devices: they are avoided by stylists and sophisticates: yet they do constitute a neat, potentially subtle variation and a useful grade in the graduated scale.

Let us now consider three or four sentences in each of which two or more of the interpolatory, interruptive, interjectional punctuation-marks occur, naturally and logically and yet not without a sense of aesthetic and intellectual values. (I have permitted myself the indulgence of inserting a question mark and an exclamation mark, un-accredited though they be.)

In the Middle Ages, tyranny occasionally became diabolical (can such things happen?) – arbitrary to a degree that verged upon madness – and some fine men, a grave loss to any country at any time, were sacrificed to a Moloch that; even in an ostensibly religious period; far exceeded that sacrifice of the first-born: the sacrifice exacted by the priests of the Ammonites: which was usually all that the ancient Semitic cults permitted . . . or perhaps deemed prudent.

This very salutary thought – that in the midst of prosperity we are still mere human beings – caused him, a person little given to reflection, to ponder awhile the transiency of things (Sic transit gloria mundi) and the marked precariousness of the tenure allowed to every living creature.

If you are any sort of judge; I myself regard you as an excellent judge; you must see that, in the circumstances (the very odd circumstances!), nothing else – at least, nothing advisable – can be done.

Chapter 9

QUESTION MARK AND EXCLAMATION MARK

T H E *question mark* is known also as an *interrogation mark*, occasionally *interrogation point*, and alternatively as *mark* or *note* or *point of interrogation*. The *exclamation mark*, occasionally *exclamation point*, is alternatively *mark* or *note* or, rarely, *point of interrogation*. Both *exclamation point* and *interrogation point* are much commoner in the United States than in Britain, where the predominant terms are *exclamation mark* and *question mark; question mark* often occurs also in the U.S.A.

Both the question mark (?) and the exclamation mark (!) are supernumeraries or, at best, supplementaries. Although strictly they are rhetorical or elocutionary rather than punctuational, yet, the one consisting of ? over a . or period, the other of a ! over a . or period, they do normally serve as periods or full stops. In short, they have a double function: rhetorical and punctuational. The ? of ? represents, I think, a *q*, short for Latin *quaere*, imperative of *quaerere*, to ask, to query*; the ! of !, probably a pointer, perhaps a dagger. Bilderdijk†, however, thinks ? to consist of the *q* and *o* of L. *quaestio*, a question, the former placed over the latter, with the *o* subsequently diminishing to a dot; and ! to consist of the Latin *Io*, the *I* being set over the *o* and the *o* diminishing to a dot here too. But it is to be noted that *Io* is usually written *io* (from Greek *iō*); on the other hand, Bilderdijk's theory is supported by the fact that *io* is an exclamation of joy or triumph.

A few examples will clarify the use of these two marks:

> When shall I see you again? – Never!
> Why? I asked. – Because it suits me never to see you again, heaven help me!
> Hurrah! Hurrah! Hurrah!

---

* 'Is there not some probability of the question mark's being a simple inversion or reversal of the Greek question mark [;]?': J O H N W . C L A R K, in a communication dated 24 November 1952.

† The Dutch writer Willem Bilderdijk (1756–1831) published in 1820–23 a four-volumed work (*Taal*) in which he dealt most learnedly with questions of poetry and language.

> Why? When? Where? How?
> (Many writers, I among them, prefer to write: Why? when? where? how?)

But:

> Where is he, I wonder?
> Where was he, I wondered.
> Where is this going to lead me?
> Where was this going to lead him, he asked himself.

Compare: It can't be the same man!

with: But it couldn't be the same man, I thought.
>   Could it – oh! could it – be the same man? But surely he was
>   dead?
>   (If the second sentence is to express exclamation rather
>   than question, it is to be written: But surely he was dead!)

Occasionally one feels the need of a mark that will indicate what we often express in conversation, or perhaps in self-communion: a mark that serves the dual purpose of question and exclamation. A sound rule is, Use the mark appropriate to questioning or to astonishment, according as the one or the other predominates. Where the two are equal, I compromise by writing ? ! , as in

> Where on earth can he have gone?!

But more of this in the next chapter: Compound Points. And yet more in Chapters 15 and 16.

Commands are usually, and wishes and assertions often, indicated by exclamation marks.

> Go!
> Go to your room and stay there!
> I tell you I did see him!
> I wish you'd go away!
> I wish you'd go away, you silly little man!
> Whatever you, Bill Watkins, may say, I say that he's a traitor!

One has only to add what may be called the critical question mark and the critical exclamation mark. These occur when either the author himself or an editor draws attention to an element of doubt or to matter that strikes him as amazing or surprising or perhaps merely regrettable; much the same thing applies to a proof-reader's query about the correctness or relevance or propriety (whether moral or aesthetic) of a word, a figure, a phrase or a sentence.

The author sets his query within ordinary parentheses:

The man, who seemed to be a Sumatran (?), asked for food.
I think that there were 69 (? 68) sheep in the field.

An editor or any other outsider would be wise to use square parentheses and thus preclude ambiguity:

He swore that 965 [? 964] was the figure that had been mentioned in this conversation he had overheard.

A proof-reader, if he knows his job, places the question mark in the margin.

The exclamation mark is used in a similar manner:

The marvel of the age (!) proved to be no marvel. (Author's.)
I think myself a good soldier [!] and an able politician. (Editor's.)
He claimed to be 120 (!) years old and to have met Lincoln. (Author's.)

A proof-reader usually avoids exclamation marks: he leaves that to the publisher: most publishers, equally polite, merely query, they do not exclaim, although a particularly shameless statement may provoke them to a double or even a triple query.

Chapter 10

'TWOPENCE COLOURED': COMPOUND POINTS OR MULTIPLE PUNCTUATION; PLURALITY OF DOTS

THE FIRST thought of the unthinking will be: But surely no chapter is required? Why not a paragraph at the end of Chapter 9?

The matter is not quite so simple as that. Indeed, to avoid confusion, the chapter must first of all be divided into two parts, Punctuational and Non-Punctuational; then we must bear in mind that the latter has to deal not only with several of the marks or points or stops used in punctuation but also with asterisks. We shall be wise to consider first:

I: NON-PUNCTUATIONAL PLURALITIES

§ 1: Asterisks

The asterisk (*) qualifies for a place on two counts. First, it varies the dash, or a dot or dots, employed to signify either that a letter or letters are missing from (say) an inscription on stone or from a word in an ancient manuscript – or indeed, a modern manuscript or even a typescript or a printed book, damaged by fire or water or mould – or that a letter or letters have been intentionally omitted from an objectionable word. Thus:

> d**n or d***, for $d - n$ or $d - $, damn
> ku***mis, obviously $kuklamis$, the Greek $\varkappa\nu\varkappa\lambda\alpha\mu\iota\varsigma$, cyclamen
> Th** *an fell grievously ill (That man . . .).

Second, the asterisk is plurally used either to imply that an interval of time has passed between the matter preceding and the matter following the line, or partial line, of asterisks; or to draw attention to an abrupt or otherwise considerable transition. In the second variation, it constitutes a substitute for a double space or for a section-heading (e.g.: § 3). Thus:

(1) . . . and after a long and painful illness, John X. died.

   *   *   *   *   *   *

After the funeral, the heir set about putting the estate in order.
(Often only three asterisks are used.)
(2) On this subject, Milton is thought to have said the last word.

   *   *   *   *   *   *

On matters of religion, Milton was a very formidable controversi-
alist. . . . .

The single asterisk, by the way, serves to announce a footnote,
thus: An asterisk * is a well-established device . . . The footnote will
begin thus: * Asterisk is a word coming from Greek and literally it
means a little star.

It may also indicate that there is an answering note in the margin.

Singly a word, paired a word-group or even a passage, the asterisk
occasionally serves to indicate that the word or words have a special
character (elsewhere defined). Thus, in:

* colon, * comma, * period, * parentheses, dash, full stop

the asterisk is clearly intended to show that the asterisked terms are
Greek in origin.

And in:

an eye for an eye, *land of Nod*, far and wide, from top to toe,
from Dan to Beersheba:

the asterisks set off phrases of Biblical origin.

§ 2: Dashes

The non-punctuational uses of the single dash have already been
treated (Chapter 8, division II). There remains the question of two or
more dashes employed otherwise than for punctuation.

The only important non-punctuational function that two or more
dashes have is to indicate that two or more words have been omitted,
usually for reasons of propriety, or that two or more words are missing
from the text.

– – it! I asked you not to do that.

§ 3: Dots

To indicate either an interval of time or an abrupt or otherwise notable change of subject, one or two lines of dots are occasionally used instead of asterisks (as in § 1). Strictly, this use lies midway between the punctuational and the non-punctuational.

Like asterisks, dots often serve to indicate the omission of letters from a word – or to indicate the number of letters missing from a word in, for instance, a manuscript. Thus: d..n, damn; d...ation, damnation; he wen. t. t.. ..ir, he went to the fair.

Sometimes, however, dots are used to indicate the omission or the loss of entire words: the spacing and the context, considered together, will show when words, not mere letters, are missing. Thus:

John . , the torn, soiled document tells us, went to Edi...... [? Edinburgh] in the year 17.8 [? 1798], and there he met . . , a wea.... [? wealthy] wido., and . . . . . 1799 [? married her in the year 1799]. Req....... . p...! [Requiescat in pace!]

Three dots usually indicate that certainly three, perhaps more, words – but not a complete sentence – have been omitted; and they are usually written close . . ., not spaced . . .

Six dots . . . . . . indicate that a complete sentence or several complete sentences have been omitted or are missing.

A complete line of dots, taking the same space on the page as a line of handwritten, typewritten or printed words, will indicate the omission of a paragraph; complete, except that the line starts where the first word of the paragraph would start. Two such lines would indicate the omission of two paragraphs; three, that of a passage.

II: PUNCTUATIONAL COMPOUNDS AND PLURALITIES

§ 1: Dots

One kind of plural dots used punctuationally has been mentioned in Chapter 8, division III (the use of separative dots (. . . matter . . .).

Another kind consists of three or more (usually six) dots used to intimate that here is a pause in the action, a hiatus in the thinking, a hesitation in the dialogue.

He did not know what to do ... To whom could he turn? ... Where seek refuge?

Night fell ... The boy soon went to sleep. All now was silent ... (Or ......)

At midnight he knocked. The door opened ...... The sun was shining brightly when he continued his journey.

Let me see! ... Yes, perhaps that's how it happened ... But perhaps not ... Ah, yes! I have it now.

But not only interval and hiatus, hesitation and reflectiveness, are shown in this way. Multiple dots are equally suitable – many would say unsuitable – for the expression, or at least the intimation, either of suspense, when they are called Points of Suspense, or of reverie; also, they have long been a device, favoured by novelists, to imply that the lovers are progressing satisfactorily – after all, these dots are, to some people, so much less objectionable than verbal innuendo, and they do draw a veil that is opaque.

§ 2: Leaders

Leaders have, by Webster, been defined as 'a row of dots or hyphens [preferably: short dashes], used in tables of contents, indexes, etc., to lead the eye across a space to the right word or number'. Thus:

Chapter	Page
I...	I
or: II -	23
Sonnet, by Wordsworth	97
or: Ode, by Dryden- -	169
Greek ....hudōr	
Latin - aqua	
German ....Wasser	
English -water	

§ 3: Plural Queries and Exclamations

Like the multiple dots of interval, suspense, reverie, the double and triple question mark and exclamation are to be used in the strictest moderation – if at all.

Obviously they could, in the hands of a scrupulous and subtle writer, serve to express delicate gradations, from unease through doubt to fear; from mild astonishment to sharp surprise to blank amazement: but it is unlikely that he would use them at all.

However undistinguished we are, however badly we write, we should do well to avoid this sort of thing:

Lo! a chest of gold (!!) – a large chest too (!!!): who would have expected it? Who would have hoped for such a thing?? What greater extravagance could we have dreamt of???

§ 4: Compound Points

All compound points consist of pairs, and one member of every pair is a dash. Obviously the possible combinations are these:

the comma dash   , –
the semicolon dash   ; –
the colon dash   : –
the period dash   . –
parentheses and dash, whether double – (   ) – or single – (or, of course,   ) –
question mark and dash   ? –
exclamation mark and dash ! –

In the first four, we have a true punctuation mark strengthened by a dash; in some instances the strengthening connotes abruptness. In ? – and ! – we have a rhetorical or elocutionary symbol followed by a dash – an entirely ordinary dash.

Let us see what the ever-helpful Webster has to say. 'The dash is used following a colon to introduce explanatory or quoted matter, especially as a separate paragraph, following commas [better: a comma] to set off parenthetical matter, and following a period to separate a heading from the rest of the paragraph.' (I should substitute a semicolon for the comma in 'paragraph, following' and again for that in 'matter, and', both to prevent ambiguity and to ensure a properly balanced distribution of weight.)

Webster, always scrupulous in these matters, goes on to say that 'Most authorities, however, object to the use of the dash to reinforce another mark of punctuation'. In the U.S.A., that may be so; for Britain, substitute 'some' for 'most'. Certainly the compound points (, – ; – : – – ( ) –) are to be used with caution and moderation.

An example or two, both of the compound points proper and of the rhetorical compounds (? – and ! –), will serve to clear an atmosphere rendered murky with much dispute and a little acrimony.

Comma Dash: I saw little of him, – intentionally, for I didn't like the man, – all the four years I lived in the same small town.

I saw little of him, – but then, why on earth should I have seen much of the man?

Semicolon Dash: '*Colon.* The character [:] used in writing and printing as a mark of . . . *b* Separation between the clauses of a compound sentence, especially in the absence of a conjunction and when the clauses balance each other in form or express an antithesis or when one contains a semicolon; – a use now for the most part taken over by the semicolon' (Webster, 1945 reprint of the 1934 recension). –

The semicolon dash as used here, denoting a pause for which a simple semicolon might to many (including myself) appear inadequate, is customary throughout the 1934 recension – the 2nd edition – of *Webster's New International Dictionary.*

Colon Dash: The device is as simple as this: –

A stock to hold it by, a blade for offensive use, a sheath to protect – and perhaps to conceal – it.

The inventory set forth the following goods: –
1 easy chair, 4 table chairs, 2 deck chairs, 1 baby's chair, 1 settee, 1 sofa, 3 beds, 1 cot.

Period Dash: I hear that you asked to see me. –

Yes; it's rather important.

He brought in several new laws. –

In so lawless a country a few more sensible laws could do nothing but good. – The most necessary of these was designed to ensure the protection of farmers against bands of brigands.

I think that all politicians need a sense of humour. It is difficult to see how they can succeed without it. – It is, perhaps, equally difficult for anyone else. – They need it every day and in a bewildering variety of situations.

Parentheses and Dash or
   Dashes: The fugitive seemed to be a man of distinction –
               (much later they learned that he was the
               famous statesman) – and he behaved courte-
               ously and considerately.
               The novel bore a title – Jim the Outcast (or, the
               subtitle informed me, A Lone Wolf) – un-
               familiar to our usually well-informed circle.
               There lay the weapon (Fred Holway's) – a
               dagger.
               I saw the weapon (a horrible object) – but too
               late to snatch it from the desperate criminal.

Question Mark
(or Exclamation Mark)
   and Dash: Where was it, do you know? – I'm sorry, but I
                 don't.
                 But come, man, you simply couldn't fail to notice
                 something conspicuous like an elephant! –
                 Well, I didn't. Daydreaming, I fear.

What, then, is the verdict? – That you use compound points only
where they are unavoidable. But, you may ask, are they ever unavoidable? To that pertinent question one cannot make a dogmatic
answer. One can, however, go so far as to say this: If you desire to
punctuate in a manner that passes beyond the humdrum, you will
find that occasionally the period dash (. –), the comma dash (, –)
and the semicolon dash (; –) are, in fact, unavoidable. Uusually,
however, a simple colon or even a single dash will satisfactorily perform all the duties of a colon dash (: –).

§ 5: Other Compound Points

There are other possibilities. Theoretically at least, they are more
than possibilities. Let us glance at a few of them:

Why?, rather than Who?, was the question he had intended to ask;
and You fool!, rather than You knave!, was the comment he had expected
to make. As it happened, he confined himself to You silly ass!; You fool!
seemed to be too strong; nor could he nerve himself to exclaim, You
knave!: yet that self-restraint can hardly be construed as weakness.

But a sensible writer would punctuate thus:

Why, rather than Who, was the question he had intended to ask;

and You fool! rather than You knave! [or: You fool, rather than You knave,] was the comment. [The rest as above.]

In brief, avoid ludicrous collacations: above all, avoid all unnecessarily awkward collocations. To prove how ingenious you are in remaining lucid in the midst of complexity is all very well; in one sense it is admirable: but the good writer and, no less, the ordinary citizen find it simpler to avoid the complexities.

§ 6: Multiple Points

'Multiple' is here a convenience for 'more than two'; 'multiple', therefore, is pragmatically equivalent to 'three', seldom to 'four', almost rarely to 'five'. To write about this 'multiplicity' would be idle; to give no examples would be fatuous.

This boxer – nicknamed The Rotten Egg (!), by some The Bad Penny (who knows why?) – got into trouble with the police.

When this happened, he was fuddled, yet he remembers thinking, That's a queer thing, that is! (He had never seen anything like it.) I wonder who did that? He must be a queer fellow. I know I'm queer myself, but not quite so queer as that! – Where was he? (He gets fuddled sometimes, you know. – But perhaps you don't know. Why should you?) – Oh, he remembered, I recall how it was.

It would be easy to find examples still more complicated. But such examples, lacking (as at this stage they must) quotation marks and italics, would, in the main, be artificial. (See Book III, the chapter entitled Alliance of Punctuation and Quotation.)

Chapter II

PUNCTUATION AT ALL POINTS; RELATIVE VALUES OF THE POINTS

§ 1: Punctuation

'PUNCTUATION AT all points' has to be understood to mean either '. . . as far as it can be complete without the accompaniments – capitals, italics, quotation marks, paragraphing, indenting, etc.' or, if you prefer, 'Punctuation unaccompanied and unallied'.

An airy discourse might be quite interesting – as an example of airy discourse – but it would have little (if, indeed, any) practical value. Such value comes both more easily and more pertinently, more attractively and more effectually, from a set of illustrative sentences, with explanatory or precautionary comment only where necessary; but, wherever necessary, with that comment.

The word breakfast, now always written as one unbroken word, was at first written break-fast. The natural development of compound words, however, is that they begin as two or three separate words – for instance, care free and free for all; then take a hyphen, as in care-free and free-for-all; and end as single, unbroken words, such as carefree and theoretically freeforall. In practice, freeforall does not exist: but it easily might. Most of us, I suppose, have seen ne'erdowell (even neerdowell) alongside the more usual ne'er-do-well.

(For the vexed question of hyphenation, see Chapter 17.)

This aborigine was brave; he possessed manual skill, mental stability, moral principles; he was prepared to accept new ideas – however strange, however odd, they seemed to him – at least to the extent of examining them and assessing them: yet, nobody knows why (– least of all the aborigine), he could not bake bread.

Ambiguity, however, is found not merely in single words but also and especially in phrases and clauses and notably in sentences, whether single or compound, simple or complex. On ambiguity in general, the best critical study has been written by William Empson, whose Seven Types of Ambiguity – a title moulded upon T. E. Lawrence's Seven Pillars of Wisdom? – provide the argument of the following paragraph; direct quotations being set within inverted commas.

If it be possible (but is it?) he will; that is, if all goes according to plan, he will; finally escape from the power of those fiends: men unlike men;

90

men much like fiends. (*Or:*...those fiends – men unlike men, but much like fiends.)

Charles Lamb and his friend Ayrton were playing whist. The latter, taking a trick by trumping, exclaimed, Ah! when Greek meets Greek [– compare *Greek*, a cardsharper –], then comes the tug of war. But, Lamb replied, when you, Ayrton, meet Greek you cannot even read it.

Until dawn breaks, all is uncertainty and a chill sense of fear (never quite becoming panic); dawn breaking, the half-light is deceptive, and the time is ripe for stratagems; until the evening twilight all then is bustle and plan and counterplanning: and at that second dusk, the weary soldiers begin to long for rest and quiet and peace: but of peace and quiet and rest, they will find nothing but an ironic simulacrum.

James McNeill Whistler – in full, James Abbott McNeill Whistler – who lived in 1834–1903; and Oscar Wilde, who, born in 1856, lived only until 1900: these were fellows less humorous than witty. On one occasion, Whistler said something particularly clever and Wilde appreciatively remarked that he wished he himself had said it; Oh, you will, Oscar; you undoubtedly will. – Beside that witticism, set this one, perpetrated by Wilde at Whistler's expense, although not in his presence: With all his faults, he has never been guilty of writing poetry. Now, wits still exist: but they are not publicized as they were during the approximate period 1890–1913.

§ 2: Relative Values of the Points

If we exclude the two supernumeraries, the question mark and the exclamation mark, as being primarily rhetorical and elocutionary, although with the caution that in their syntactical role they stand approximately on a level with – the exclamation mark slightly under, but the question mark dead-level with – the period; and if, further, we note that a reinforced question mark (? –) and a reinforced exclamation mark (! –) stand exactly level with a reinforced period or period dash (. –), we can then establish, with all the fallacious exactitude that characterizes a statistical table, the relative value of the points or stops or punctuation marks.

In a general way, we need to add very little to the general remarks made, here and there, in the preceding chapters. To drive home the practical value of the ensuing tables, it will, however, be necessary to give a few exemplary sentences.

Either we accept only the single points (, ; : .) and complementaries (– and ( )) or we accept the addition of the reinforced stops

(, – ; – : – . –). To satisfy the typographical purism of the simpli-
cists, the relative values of the unsupported stops may be set forth
in the following merely approximate table, based upon a fundamental
10 for a period:

<pre>
parentheses - - - - - -   1 or 2
comma - - - - - - - - -   2 or 1
dash - - - - - - - - -   3–5
semicolon - - - - - -   6
colon - - - - - - - - -   8
period - - - - - - - - - 10
</pre>

The value of a dash varies considerably, according to the context;
its normal value is 4 rather than 3 or 5. Usually parentheses are
slightly smoother than even a comma and indicate a slightly shorter
pause; but the pause after a long parenthesis is approximately equivalent to that after an important comma; only a very weak comma is
equivalent to average parentheses. Perhaps the relationship between
parentheses and comma would be more exactly expressed by:

<pre>
parentheses - - - - - -   1 or 1½
comma - - - - - - - - -   1½ or 2
</pre>

The full scale of both simple and reinforced stops might be
approximately determined thus:

<pre>
parentheses - - - - - -   1–1½–2
comma - - - - - - - - -   2
dash - - - - - - - - -   3
comma dash - - - - -   4
semicolon - - - - - - -   5
semicolon dash- - - -   6
colon - - - - - - - - -   7
colon dash- - - - - -   8
period - - - - - - - - - 9
period dash - - - - - -   10
</pre>

Only rarely do parentheses constitute as strong a point, demand
a pause as long, as does the comma. The semicolon is syntactically
and logically more potent than the comma dash, although it is less
abrupt: and in the same modified way is the colon more potent than
the semicolon dash, the period than the colon dash. As the period
dash – in a sense, the one definitively final stop – is the strongest of
all points, and is, by the addition of a dash, more weighty, both syn-

tactically and rhetorically, than the simple period, so, for the same reason and to the same degree, is the colon dash more weighty than the simple colon, the semicolon dash than the simple semicolon, and the comma dash than the simple comma.

The 'exact value' of the individual points is arbitrary: there can be no single exact value, for every point varies in syntactical importance and in elocutionary duration according to the almost infinite potential variations of the contexts. But the relative importance, whether syntactical and logical, or elocutionary and rhetorical, is not arbitrary. Except for those persons who must, even at the cost of being wrong, differ from others, those two scales of rising values are correct.

It is not easy to exemplify all the simple and compound stops, together with the supernumerary question and exclamation marks, within the compass of less than perhaps a dozen sentences, arranged in two or three paragraphs. The very difficulty perhaps renders it all the more desirable that one should, as economically as possible, attempt the exemplification.

That being so – and who could doubt that it was so? – we could not shut our eyes to the danger of invasion; as many notable authorities think, a very considerable danger. The hour, however, brings the man: destiny brought Winston Churchill (refuser of all titles). Winston Churchill brought victory. – It also brought detractors; but then, success always arouses envy among the little men; – indeed, without the bitter solace of a carefully tended envy, these petty minds would be driven either to anarchy or to suicide!

In literature, as in art and music (and even in science), there would appear to be cycles, – there is almost certainly the swing of the pendulum. In literature an Elizabethan Age is followed by a Civil War, a Restoration, an 18th Century, which happily passes into a 19th Century; then – less happily – into a 20th; in science a rather different course is observable; in religion, yet another: in all, however, we see that a mighty national effort, much like an exceptional personal effort, seems to require a long period of recuperation. Among other causes that contribute to the appearance (perhaps only the delusion?) of cycles and pendulous oscillations are these:–

Long and exhausting wars; periods of great prosperity; apathy in spiritual matters; the onset of materialism; a series of vast physical disasters, such as earthquakes, hurricanes, floods, fires; and the incidence of that not entirely imaginary law – The cussedness of the universe tends to a maximum.

Chapter 12

'NOT TOO LITTLE, NOT TOO MUCH':
CLOSE PUNCTUATION AND OPEN
PUNCTUATION;
OVER-PUNCTUATION AND
UNDER-PUNCTUATION

OVER-PUNCTUATION AND under-punctuation, or overstopping and understopping, form the extremes of the two systems known either as heavy and light punctuation or as full and slight punctuation (the Fowler brothers' dichotomy), or again – though perhaps rather in the United States than in the British Commonwealth of Nations – as close and open punctuation, are analogous to industrial over-production and under-production. Neither fault is quite so easy to avoid as, by those who rarely have to punctuate and never have to produce, we are told it is.

Let us see what four authorities say about the matter.

In *The King's English*, 1906, the brothers Fowler, H. W. and F. G., make 'three general remarks':

'The work of punctuation is mainly to show, or hint at, the grammatical relation between words, phrases, clauses, and sentences; but it must not be forgotten that stops also serve to regulate pace, to throw emphasis on particular words and give them significance, and to indicate tone. . . . .

'Secondly, it is a sound principle that as few stops should be used as will do the work.' Having remarked that 'Whereas slight stopping may venture on small irregularities, full stopping that is incorrect is also unpardonable', they conclude the paragraph by saying, 'The objection to full stopping that is correct is the discomfort inflicted on readers, who are perpetually being checked like a horse with a fidgety driver': but better a slight irritation than the grave doubt which often results from the ambiguity caused by understopping.

'Thirdly, every one should make up his mind not to depend on his stops.' They do not take the place of words, nor yet of construction: properly used, they should merely clarify the former and therefore simplify the latter.

It may have been noticed that the Fowlers employ rather more

94

numerous stops than many later writers. Few even of those writers would care to claim that they write better than the Fowlers did.

'Punctuation is *close* when the points, especially commas, are used freely to mark the grouping and the separation of phrases, clauses and other structural elements of the sentences, especially when clearness and precision are the first requisite, as in this Dictionary; it is *open* when points are omitted wherever possible without ambiguity. In correspondence, *close punctuation* designates the use of punctuation marks at the end of each line of the address and of the conclusion of a letter; *open punctuation*, now more common, especially in business correspondence, designates the omission of punctuation marks at these places' (*Webster's New International Dictionary*, 2nd edition, 1934). – Compare *You Have a Point There*, Chapter 3, The Comma, § 11, Commas in Addresses, Letter-Headings, Letter-Endings.

In *Modern English Punctuation*, 2nd edition, 1949, Reginald Skelton writes, 'The term "overstopping" is preferably confined to cases where the punctuation, though palpably excessive, is technically correct or very nearly so, as in the following: –

Jeannie, too, is, just occasionally, like a good girl out of a book.
Shakespeare, it is true, had, as I have said, as respects England, the privilege which only first-comers enjoy.
I return, herewith, the S - Insurance cheque, value £35, in settlement of your fire claim, duly endorsed on behalf of the Council.'

Concerning these three examples – the first two, by the way, come from *The King's English* – the author has remarked:

(1) 'Omit all the commas, or at least the first pair.'
      (*Too*, like *also*, very rarely requires commas.)
(2) 'This sentence can only be remedied by recasting it, e.g. "It is true that Shakespeare, as I have already said, had the privilege which only new-comers to England enjoy".'
      (The interpretation is questionable. But we'll pass that.)
(3) 'Drop all the commas except the last.'
      (I should retain also the commas before and after 'value £35'. One suspects that the cheque, not the fire claim, had been endorsed.)

Understopping, says this writer, may be seen in the following quotation, 'where all seemingly unessential commas are avoided: –

To reach it they had to go through the casing which was so low that they had to lie at full length to move in it . . . Every time the bomb was moved there was a loud twanging noise as of a broken spring which added nothing to their peace of mind.'

In both sentences the omission of the comma before *which* is contrary to usage and is destructive of clarity. The author's fully pointed version runs –

To reach it, they had to go through the casing, which was so low that they had to lie full length in order to move in it . . . Every time the bomb was moved, there was a loud twanging noise, as of a broken spring, which added nothing to their peace of mind.

As that author has well said, 'Punctuation should be consistent with our mode of speech; no one could deliver such long sentences * without a break. Moreover, the avoidance of commas amounts to a denial of the main purpose of punctuation, which is to enable us to seize the writer's meaning easily and quickly . . . For although this slowing-up effect is scarcely perceptible in the individual instance, its cumulative effect, when systematically practised, is by no means negligible.'

'A further objection to systematic understopping,' he says, 'is that it inevitably leads to the occasional inadvertent omission of commas which *are* "absolutely necessary", for the prevention of a momentary misreading.'

In his *Good English: How to Write It* † G. H. Vallins has a chapter entitled 'Points of Punctuation' and there he remarks that 'Punctuation, like syntax itself, has tended to become more formal and scientific'. He includes no specific section on over- and under-punctuation, but he does draw attention to the error involved in the following sentences –

. . . while light conversation, punctuated by squeals of pain is to be expected.

---

* Mr Skelton's two other examples are these –
Only the announcement of retribution and the application of reprisals wherever possible can stop the rising tide of madness of the assassins and save hundreds of thousands of innocent victims from certain death.
The annual produce of the land and labour of any nation can be increased in its value by no other means but increasing the number of its productive labourers or the productive power of those labourers who had before been employed.
† Pan Books edition, January 1951; André Deutsch Ltd's considerably enlarged edition, May 1952.

There is something wrong with him which, with careful handling may be put right.

The new scheme instils a fresh interest in education and at the same time, engenders the beginnings of a sense of social responsibility.

As Mr Vallins rightly says, all three sentences require either no comma (open punctuation) or two commas (close punctuation); the latter thus:

. . . while light conversation, punctuated by squeals of pain, is to be expected.

There is something wrong with him which, with careful handling, may be put right.

. . . and, at the same time, engenders . . .

In the four authorities considered above, the excessive use and the excessive avoidance of the comma have naturally predominated over the excess and dearth of other points – to which, much the same remarks apply. It is, therefore, not surprising that in his article, 'A Vicious Fashion in Punctuation' (*The Journal of Education*, January 1942), Mr V. H. Collins*, author of that very useful study of synonyms, *The Choice of Words* (1952), has confined himself to the comma.

Moreover, he further restricts himself to an examination of the practice 'of inserting a comma between an adverb or adverbial phrase and the words directly following it that it qualifies. The practice generally occurs at the beginning of a sentence. Here are some typical examples selected to represent some of the most common types of sentence in which it is found.

1. In March, the Greek army was reinforced.
2. At Boulogne, a meeting was held between the two ministers.
3. Before 1914, several warnings had been given.
4. On his return, he consulted his solicitor.
5. Moreover, the morale of the army was being affected.
6. Lastly, I come to the economic factor.
7. Of course, such an operation needs time.
8. By these means, the desired result was obtained.
9. On the other hand, the overland journey was dearer.
10. After this, we can safely say . . .
11. In this way alone, I had an advantage over my enemy.
12. At the end of the war, Great Britain had an immensely strong navy.†

* Mr Collins and the Oxford University Press have generously allowed me to quote freely from this article.
† Mr Collins prints all these sentences in italic.

'Take example 1. Nobody in his punctuation-senses would think of writing *The Greek army was reinforced, in March*. On what principle, and with what advantage, is a comma interpolated merely because *in March* precedes instead of follows the subject of the sentence and its verb?

'In not one of the examples is the comma necessary or serviceable. In a few instances a comma might perhaps be defended, on the grounds that it indicates emphasis. But good writing should secure emphasis by the construction of the sentence – not by stops, any more than in our grandparents' letters by the underlining of words.'

Then why not write 'In a few instances a comma might perhaps be defended on the grounds that it indicates emphasis' – that is, without a comma after 'defended'? Of the twelve sentences chosen by Mr Collins, I should certainly punctuate two of them and perhaps punctuate a third. Thus:

5. Moreover, the morale of the army was being affected.
9. On the other hand, the overland journey was dearer.

And, if I intended to emphasize *of course*:

7. Of course, such an operation needs time.

Like *however* the conjunction, *moreover* requires a comma or a pair of commas. Compare sentence 5 with

However, nothing can be done about it –

and the more usual

Nothing, however, can be done about it

with

Nothing, moreover, can be done about it.

Mr Collins, who ranks among the more intelligent of our writers upon language, has noted *however* the conjunction and distinguished it from *however* the adverb. He opportunely adds that 'most of the other exceptions are where an adverb consists of a word that can be used also as another part of speech. Here again a comma is needed to avoid false scent * as in the following examples: –

(a) Besides, these were not yet ready.
(b) Shortly after, he was told that it would be dangerous to remain.
(c) Further, violence often defeats its object.

---

* Most stylists would point *scent* with a comma.

'In these sentences a comma is desirable to show at once in (*a*) that *Besides* is not being used as a preposition governing *these*; in (*b*) that *after* is not introducing a temporal subordinate clause; in (*c*) that *Further* is not an adjective qualifying *violence*.'

Having noted that *by the way* used metaphorically and its loose synonym *incidentally* require a comma because they stand outside the main structure of the sentence and constitute the writer's aside (equivalent to *I might*, or *I should, add that*), Mr Collins adduces several other examples requiring a clarifying comma * –

(*a*) Further, on examination a discrepancy was revealed.
   (Unless there were a comma, *on*, which is here a preposition governing *examination*, might at first seem to be joined to *Further* to form a combined adverbial phrase.)
(*b*) Before long, suspicions were bound to arise.
   (The comma here shows at once that *long* is not an adjective qualifying *suspicions*.)
(*c*) After all, his work had to come first.
   (The comma shows that *all* does not equal *all of* (his work).)
(*d*) By the end of 1916, 273 deaths had occurred.
   (Without a comma the collocation of numerals might be confusing.)

In a private communication,† Mr Collins asks me to 'damn the nasty practice of separating with a comma a subject from its verb, and a verb from its object' (or presumably its complement). 'I don't refer to parenthetical phrases, etc., with two commas.'

This is the sort of thing he means:

He, very ably, made the whole thing sound as simple as in fact it was
He will be, undoubtedly, very much afraid
'The charm in Nelson's history, is, the unselfish greatness'(EMERSON, quoted by the FOWLERS)
He saw, with misgiving, that the wall might topple over
He heard, with elation, the wedding bells.

Not one of those pairs of commas is necessary. In addition to being unnecessary, those commas destroy the natural flow of the sentences; the Emersonian example is intolerably pompous.

We have covered most of the ground. But whenever I ask myself

* The remarks after (*a*) . . . (*d*) are Mr Collins's.
† The comma after 'communication' is required stylistically, even though neither syntax nor logic nor clarity demands it

whether I have indeed covered most of it, I turn either to H. W. Fowler's *Modern English Usage* or to the Fowler brothers' *The King's English*. The latter book chasteningly warns me that I have yet to mention * (1) *perhaps* and *probably*; (2) *indeed* and *assuredly, certainly, indubitably*, etc.; (3) *thus*; (4) *apparently* and *seemingly*; (5) *namely*; (6) *therefore* and the conjunctival *thence* and *hence*; (7) conjunctival *now* and *then*; (8) conjunctival *for* and *because*; (9) *and*; (10) *yet* and *nevertheless*, conjunctives; (11) *in the main* and *for the most part*. In the first four of the following sentences every comma or pair of commas is unnecessary, as, in No. 5, the comma after 'namely',

(1) I shall, perhaps, be there [*or*, I shall be there, perhaps]; probably, I shall not.
(2) You will, indeed, find him much changed. Certainly [*or*, assuredly or indubitably], he has much changed.
(3) Thus, his novel made him many friends.
(4) He has, apparently [*or*, seemingly], done very well for himself already.
(5) They lost all their effects, namely, two suitcases, a brief case, a bandbox and two brown-paper parcels.

(6) Of the 'many words that are half adverbs and half conjunctions, like *therefore*', the Fowlers have aptly remarked, 'We have the right to comma them off if we like; but, unless it is done with a definite purpose, it produces perplexity as well as heaviness', as in this quotation from Trollope:

> Both Tom and John knew this; and, therefore, John – the soft-hearted one – kept out of the way.

Compare:

> Troy fell in ruins. Thence [*or*, Hence], the tears.

(7) But the purely conjunctival *now* and *then*, as distinct from the purely adverbial *now* and *then*, do require commas, to make it, even to the most moronic, clear that here we have conjunctions, not adverbs equivalent to 'at this time' and 'at that time'. Contrast:

> Now I think of it, he did act suspiciously

and:

> Now, if you think of it, he did act suspiciously
> (= But, if . . .);

---

* The Fowlers mention nine of these terms.

> Then I had to behave oddly. –
> *or:* I had to behave oddly then.
> Then, he did not know about it. –
> *or:* He did not know about it, then.

(8) In the following sentences, the commas after *for* and *because* are purely elocutionary. They may be necessary for the guidance of pupils reading aloud: but when did the needs of such pupils constitute a criterion of punctuation?

> I don't know. For, I have no means of knowing.
> You must not feel like that – because, *you* were not responsible for the safety of the party.

(9) The merely elocutionary *and* is still worse –

> They planned to rob the bank; they formed a party to commit the crime; and, they committed it.

(10) Both *nevertheless* and the connective, as opposed to the adverbial, *yet* stand in no need of commas. The following sentences are therefore faultily punctuated:

> I don't like the man. Nevertheless, I shall judge him solely on his merits.
> I don't like the man, but, nevertheless, I shall . . .
> You failed miserably. Yet, you were bound to fail.
> You failed miserably: and, yet, you were . . .

(11) Such adverbial phrases as *in the main, for the most part, on the whole, all in all,* require a comma after, or before and after, only when their lack would set up an ambiguity.* Contrast the following pairs:

> In the main the army was very powerful
> In the main, army needs were greater than naval.
>
> On the whole their fears seemed to be excessive
> On the whole, ways and means took up the most time.

All in all seldom, *for the most part* never, creates ambiguity:

> For the most part they behaved well
> All in all they behaved well.

But:

> All in all, things went very well.

---

* This feature either corresponds with or at least resembles a contingency treated by Mr Collins.

There are many other relevant instances; but since most of them are analogous or else similar to those noted in the sub-groups (1)–(3) we have just examined, we need not deal with them separately. We have seen enough to convince us – or at least suggest to us – that, here as in all other questions of punctuation, the middle way is not merely the safest; it is the best.

Once or twice we have, in the opinions expressed by the five authorities we chose for quotation, found either stated or implied a belief that punctuation is a necessary evil and that it deals with the merest mechanics of writing. To some extent, that is true; but only to some extent. The truth is wider, more helpful, more valuable.

To everyone who writes pedestrianly and humdrumly, punctuation must be a humdrum thing: part of the mechanics of writing. To him who tries to write well, still more to him who does indeed write well, punctuation forms not a part of the mechanics of his art, but an integral part of his art as a whole.

What has happened so to affect the attitude of all sorts of men, the stupid, the normal, the clever, the brilliant and the profound, is perhaps this. Unless punctuation is noticeably bad – that is, incorrect or inadequate or excessive, sometimes both incorrect and inadequate, or incorrect and excessive – or noticeably excellent either in its precision or in its subtlety, they do not think of the punctuation at all; and, taking it for granted, they inevitably tend to depreciate it.

Some of those who urge that punctuation should be as open (that is, as light) as possible have clear and logical minds; they rejoice, or say they rejoice, in legal English. 'In legal documents, where clearness of reference is the first essential, punctuation-marks are systematically omitted precisely because this omission necessitates a constructional expression the meaning of which cannot be mistaken' (T. F. & M. F. A. HUSBAND, *Punctuation: Its Principles and Practice*, 1905). That is a myth. I have seen various legal documents: and every last one of them would have been the better for at least a little punctuation.

The upholders of an extremely open punctuation forget a very important fact. That sort of punctuation serves fairly well for simple description, simple exposition, simple narrative, but it proves horribly inadequate for the more subtle and sophisticated and aesthetic kinds of description, exposition, narrative – let alone for poetry, drama, belles-lettres, several kinds of history, most philosophy, much science.

Communication is the primary purpose, therefore clarity the primary need, of writing; but equally they are far from being the only purpose and need. For many kinds of writing, punctuation is all the better for being fairly close, although not very close. *Mēden agan*: Nothing too much!

The exact amount of punctuation depends upon both the subject and the manner. But, whatever the manner, whatever the subject, whatever the amount, punctuation is important. At the lowest estimate, it is obviously far more important than spelling; yet it receives much less attention, perhaps because it is much more difficult. You will find that virtually all depreciators and literally all deriders of punctuation are themselves indifferent or, at best, humdrum punctuators.

Book II
ALLIES AND ACCESSORIES

Book II

ALLIES AND ACCESSORIES

Chapter 13

CAPITAL LETTERS *

A *capital*, elliptical for a *capital letter*, derives from Latin *capitalis*, of, at, for, with the head, itself from the stem *capit-* of *caput* (genitive *capitis*), the head. A capital or upper-case letter is distinguished from a small or lower-case letter of either a style of writing or a font of type by having greater height and usually a different form. (Small capitals have the form of capitals but the height of small letters.) The verb is 'to *capitalize*' or 'to *capital*'.

'Closely bound up with punctuation is the use of capital letters. Here again we are in a somewhat vague, indeterminate world.' Outside 'fairly well-defined limits, the writer has to walk warily in a kind of no-man's-land'. In short, 'the good writer will observe the main conventions; but beyond these he has the privilege and responsibility of deciding between . . . capitals and small letters. His use of capitals, like his punctuation generally, should exactly correspond with his meaning.' (G. H. VALLINS, *Good English: How to Write It.*)

Apart from the use of a capital for the first letter of the first word in a sentence, the most important group of capitalled words consists of Proper Names. Other important groups are the Punctuational, the Rhetorical, the Abbreviational, and Trade Names.

To classify the various words and word-groups requiring a capital is surprisingly difficult. By far the most comprehensive classification I have seen is that which was established in the 1934 recension of *Webster's New International Dictionary*; yet to even that classification I find that four or five additions – one of them, important – have to be made. Without benefit of Webster I should, however, have probably overlooked one or two of the sub-classes in the following survey, arranged functionally rather than, as Webster's, itemizingly. In this

---

* Capitals in relation to titles of books and articles will be dealt with in Chapter 19.

arrangement I have aimed less at being impeccably logical than at serving the public's convenience: there exist too many overlappings for me to achieve anything more than a partial and specious logic.

I: PUNCTUATIONAL

(1) A capital is used for the first letter in every sentence:

He was a brave man.
A brave man, such as Lord Roberts, is rather taken for granted in the Army.

(2) Not only after a full stop, which strictly ends, not announces, a sentence but also, at least normally, after a question mark or an exclamation mark, is an initial capital required.

What did you see? And what did you do?
That's not the way to treat a lady! Even if she's no lady.

(3) After a colon, especially if it announces a definition, a formal description, a list, or a speech.

As an example of the definition that could apply to only one thing and is yet ludicrously inadequate is this: Man is the only animal that reads.
I replied: You can't do that, at least not here.

(4) But then, all 'internal' sentences – sentences consisting of a speech or a full-sentence quotation – begin with a capital, whether the stop preceding the internal sentence be a colon or a dash or a comma; thus:

I asked him point-blank, Then why do it?
I asked him, after much hesitation on my part and much embarrassment on his – Then why do it?

Only when the quotation merges either almost indistinguishably or very neatly with the main body of a sentence, or at worst with the general trend of the discourse, is the initial capital abandoned. To do that, however, the writer, unless he be 'concealing' the quotation, has to employ quotation marks. (See Chapter 15.)

Closely allied to the punctuational capitals are the

II. RHETORICAL

(1) Two words conventionally receive the capital. These are the vocative *O* and the exclamatory *Oh*.

I ask, O King, that my life be graciously spared
Tell me, O my son, how you contrived to spend so much money in so short a time.

The exclamatory *O* is more often written *Oh* or *Oh!* If *Oh* is used in direct address, it takes a comma:

Always – Oh, how conscious I am of this! – something goes wrong.
Soon I must be going – Oh, Bill, would you help me to pack my things?

In modern practice, however, both the vocative *O* (or *Oh*) and the exclamatory *Oh* (or *O*) are frequently written *o* or *oh*. Here we have logic overcoming convention.

The only other truly rhetorical use of capitals is that for personification: an inanimate object or an abstract idea represented as a person, as in Webster's excellent example:

Of old sat Freedom on the heights.

Compare: Faith, Hope and Charity

and: That was Chaos; this is Life.

Such an example as –

To mankind, Spring comes as a renewal –

stands on the borderline between personification and calendar (see Proper Names below).

III: TYPOGRAPHICAL

First there is the nominative of the First Person: *I*: the only pronoun that, in English, takes a capital, unless the reference be to the Deity (VIII: RELIGIOUS). Yet Middle English had *i*, *ich*, *ic*, from Old English *ic*, and no other modern Indo-European language thus dignifies its 'I' with a capital. The capital *I* was established by early printers, mainly to avoid the ambiguity that had been caused by a confusion of such variant forms as *i*, *j*, *I*; more precisely, the use of *I* (for 'ego') was a specialization of writing a 'long' *i* when the letter stood alone.

The other capital that can fairly be described as typographical is that which comes at the beginning of every verse-line, irrespective of whether or not the line-beginning corresponds to the sentence-beginning. Thus:

> Lars Porsenna of Clusium,
> By the nine gods he swore,
> That the great house of Tarquin
> Should suffer wrong no more.

Modern poets, however, tend to capitalize verse in the same way as they capitalize prose; this innovation extends also to personification. Here, again, we have logic and good sense expelling a needless convention. The matter is divided into verse-lines: what more guidance could anyone expect and what other guidance could he need?

IV: LITERARY

This admittedly arbitrary heading serves very conveniently to introduce a set of terms comprised by the divisions of a literary work. An example will say all that needs to be said:

> In *The Rise and Fall of Fission*, Book III, Part ii, Chapter 2, Section *c*, we find a puzzling reference to *Don Juan*, Canto II.

Often, however, when the reference is simple, a capital letter is optional; a small letter occurs at least as frequently, as in the second word of:

> *Fission*, ch. 18, will provide you with all you need.

This is therefore a matter, not for posing a principle, but for decision by individual taste.

Literary rather than typographical or rhetorical is the double convention regulating the way in which one begins a letter –

> DEAR SIR OR MADAM,
> 　　　　　　　　　This may seem to be an unconventional
> approach. As it happens ......

The word or words other than 'Dear' or 'My dear' (My dear Mother – Father – Sister – etc.) take a capital or capitals (My Lord Duke); so also does the first word of the letter proper.

V: LEGAL

Although it is not obligatory, it is advisable, for laymen to write of one's last will and testament as one's Will. Occasionally the capital letter forms a safeguard. Manifestly a useful distinction exists between these two sentences:

His will has not been made known.
His Will has not been made known.

VI: COMMERCIAL

A trade name – 'better called a *trade-mark name*' (Webster) – takes a capital when it constitutes a name either invented or arbitrarily bestowed, whether by the manufacturer or by that merchant who markets it, to distinguish a process or an article produced or sold by him. The broader term *trade mark* (or *trade-mark* or *trademark*) covers not only a word or words or an initial or initials, but also symbols and devices; that word or those words, that initial or those initials, are likewise written with a capital.

He owns a Rolls Royce, a Cadillac and a Ford.
(In each instance, 'car' is understood.)
Her Hoover is worn out.
(Here 'vacuum cleaner' is understood.)
The Kodak he uses is different from my Leica, but that does not make it better.

For such terms a small letter is permissible only when, for example, 'kodak' is used for any small hand camera. But be careful: trade-mark names are protected by law: they must never be used in infringement or in any other unfair competition.

VII: OFFICIAL (other than titles of honour)

These fall into four sub-groups:

(1) Such words as *ward, district, county, apartment, province, state, presidency, territory, dominion,* take a capital when they refer to a definite, officially recognized division whether political or administrative. Thus, Cape *Province* (*C.P.*) of South Africa, or Wellington

Province, New Zealand, or the *Province* of Ontario, Canada; such or such a *Ward* of New York City; the *State* of Washington, the *District* of Columbia; Tanganyika *Territory*, East Africa, and the Northern *Territory*, Australia; Madras *Presidency*; the *County* of Yorkshire, and the plural York *County* of the United *States* of America; the *Dominion* of Canada, the *Dominion* of New Zealand; the *Commonwealth* of Australia; the *Department* of Seine-et-Marne; the *Condominium* of the New Hebrides in the S.W. Pacific.

(2) Such governmental and municipal titles as Member (of Parliament, the House of Representatives, etc.) – Senator – Minister – Governor, Governor-General, President; Councillor – Mayor, Lord Mayor. The corresponding adjectives, when used specifically, as in: the Presidential election.

(3) The Army – the Royal Navy, the United States Navy – the (Royal) Air Force.

(4) Names of the Units of the Fighting Services; for instance, H.M.S. *Apollo*, U.S.S. *Missouri* – The 1st Army, the 2nd Army Corps, the 29th Division, the 7th Brigade, the 3rd Battalion, the 2nd Company; the 2nd Battery; No. 1 Wing, Group 2, 2nd Squadron, No. 1 Flight; Air Raid Post, No. 3.

VIII: RELIGIOUS

Beginning with the Deity, we write God – God the Father, God the Son, God the Holy Ghost; God Almighty – the Almighty – the Eternal Father; Allah; the Buddha; Christ, Jesus Christ – the Redeemer or Saviour – the Son of Man; the Holy Ghost, the Holy Spirit; Mary the Mother of God. Pronouns and possessive adjectives referring to God, or to Christ, likewise, take a capital, thus: God in His infinite mercy; . . . Jesus Christ, Who so loved the world; He giveth and He taketh away.

The Bible and the parts of the Bible, like other sacred books, take a capital: the Bible (or, The Bible); the (or The) Talmud; the (The) Koran or Alcoran; the (The) Vedas; the (The) New Testament – the Scriptures – the (rarely The) Good Book – the (The) Book. So do the directly derivative adjectives, when applied literally, as in: Biblical criticism – the Talmudic text – Koranic imagery – Vedic philology; Scriptural, but often scriptural, authority.

Religions and sects or, as we now call them, denominations; their members; religious orders, confessions, masses, communions; a specific cathedral, basilica – church, chapel – mosque; observances and festivals, forming a link with the calendar (group IX); – all these are dignified with capitals, thus: Christianity, Judaism, Mohammedanism, Buddhism, Confucianism; the (Holy) Church (the Christian religion); Christians, Mohammedans, Buddhists; the (Holy) Catholic Church – the Church of England – Presbyterianism, Methodism; Catholics, Anglicans, Presbyterians, Methodists, Baptists; the Benedictines, the Jesuits; the Augsburg Confession (or the Confession of Augsburg) – the Confession of Dositheus; the Creed of Constantinople, or the Constantinopolitan Creed – the Apostles' Creed, often simply The (or the) Creed; the Mass – Holy Communion – the Holy Sacrament; the Vatican, Westminster Cathedral, Westminster Abbey, York Minster, the Basilica of St Sophia – the Church of St David – the Royal Chapel; Christmas(tide); Easter, Lent; Shrovetide, Shrove Tuesday; Palm Sunday.

IX: CALENDAR

This group is obviously linked with the preceding. The days of the week, like the months of the year; Saints' days, like quarterdays and religious festivals; specific holidays, whether civil or religious: all these take a capital. Thus: Thursday, August 7, 1952; St Patrick's Day; Good Friday, Easter Monday, Whit Monday, Independence Day, August Bank Holiday, Labor (Labour) Day, Anzac Day, 'Vendémiaire (vintage) began on September 22'.

X: HISTORICAL

This group embraces the following varieties of historical fact and theory –

(1) Eras, epochs, ages, periods, whether strictly historical or prehistoric or geological or imaginary (mankind's indefeasible optimism), as in: the Christian Era, the Mohammedan Era; A.D., B.C.; Neolithic, Palaeolithic; Jurassic, Devonian; 'the Niagara epoch of the Silurian period'; the Crusades; the Middle Ages, the Dark Ages; the Golden Age, the Millennium.

(2) Treaties and pacts, laws and acts, important events, all these

take a capital, as in: the Treaty of Versailles; the Justinian Code, the
Salic Law, the Acta Martyrum; the Battle of Salamis – Waterloo –
Gettysburg.

(3) Parliaments, congresses, councils, other legislative bodies;
municipal bodies; political parties; organizations and institutions political, administrative, religious, scientific, etc.; exhibitions, expositions,
shows; all these collectivities assume – some of them arrogate to
themselves – a capital. Thus: the Parliament of Britain, Barebone's
Parliament, Library of Congress, the Congress of Vienna, the
Chamber of Deputies, the House of Representatives; Council of
State, Council of Ephesus, the Governor's Council, the London
County Council (L.C.C.); the Whigs and the Tories, Republicans
and Democrats, Conservatives and Communists, Liberals and Social-
ists; the Engineers' Union; the Rotarians, the British Legion; the
French Academy; the Benevolent and Protective Order of Elks, the
Free and Accepted Masons; the 1851 Exhibition, Chicago's Century
of Progress Exposition, the Agricultural and Pastoral Show (of this
district or that).

XI: GEOGRAPHICAL AND TOPOGRAPHICAL

With the political divisions treated at OFFICIAL (VII, 1), compare
such definite geographical divisions as the Southern Hemisphere, the
Old World and the New, the North and the South, East (or the
Orient) and West (or the Occident), Asia and America, England and
Virginia, York and New York. Note also that, when they form part
of specific names, generic terms take a capital like the rest of the
name; also that two or more generic terms may form a specific geographical name; thus: the Holy Roman Empire, the British Commonwealth of Nations (the British Empire), the United States of America;
the Red Sea, the Black Sea, the Yellow Sea – the Atlantic Ocean, the
Pacific Ocean; the County of Yorkshire – Cook County, in the State
of Minnesota; Cape Cod, the River Nile, Lake Victoria Nyanza,
Mount Everest.

That general principle extends to topography, thus: Oxford
Street, Fifth Avenue, Kensington Gore.

XII: SCIENTIFIC AND TECHNICAL

(1) In zoology and botany, every genus (but no species) takes a capital. In binomial scientific names – names consisting of two terms – the first term represents the genus, the second the species, thus: Houstonia caerulea. Breeds of horses, cattle, sheep, pigs, etc., take a capital: the Arab, the Percheron, the Shetland pony.

(2) Likewise the New (or Scientific) Latin names for the zoological and botanical categories higher than a genus, i.e. for family, order, class, and, highest of all, phylum in zoology or division in botany, – these take a capital.

(3) The names of the planets and asteroids and stars, of constellations, of comets and meteors, and even of the earth, moon, sun when they occur in astronomical lists, take a capital: 'The most important planets are Earth, Venus, Mars, Mercury, Jupiter, Saturn, Uranus, Neptune and Pluto'; 'Among the constellations we may name Ursa Major and Ursa Minor, the Great Bear and the Lesser Bear'; 'Stars include such shining examples as Sun and Moon, Betelgeuse and Sirius'; Halley's Comet.

(4) Technicalities. Wherever a term, whether single word or several words, is used strictly as a technicality, it takes or tends to take a capital: certainly a capital is taken whenever a technicality would, if lower-cased, be ambiguous, but, if upper-cased, entirely clear. Thus:

When he speaks of a proper name he does not necessarily mean a Proper Name; probably all he means is a suitable name. Likewise, when he says that to call a woman a slut is to use a common word, he isn't thinking that it is also a Common Noun.

English grammar is now treated under the three main heads of Phonology, Accidence, Syntax.

The kingdom has in war-time been well served by the Defence of the Realm Act; in time of peace, the Crown has recourse to Act of State.

Mr Skelton has in his *Modern English Punctuation* drawn attention to what might be called semi-technicalities. To ensure that a phrase or other word-group be read as an entity or be treated as a single term – in short, to unify the words of a phrase or a group – the easiest way to do it is to capitalize the essential words, thus:

It may be a nuisance to learn, but it is at least a convenience to know the Parts of Speech.

What Every Cricketer Should Practise is hardly less exciting than What Every Footballer Should Avoid.

You surely see that Physical Training has its importance.

XIII: PROPER NAMES

(1) By the term Proper Names we mean especially the names of places (Asia, Scotland, Chicago, the Mississippi, Mont Blanc) – compare, therefore, group XI, Geographical – and the names of Persons (John, John Smith, Sir John Smith; the way of Martha and the way of Mary).

(2) But also certain things, e.g. the titles of books, newspapers, magazines; stars and planets; ships and airships and regiments; days and Saints' days; etc. Most of these have been particularized in groups I–XII.

(3) Titles of honour joined to a Proper Name: Queen Elizabeth the Second – Queen Elizabeth – the Queen (= the queen now reigning); President Roosevelt or familiarly the President (either Theodore or Franklin Delano while he was President of the United States of America); the King of England; the Emperor Augustus.

(4) Epithets serving, either wholly or in part, as Proper Nouns, as: the Iron Duke, the Iron Chancellor; William the Conqueror, William the Silent; Farmer George; the Swan of Avon; the Sage of Baltimore – Chelsea – Concord – Highgate; the Apostle of Free Trade – of Temperance; Father Abraham, the Father of His Country.

(5) The names of races and nations, peoples and tribes, like the names of languages, take a capital:

The French speak a Romance language.

He wishes to learn French; that won't be very easy for him to do at all thoroughly, for he has no Latin.

The German people consists of Saxons, Bavarians, Prussians, Hanoverians, and certain other tribe-survivals.

The language of the Shawnees is Algonquin.

(6) The derivatives of Proper Nouns usually take a capital when these derivatives are used literally or primarily, as in: Georgian poetry, i.e. English poetry of the reign of King George the Fifth; Spanish pride; 'The English language is becoming Americanized, for the number of Americanisms current in Britain is increasing daily'; a meeting-place, Gallice (or Gallicé or Gallicè) rendezvous.

(7) Note that a Common Noun, by being individualized or particularized – i.e. rendered specific – in meaning, becomes virtually a Proper Name. Thus:

I must speak to Father about that. (My father.)

The President is expecting me. (The president in power at the moment.
– Compare sub-section 3 above.)
   But Sonny (= my son, your son, his son) won't like it.
   Yes; Uncle will agree, but Aunt, if I know her, will refuse.

   .(8) Nicknames and pet-names take a capital: they too are virtually
Proper Names.

Chapter 14

ITALICS

EMPHASIS; DIFFERENTIATION AND DISTINCTION; QUOTATION

ITALIC WRITING is ordinary writing underlined; italic (originally Italic) printing is in a different type from roman (originally Roman) or ordinary type, in that it is lighter and also in that it slopes to the right. Words so written and printed are said to be *in italic* or *in italics*. To write or print words thus is to *italicize* them. *Italic type* is so called because it was designed and first used in 1501 by an Italian printer, Aldo Manuzio, whose name was latinized as *Aldus Manutius*.

'Italic letters,' says Webster, 'are now used chiefly to distinguish words for emphasis, importance, antithesis' and particularization. But that is to say rather too little. The chief purposes of italics may be set forth under eight heads.

One preliminary remark, covering all eight classes of italics, has to be made. If within a word-group or a phrase, a clause or a sentence, written in italics one wishes to emphasize a letter or a word or a phrase, one has to use roman type – or, in handwriting and typescript, to omit the underlining of the letter or word or phrase.

In all my life (he said) *I have never succeeded in doing exactly what I most wished to do.*
The word is spelt *human*, not *humane*.

§ 1: Emphasis

Italics are most often used to indicate the word, the word-group or phrase, even the sentence upon which the writer wishes to lay the greatest – or, at the least, a great – emphasis. A good writer italicizes for this purpose only when he cannot obtain the required degree of emphasis in any other way. Stylistically, emphasis is best obtained by either structural, i.e. syntactical, or rhetorical means. Too many writers use italics in a manner purely elocutionary. Italics, according to *The King's English*, are a confession of weakness. That statement, however true of most elocutionary and some rhetorical uses, obviously does not apply to §§ 5–8.

> He *hates* me.
> It's the only way it *can* be done.

Compare: He hates me very much.
> Only in this (or, that) way can it be done.

§ 2: Importance

Closely akin to emphasis is importance: importance of subject matter, not merely the importance, in the writer's eyes, of some aspect of the subject.

> Whom do you think I saw in Odessa? *John Kremlin Smithers*, whom the brigands were supposed to have killed in Georgia late in 1951.
> At the University of Cook Province my daughter is studying French, English and – who would have guessed it? – *cookery*.
> He was brave, kind, *good*.
> He believes in the principle, *First* things first.

§ 3: Antithesis

Antithesis constitutes a device at once elocutionary and rhetorical and stylistic. But, if well worded, it is so effective stylistically that it should not need italics to weight it still further: too often italics here resemble a comedian's hopeful laugh at the end of the joke he has just made or is about to finish making. Those persons who cannot perceive an antithesis will not feel much more keenly if you knock them on the head with italics; you might easily stun them.

> To Dives the *world*, to Cleopatra the *flesh*, to Mephistopheles the *Devil*.
> *You* may like it, but *he* dislikes it intensely.

Compare: To Dives, the world; to Cleopatra, the flesh; and to Mephistopheles, the Devil.
> Although (or, Whereas) you may like it, he, on the contrary, dislikes it intensely.

§ 4: Particularization

Here the writer so strongly wishes to single out a word, a phrase, a clause, that he italicizes it and therefore ensures that you notice it and remember and perhaps even ponder it, as in: I think that *hubris* is the word you want.

Compare: In that turbulent group of fellows I was able to discern only
John and Bill and *Jim*.
Particularization can be effected best by some structural or syntactical device –

with: In that turbulent group of fellows I was able to discern only
John and Bill and notably (or, especially) Jim.
Particularization, you will readily understand, can be best effected by a structural or syntactical device.

Uniting the purposes of Importance and Particularization is the sign-posting that determines the use of italics in:

*A*pt *a*lliteration's *a*rtful *a*id.

§ 5: Technicalities, Slang, Dialect

For reasons of clarity or perhaps convenience a writer will set off in italics any and every highly technical, every slangy or dialectal word or phrase in his narrative, description or exposition; in dialogue there is less justification for italics, because into all except the most formal dialogue such words and phrases fall naturally enough.

Here, then, was the *trainasium* of which we had heard so much.
This was that uneasy period of what certain American journalists called the *phoney* war.
We went, just as hard as we could *tivvy*.

§ 6: Foreign Words and Phrases

Foreign, including Greek and Latin, words and phrases not yet acclimatized in English are, by the use of italics, clearly shown to be almost shamelessly exotic and quite spectacularly un-English. Unacclimatized foreignisms should, indeed, be displayed as such, for some Britons and Americans and many foreigners would otherwise fail to think of them as other than English. But why use them at all?

He wore his *fin de siècle Weltschmerz* and *accidia* with a most engaging *panache* and *hauteur*.

To him the *status quo* was sacred: *laudator temporis acti* he was, nor did he care who knew it.

Mēden agan sums up his philosophy. Not for him the excesses of *hubris*, nor the allurement of *kudos*.

§ 7: Titles of Books and Periodicals

For a full treatment, see Chapter 19. Here we need only remark that the titles of books, newspapers and magazines are shown more often by the use of italics than by any other means.

I see in *The Times* that X. died yesterday.
Gone with the Wind is almost too famous.

But be sure to give the full title, not merely a part of it, in italics. One so often sees this sort of thing:

Carlyle wrote several great works. My favourite is the *French Revolution*. (For *The French Revolution*.)

§ 8: Quotation

One of the ways in which to indicate either speech or quotation is to italicize the word or words.

Exclaiming *hurrah*, he threw his hat into the pond.
(Note that 'Exclaiming' renders it unnecessary to put an exclamation mark after *hurrah*.)
He coldly said *Good-day to you, Sir*, and turned abruptly to his companion.
The exact quotation is *to fresh woods and pastures new*, not *to fresh fields* . . .

Chapter 15

QUOTATION MARKS OR INVERTED COMMAS
WHETHER ABSOLUTE OR RELATIVE

LIKE ITALICS and (Chapter 17) hyphens, quotation marks are to be used as sparingly as possible. They should light the way, not darken it.

In handwriting and typing, they are usually indicated thus: "......" or '......', although many people take time to make their 'quotes' resemble those of printing: "......" or '......'.

Formerly "double quotes" were obligatory. Nowadays 'single quotes' are fast becoming very common. An inner quotation differs from the main quotation, in that primary '......' takes secondary "......" and primary "......" takes secondary '......'. 'The more logical course would seem to be that single marks should represent the first quotation and double the one contained in it. Consistency would then require that single marks only should be used in ordinary quotation,' as T. F. and M. F. A. Husband say in their very good, long-forgotten little book, *Punctuation: Its Principles and Practice*, 1905.* (See also § 8.)

§ 1: Strictly Quoted

Quotation marks – too sweepingly stated, by a notable authority in 1893, to be 'now called *inverted commas*', an inaccurate term and an unrevelatory – are primarily used to indicate the exact words of a speaker or of a text. Obviously 'He said that "he was not a fool" ' is incorrect if the second 'he' refers to the speaker. Unless the speaker were referring to a person other than himself, the speaker's words were 'I am not a fool'.

Examples of correct usage (but not of the most complicated usage – see Chapter 22) are these:

You have declared, 'I am Tecumseh Siwash'. But can you prove that you are?

---

* In a footnote they remark, 'The Clarendon Press follows this method'. So do most writers – at least, most of those writers who can get their own way.

You say, 'I am Tecumseh Siwash. Why should you doubt my word?' But I do doubt it.

Someone has said, 'The wind bloweth where it listeth'; not 'The wind bloweth where it listeth!': there was no occasion for an exclamation mark.

'I cannot,' he replied, 'incur a debt for you. But if you like' (to myself I breathed, 'Oh, I do!') 'I shall speak in your behalf.'

'You, John, have followed my advice, "Take nobody's word for it. Check everything yourself!" But have you, my dear boy, noticed that my dictum requires the rider, "What you yourself have written will, after a lapse of years, itself need to be checked"?'

§ 2: Emphasis and Importance

If a writer wishes to emphasize the importance of a word or a word-group, he can theoretically do so by using quotation marks. In practice, however, he very rarely does this for any purpose other than those to be set forth in §§ 3–7.

There is one exception, yet even that could be included in § 4. Particularization: any word named as a word. Thus:

He objects to all misusages, but especially to 'anticipate' used as a synonym of 'expect'.

§ 3: Antithesis

The use of quotation marks to point an antithesis is comparable to the use of italics for that purpose; it is comparable also to their use for particularization. Usually such quotation marks betoken a mind pernickety rather than penetrating, and apparently and superficially rather than really subtle: in other words, such marks are to be avoided. But to show what I mean:

'Moral law' he revered, 'ethical obligation' he resented.

The 'cause of justice', he thought, is a 'just cause'.

He concerns himself more with 'measures' than with 'mankind'.

§ 4: Particularization

One kind of particularization has been mentioned in § 2, second paragraph: words named as words. Another kind occurs in:

He liked to think that now he would be free to study the history of such moral ideas as 'reverence', 'reputation', 'respect'; above all, 'respect'.
Of all the subjects proposed to him, he chose 'the penalties of selfishness' as the most likely to appeal to his judges.
Abstract nouns, especially 'veneration' and 'virtue', have a long and often intricate semantic history.

Particularization of a word usually amounts, in practice, to definition or clarification and, most importantly, to a sharp transition from vague generalities to sharp particulars.

§ 5: Technicalities, Slangy, Dialectal, Illiterate Expressions

Here we have an alternative to italics: compare the preceding chapter, § 5.

This is the process – some call it the principle – known as 'ease of pronunciation'.
He threatens to 'tan your hide' if he catches you stealing apples again.
She's 'no oil-painting', it is true, but, as you know, she has 'a heart of gold'.

§ 6: Foreign Words and Phrases

For 'italic(s)' in § 6 of the preceding chapter (see pp. 120–1) substitute 'quotation marks' and you have all that can usefully be said on the matter.

Lucy found his 'savoir-faire' and 'je ne sais quoi' almost irresistible. She remembered that her own ideal was one of 'sans peur et sans reproche'.
Such a phrase as 'longo intervallo' exemplifies that all-pervasive duality which characterizes every long-established language: the verbal counterpart of the space-time continuum of modern physics.

§ 7: Titles of Books and Periodicals

In 1905 the Husbands wrote, 'It is no longer usual to put within inverted commas titles of books, names of newspapers, periodicals, etc. These are now generally printed in italics.' *The Quarterly Review* has retained its ancient practice: and there is this to be said for it, that where such titles abound, it does prevent the page from developing a sort of chequerboard effect.

For one set of titles, however, many writers do use quotation marks.

He must have read that newspaper article – 'How to Flee Fleas' – in *The Funmaker.*

See *The Thrice-Yearly Review,* 'Anabasis Xenophon's March from A. to B. in Lesser Utopia'.

In those two sentences, as the blindest will have seen, quotation marks have been rightly employed: they are clear, where italics might be ambiguous; they distinguish the part from the whole; and they preserve a sense of proportion, to mention only three of half a dozen reasons. They might be compared to the use of quotation marks to distinguish a nickname from a proper name, as in:

James 'Hobo' Stevens *or* James ('Hobo') Stevens.

§ 8: Typographical

The subject of quotation within quotation has been mentioned in the preliminary remarks at the head of this chapter. The simplest rule is: Alternate! Single, double, single, double. To go beyond single-double is rarely necessary and should, whenever possible, be avoided; to go as far as single-double-single-double is to incur a charge of insanity. The worst offender, so far, has been George Moore.

If "double quotes" be preferred to 'single quotes', the alternation is double, single, double, single. The majority of thinking people now prefer 'single quotes'. Two examples will suffice.

'I don't much care for your addiction to such horrific words as "eventuality" and "transpire",' he said, far more in sorrow than in anger.

The text reads: 'Dr X. Y. Z. is reported to have said, "I think that anyone who uses 'eventuality' and 'transpire', for 'event' and 'to happen', ought to be deported". He seemed to be grieved at this evidence of man's frailty.' From this point onwards, the text has been rendered indecipherable by the tears shed by the worthy Doctor.

In a consecutive quoted passage, where the quotation runs to two or more of those stylistic divisions which we call paragraphs * (Chapter 20), the quotation marks are to be repeated at the beginning of every relevant paragraph and, of course, at the end of the discourse. Most writers also put quotation marks at the end of every paragraph; this is a matter of taste; I myself use only one end-of-paragraph quotation mark – at the conclusion of the quoted passage.

---

* An anticipation, true, and therefore abhorrent to me; yet hardly to be avoided.

Chapter 16

MODES OF EMPHASIS

THERE ARE two ways in which to emphasize: by punctuation, italics, quotation marks, etc.; and by syntactical or stylistic device. Strictly the latter does not concern the purpose of this book; nevertheless I shall very briefly deal with it.

I: PUNCTUATIONAL*

§ 1: Italics

Emphasis by italics has been treated in Chapter 14, § 1 (p. 118). An additional example or two may help.

Why, man, you look *ill!* – Well, I don't *feel* ill. (Or: Why, man! you ......)

It is one thing to *promise*, quite another to *fulfil*.

§ 2: Initial Capitals

The use of initial capitals for semi-technicalities has been treated in Chapter 13, group XII, sub-group 4 (see p. 115): the capital letters invest these terms with some sort of importance, hence with some degree of emphasis: yet they do not afford true examples of emphasis-by-capitals.

Perhaps the most spectacular, certainly not the least reprehensible, use of capitals occurs in the letters of those gushing females who very often speak and quite often write in capitals, thus:

MY DEAR FOOTSIE,
            I have Fallen in Love with the most wonderful Man. He is of the Strong Silent Type, but believe me, darling, he's far from Dumb!

---

* Here, the adjective corresponding to 'Punctuation and Its Allies'.

Well, Florence, how nice to see you! Now we'll be able to have a long, cosy Heart-to-Heart Talk.

But I sha'n't be able to offer you much in the way of food or drink, what with all this Rationing and, worse, all this perfectly dreadful National Austerity.

Let us exchange these occasionally delightful, rather more than occasionally maddening feather-brains, for a practice not very different from that mentioned at the beginning of this section. There we referred to semi-technical terms: here we have terms that, in themselves entirely non-technical, achieve all the deceptive dignity of technicalities merely by occurring in a serious context – for instance, a manual on rhetoric, a text-book on birds, a formidable work on geology; a governmental directive or a departmental memorandum; or even, at the opposite end of the scale, a formal circular.

Providing these serious-minded and decorous capitals be used sparingly, one can hardly object to them. I should, in a genial mood, condone, although I should not myself use, the capitals in –

Dramatic critics with a Classical education and an adequate idea of their own importance tend to employ – sometimes they do well to employ – such terms as Catastrophe and Catharsis, Development and Resolution, Protagonist and Antagonist.

That is a country where you will see the Clematis and the Vine, the Apple and the Peach, the Oak and the Willow, the Fir and the Pine.

But I should neither use nor condone such excesses and such inconsistencies as these –

In his autobiography he speaks wistfully of Childhood, sympathetically of Adolescence, reverently of Marriage and understandingly of Life. He admits, however, that he awaits with impatience the Life Eternal and Bliss Everlasting.

Every Literary Work has a Beginning, a Middle, an End. A few Works have also a Prologue and an Epilogue – as it were, a Prescript and a Postscript.

To emphasize everything is to emphasize nothing: and to Use Capitals for Every Noun, Every Verb, is as bad as to *Italicize* every *Significant Member* of a sentence.

Compare §§ 3 and 7: Small Capitals, Multiple Emphasis.

§ 3: Small Capitals

Under the somewhat telegraphic 'small capitals' I shall include not only words written or typed or printed entirely in small capitals (THUS) but also words that, normally bearing an initial capital (Europe), are capitalized throughout and therefore have to consist of a large initial capital and, for the remaining letters, small capitals (EUROPE).

Manifestly, such capitals are to be used with the utmost discretion and in scrupulous moderation. The sort of emphasis they should subserve is that which, reduced to practice, may be summarized as: the guidance and convenience of the reader. Thus –

Although, perhaps rather because, this vast scientific work by many authorities inevitably contains an almost bewildering multiplicity of facts, the main trends and the most important laws are picked out in small capitals. Thus, in the chapter on Darwin, we refer to EVOLUTION; in that on Rutherford, to the ATOM; in that on Fleming, to PENICILLIN. Likewise, in the chapters on evolution, the atom, penicillin, the first reference to each of those great scientists will bear the notation DARWIN, RUTHERFORD, FLEMING.

Whereas references to merely illustrative words will be made in *italic*, all references to keywords, whether the reference be important or casual, will be either in small capitals (as ROOT) or in large and small capitals (as NOAH).

For a warning, see § 7, Multiple Emphasis.

§ 4: Quotation Marks

The use of quotation marks for emphasis has already been mentioned in Chapter 15, § 2, and also in §§ 3–7.

Little remains to be said, for the main purpose of quotation marks in their role of emphasizers is to make the word or words stand out from the context. Their only other relevant purpose is to emphasize the idea-aspect of the words concerned: hence, one must guard against their excessive use, for they tend to render the near, remote, and the earthy, ideal, and the worldly, spiritual, and, in short, the objective, subjective. – One or two crafty writers have, by a clever use of quotation marks, succeeded in giving to the pedestrian and even the gross an air of distinction and even of philosophy. Remoteness and apartness are effects that a good writer very rarely wishes to achieve.

The following example of emphasis by means of quotation marks may help to clarify a rather nebulous practice:

If you employ the designation 'real idealism' instead of its synonym 'ideal realism', you tend to set up an ambiguity that does not attach to the latter. Strictly an ideal realist is one who, possessing an 'idealistic epistemology' or 'idealistic theory of the validity and limits of knowledge', is, as metaphysician, a 'realist'.

That sentence is far too remote, far too intellectualistic. If we italicize 'real idealism' and 'ideal realism' and discard their quotation marks, and if we then discard all the other quotation marks, we simplify the meaning and, by destroying the wrong sort of emphasis, make the sentence more rather than less emphatic in the best sense of that word.

§ 5: Hyphens *

When they deal thoughtfully with subjects a shade more abstruse than a loaf of bread or a game of football, a few good writers will occasionally use hyphens to unify a phrase or other group of words and thus emphasize the idea expressed by those words. The group of individuals becomes a team; a number of distinct entities – apprehended, it is true, as a collectivity or a collective idea – becomes an intellectual, aesthetic, stylistic unit.

Fortunately the practice is very much simpler than the theory. Thus, whereas most of us would write:

The ideal of the mystic is oneness with God,

the stylist would perhaps write:

The ideal of the mystic is oneness-with-God.

If the collectivity be put first, i.e. made the subject of the sentence, most of us would write:

Oneness with God is the ideal of the mystic,

but the stylist would probably prefer:

Oneness-with-God is (*or*, constitutes) the ideal of the mystic.

* It seems better to anticipate Chapter 17 on the hyphen than to postpone § 5.

The relationship of the theory to the practice can be more clearly seen in a sentence no stylist would permit himself:

The idea oneness-with-God forms the very basis of mystical philosophy; that of God everywhere-and-in-everything-whether-animate-or-inanimate, the basis of pantheism; and that of God-in-the-form-of-man or, at the least, God-with-the-(better)-feelings-and-the-(superior)-attributes-of-man, the basis of anthropomorphism.

§ 6: The Dash, the Colon, the Semicolon

The dash used for emphasis has been mentioned in Chapter 8, § 15; the colon thus used, in Chapter 6, §§ 7 and 11. All we need here is an example or two, for the refreshment of memory, because the general question of obtaining emphasis by the use of this or that punctuation mark has been treated in Chapter 11, § 2, Relative Values of the Points (see pp. 91–3).

In Piccadilly I saw the very last man I had expected to see there – a true Londoner.
There is only one thing he cannot bear: sympathy.
She had to act as hostess to a group of complete strangers; strangers, mark you!

Compare the following gradation:

Yes, I think I shall enjoy life among the eccentrics.
Yes; I think I shall . . .
Yes – I *think* I shall . . .
Well, yes, I think I shall: or should I say, No, I don't think I shall?: enjoy life among the eccentrics.

Also compare the emphasis obtained by punctuating 'He was perhaps weary of it all' with commas: 'He was, perhaps, weary of it all'.

§ 7: Multiple Emphasis

The term 'multiple emphasis' has been chosen in order to cover what has been called Double and Triple Emphasis and, more simply, Excessive Emphasis. The reference is to emphasis by punctuation, capitals, italics, quotation marks, etc. – not by syntactical emphasis.

To use an exclamation mark (Chapter 9) is occasionally permissible. But the following sentences exhibit a repellent excess:

He exclaimed, I shall do as I like! *when* I like!! *how* I like!!!
This ruthless man-eater (!), this scourge of the jungle (!!), this most dreaded of all quadrupeds (!!!), had come to the district and made life there a chaos!

In the second, the parenthetical exclamations are obviously those of a critic or an editor; in the first, the writer, not satisfied with six 'shrieks', has superadded italics. To show how insidious is the temptation to sign-post one's sense of astonishment or indignation, I admit that only just in time did I refrain from putting an exclamation mark at the end of the preceding sentence.

Unless there be a paramount reason for the use of both of these modes, do not add the emphasis of quotation marks to the emphasis of italics. Thus:

The word 'décor' is a Gallicism popular among theatrical critics,

or: The word *décor* is . . . ,

but not: The word *'décor'* is . . . ,

however fascinated one may be by one's ability to accentuate the word correctly and even to use it at all.

Then there is that sort of orgiastic emphasis which is favoured by inferior writers and uncritical laymen:

He came, he *saw*, he C O N Q U E R E D

or, worse still:

He *came*, he S A W , he C O N Q U E R E D.

The sentence is itself so dramatic that it needs no emphasis: any additional emphasis strikes us as being both puerile and hysterical. This particular horror might be called ascent by typography.

With that particular sentence, compare this (cited by Skelton):

I have a great mind to whip you . . . *and I* W I L L *too*:

where 'W I L L' represents an emphasis within an emphasis – a higher degree of emphasis within a word-group already emphatic.

To see in print such excesses as those noted above will cause most right-minded persons to forswear them. They are obvious.

Less obvious, however, is the following sentence quoted by Beadnell and commented-on by the Fowlers:

My friend! this conduct amazes me!

Although the exclamation mark after 'friend' is justifiable and in accordance with usage and sense, that at the end is excessive. Strictly, even the first is unnecessary, unless it not only connotes amazement but requires a pause. I should have preferred:

My friend – this conduct amazes me:

where the dash indicates the pause and the sentence as a whole is sufficiently emphatic in itself.

Clearly one could go on almost indefinitely with variations of multiple emphasis. But if the foregoing warnings and examples have not inculcated the lesson, *Never emphasize unless you have to do so and, when you feel or, better, know that you must, emphasize as little as possible*, then probably nothing will.

That italicized sentence, by the way, could just as well have been put into quotation marks or merely set off with a dash (or a colon or a semicolon) before and after it; but whatever the mode, the sentence should begin with a capital.

II. STYLISTIC OR SYNTACTICAL

This matter, strictly irrelevant, is introduced merely as a complement to what has gone before: it will therefore be treated with a summariness bordering upon the arbitrary and mainly by examples that are representative, not exhaustive.

Inversion: Small though he was, he possessed great strength.
Small, he yet was very strong.

Repetition: He is an indifferent sportsman, most indifferent.
He is an indifferent sportsman, – yes, indifferent.
(Compare the catch-phrase nature of: He is an indifferent, *repeat* indifferent, sportsman.)

Addition: The angry man protested. Vehemently.
The angry man protested – vehemently.

Affectation: He was angry, very.
He was bitter, bitter.
(= He was exceedingly bitter.)

Chapter 17

THE HYPHEN

THE HYPHEN (-) has two main and entirely distinct functions: dividing and compounding. The former kind of hyphenation, concerning single words strictly indivisible, takes place only for typographical or other conventional reasons; the latter concerns the junction of two or more single words into a discernibly collective union.

The etymology is revealing: the Late Latin *hyphen* derives from the Greek ὑφέν, *huphen*, earlier ὑφ' ἕν, *huph'hen*, literally 'under one', hence 'into one' or 'together': from ὑπό, *hupo*, under, and ἕν, *hen*, neuter of εἷς, *heis*, one.

I: DIVISION

The chief purposes of the typographical and otherwise conventional hyphen are these:

1. For the division of a word into syllables, as *a-bout*, *ac-tu-a-ri-al* (loosely *ac-tu-ar-i-al*), *di-vi-sion* (strict) or *di-vis-ion* (accepted) or *div-is-ion* (loose but very common). To diverge for a moment: as English has, in a sense, corrupted every long vowel, so it has also departed from the normal syllabification (British) or syllabication (American) of Greek, Latin, the Romance and most other languages. Thus, syllabication is often divided thus: *sy-llab-i-ca-tion* (si-lab-i-cā-shun) or *sy-llab-i-cat(i)-(i)on* (si-lab-i-cāsh-un). But the Medieval Latin genitive *syllabicationis* was divided thus: *syl-la-bi-ca-ti-o-nis*. The ideal is: Wherever possible, begin a syllable with a consonant.

2. When stress – the emphasis characterizing pronunciation – is added to syllabification, a word is figured thus: either *si-láb-i-cà-tion* (British style) *or si-láb-i-cà-shun* (American), where no distinction is made between the weak stress of *-lab-* and the strong stress of *-cā-*; or, differentiated, *si-làb-i-ca-shun* (British) or *si-láb-i-cà-shun* (American).

134

3. Certain writers, especially of fiction, adopt for the indication of a stammer, a hesitant pronunciation, a sobbing or a gasping, this sort of figuration:

Boo-hoo, I d-don't w-want to s-s-see him
C-cyril, w-what's the m-matter with S-s-sister S-sue?
I c-c-c – just – c-can't – g-get my b-breath – at all.

In the third example, hyphens separate the stammering attempts at a recalcitrant sound, but dashes the naturally longer pauses between the gasped words or word-groups. This use of the dash is closely akin to that in:

You seem unable to understand what I'm saying. Try again: You – are – on – the – wrong – bus, old man.

Now, if within the slowly enunciated statement there occurs a long word, that word must be articulated, thus:

You – are – on – the – wrong – bus – for – the – Mon-u-ment:

with hyphens indicating the syllabification. To avoid an ugly-looking arrangement of writing or typing or type, some writers prefer:

You, are, on, the, wrong, bus, for, the, Mon-u-ment:

or even: You. are. on. the. wrong. bus. for. the. Mon-u-ment.

4. If at the end of a line, whether of prose or even, as a poetic (?) device, of verse, a word remains incomplete, a hyphen is inserted to indicate that the word is, in fact, incomplete, thus:

He thinks that at last he himself has unveiled the mys-
tery.

5. The deferent or suspensive or annunciatory hyphen is that which occurs in such contexts as these:

He uses, at will, the six-, the eight- and occasionally the ten-syllabled line.
A four- or six-cylindered motorcar.

6. Compare the use of the hyphen in quoting separately the elements of compounds. This hyphen may precede the element or follow it or do both. Examples:

In *graminivorous*, *-vorous* means 'eating'.

In *omniscience, omni-* means 'all'.

In *omnicompetent*, the second element (*-competent*) is itself a compound; *-com-* at least connotes 'with'.

II: COMPOUNDING and COMBINATION

§ 1: General

(i) In *The King's English*, the Fowler brothers have stated four principles, which may be paraphrased thus:

Hyphens should be omitted wherever reason permits the omission; that reason may be aesthetic. They rightly advocate *today, tomorrow*, instead of *to-day, to-morrow*, words never hyphenated by Americans, increasingly less by Britons.

The degrees of relationship may be implied in *walking stick, walking-stick, walkingstick – land's man, land's-man, landsman*. These three stages are known as *separate* or *distinct*; *hyphenated* or *hyphened*; *solid* (American) or *conglomerate* or *unified* or especially *continuous* (British).

Write *war casualties*, not *war-casualties*; on the other hand, *breathing-space* means an interval, *breathing space* a space that breathes; and *walking-stick* or *walkingstick* is, for reasons of sense, preferable to *walking stick*, a stick that walks, hence a person resembling that hypothetical object.

If a phrase be used as an adjective, it needs to be hyphenated, as in 'a come-hither look'; the same applies to phrases used as nouns, as 'Let's have a get-together and a heart-to-heart'.

(ii) Sometimes a hyphen will prevent us from becoming ambiguous, as in 'He sold three farthing candles', correct if he sold three candles at a farthing apiece (the *farthing dips* of the 18th Century) but incorrect if he sold candles at three farthings apiece, the correct sentence then being 'He sold three-farthing candles'. The exercise of a little sense will usually show us what to do. Webster implies the same principle when he speaks of that hyphen which occurs in the 'arbitrary use of a phrase as a conventional name of something, where there is such a transfer of meaning that the literal senses of the words do not indicate the general nature of the meaning intended (*forget-me-not; love-lies-bleeding; bull's-eye*)'.

(iii) For compounding or combination in general, it is exceedingly difficult to devise a satisfactory set of rules, because comprehensiveness is virtually impossible and because there are numerous exceptions. The following set of directions – in many instances 'rules' would be too strong a word – should provide some guidance.*

§ 2: Particular

The particular recommendations fall into eight main groups: i, miscellaneous; ii, compound nouns; iii, compound pronouns; iv, compound adjectives; v, compound verbs; vi, compound adverbs; vii, compound prepositions; viii, prefixes.

I: MISCELLANEOUS

1. Sometimes a hyphen prevents either ambiguity (compare § 1, General, paragraph (ii)). Webster adduces these most convincing examples *auto-audible, co-worker, supra-intestinal*, as you will see immediately you compare the unhyphenated forms *autoaudible, coworker, supraintestinal*.

2. If the last element of a word is a suffix or a combining-form, the word is normally written solid, as in 'anachron*ism*' and 'death*like*'.

But whereas American usage prefers 'death*like*' and 'corpse*like*', etc., British usage prefers 'death-like' and 'corpse-like'. Avoid such compound + *-like* forms as *King-Mark-like*, itself, however, preferable to *King Mark-like*.

3. Such compounds as, for the first element, have a prefix ('*undo*' – '*semi*quaver') or a combining-form ('*tele*vision') are written solid. For the exceptions, see sub-groups 8 and 9.

4. If the second element is capitalized, a hyphen precedes it, as in *Anglo-American, pro-Hitler, anti-Semitism, post-Napoleonic*.

5. If the word *self* occurs as the first element, it is usually followed by a hyphen, as in *self-love, self-conscious*.

6. The prefix *co-*, if followed by an element beginning with *o*, always takes a hyphen, as in *co-operative*; if followed by any other vowel, it usually takes, in American practice, no hyphen (*coambassador, coeducate, coinsurance, counite*), whereas in British practice it

---

* The arrangement is based upon the classification made by Webster (at **compound**) and modified by the treatment in the already mentioned works by the Fowlers, Reginald Skelton, G. H. Vallins, myself (*Usage and Abusage*) – and very considerably enlarged by the last-named.

usually does take a hyphen, as in *co-ambassador, co-educate, co-insurance, co-unite*, a notable exception being *coefficient*.

7. In American practice all other first elements ending in *o* do without a hyphen before the next element, as in *radioactive*, British usage preferring *radio-active*.

8. Either *pre-* or *re-*, followed by an element beginning with *e*, takes a hyphen, as in *pre-empt* and *re-employ*.

9. Moreover, *re-* takes a hyphen whenever the second element is employed in its literal sense and the combination has the same form as a *re-*formation in a secondary sense: thus, we write *re-form*, to form again, to avoid confusion with *reform*, to amend; compare *relay* and *re-lay*.

10. If either the prefix or the first element ends and the second element begins with *a* or with *i*, a hyphen precedes the second element as in *contra-active* and *di-iodoform*.

11. Whereas American usage omits a hyphen after *non*, as in *noncommittal, noneconomic, nonmoral*, British usage normally inserts it, as in *non-committal, non-economic, non-moral*.

12. When, as rarely happens, a triple consonant occurs in a word, there must, both for the sake of clarity and for the prevention of mispronunciation, be a hyphen before the third. The best example is that which occurs in such Scottish-county names as Caithness-shire, Inverness-shire, Ross-shire.

II: COMPOUND NOUNS

As we have seen, compounds start as separate words, then acquire a hyphen, and end as continuous (or unbroken or solid) words. That tendency has accelerated since about 1914: World War I taught many people that superfluities should be treated as such and therefore discarded; World War II increased the tempo, nor have the post-War years done anything to retard it. Americans have gone further than Britons along the lines of 'continuity' or 'solidity'. Some Britons think that Americans have gone too far: yet, ugly as certain American 'continuities' (e.g., *nonresistance*) appear, at first, to British eyes, it must be admitted that Americans have been, are being and will doubtless continue to be chargeable with nothing more reprehensible than 'intelligent anticipation'. This simplification merely accords with the general tenor and tempo of life ever since 1914. 'So why,' ask virtually all Americans and not a few Britons, ' – why resist the inevitable?'

This general tendency applies to compound adjectives as much, and to compound verbs and adverbs almost as much, as to compound nouns. It is best to ignore all those compounds which are written solid, likewise all those which are written separate (*post office*), and to deal only with those which take a hyphen.

1. *Noun and noun*. Comparatively few of these carry a hyphen, the principal exceptions being perhaps:

(*a*) Word-groups of the kind exemplified by 'Paris-Rome express' – 'London-Cape Town airway' – 'cleric-layman *or* professional-amateur *or* native-foreigner *or* Services-Civil Service dispute', where the hyphen connotes 'to' and 'and' or 'between . . . and'. The same remark applies to 'the London-Cairo-Bombay-Colombo-Port Darwin route' variation. But real trouble begins where both or all members of the combination consist of two or more words or where single words are mingled with pairs and trios, as in 'the London-New York State-Washington State-Pacific Islands-Australia-New Zealand pact': where, by the way, it is advisable to employ short dashes instead of hyphens; a practice very necessary where, in the combination, there already exist one or more hyphens, as in 'a sinister hanger-on-go-between collusion', which, of course, no self-respecting writer would permit himself.

(*b*) Where the two nouns are in apposition, each being a description of the same person or thing, where in short the two nouns are equivalent to – and – ', as in *King-Emperor, actor-manager, city-state*. Compare such hyphenated surnames as *Tewkesbury-Jones, Smith-Johnson*.

(*c*) Such standard or technical units of measurement as end in *mile, foot, inch* – *ton* or *pound* – *year, day, hour, minute, second*: as *sea-mile* (American *sea mile*) or *car-mile, acre-foot* and -*inch*; *foot-ton* and -*pound*; *light-year, man-day, horse-hour*, etc.

(*d*) *Power* merits a note to itself. British usage began with *horse power* but has since ca. 1880 preferred *horse-power*; American usage prefers *horsepower*. The combination of *power* with *man* shows that whereas Britons use *man-power* for both noun and adjective, Americans use *man power* for the noun, *man-power* for the adjective. But men of good sense are gradually deciding to regularize the position by employing *horsepower* and *manpower* in all contexts.

(*e*) Where there are three (or more) nouns and the first two (or three) are attributive, i.e. descriptive of the rest of the compound, the practice exemplified in the following compounds would seem to be the only sensible one:

horse-power (better *horsepower*) *year*,
horsepower wear-and-tear.

(*f*) Although most combinations of capital letter nouns are left separate as *I beam*, *T square*, *X ray*, at least *U-boat* takes a hyphen. When, however, such combinations are used either as adjectives or as verbs, it is customary to hyphenate, as in *X-ray eyes* and 'He had to be *X-rayed*'.

(*g*) Reduplicating nouns – and indeed reduplicating adjectives, verbs, adverbs, whether independent or derivative from reduplicating nouns – are usually hyphenated, as in

nouns: *clip-clop*, *tick-tock;*
adjectives: *topsy-turvy* (like the verb and the noun: from the adverb);
verbs: *tick-tock*, *topsy-turvy*;
adverbs: *slap-dash* (whence the adjective and the noun) but increasingly *slapdash*; American *slapdash*.

(*h*) Compounds with *doer*, *maker*, *worker* and *keeper*, as with the nouns, *doing*, *making*, *working* and *keeping* (so too with the corresponding adjectives and with the past-participial adjectives ending in *done*, *made*, *worked* and *kept*) fall into the three natural groups:

many long-established compounds are solid, as in *bookmaker*, *bookmaking*, but *book-maker*, *-making*, applied to hack work – *bookkeeper*, *bookkeeping*, but in British usage often hyphenated – *doorkeeper*, *housekeeping*;
yet some long-established compounds are hyphenated, as *ill-doer* and *ill-doing* – *mischief-maker* and *mischief-making* – *bee-keeper*, *-keeping*, but American *beekeeper*, *beekeeping*; so are many recent compounds, as *wonder-worker*;
and a few are left open or separate, as *church worker*.

But in all these *doer*, *maker*, *worker*, *keeper* and *doing* (etc.) compounds, the general principle governing the development of compounds is at work: the gradation is *hand maid*, *hand-maid*, *handmaid*. A safe modifier is what we might call 'visual euphony' or, better, 'harmony'; the aesthetic reader would not much care for a long string of unhyphenated consonants. Here, as in so many other subtleties of style, good sense and a regard for harmony will help one to decide whether a hyphen is advisable or at the least helpful.

(*i*) When the first element is in the possessive case, a hyphen is obligatory, for otherwise ambiguity would often arise. This applies mostly to plant or flower names, such as *lamb's-foot*, *mare's-tail*,

Juno's-herb, *Venus's-hair*, *Venus's-looking-glass*, *dog's-tongue* or *hound's-tongue*, and to several folk-poetry words, such as *bull's-eye*. But a few have acquired continuity, as *coltsfoot, goatsfoot, wolfsbane*.

(*j*) For compound numerals, see IV: COMPOUND ADJECTIVES.

(*k*) Certain nouns, on no easily discerned principle, are traditionally, though not irrevocably, hyphenated, as *country-dance, horse-radish, trade-mark*; but *trade-mark* has already begun to give way to *trademark*.

2. *Noun and adjective*. (*a*) Adjective-noun compounds do not usually take a hyphen: *first lieutenant, barbed wire, general manager*; but *under-secretary*.

(*b*) Noun-adjective compounds take a hyphen in the following set terms: *adjutant-general, brigadier-general, lieutenant-general, major-general; attorney-general, director-general, postmaster-general, secretary-general*, this last being the only one to be hyphenated in American English.

(*c*) In certain noun-adjective compounds, the hyphen is almost customary; yet modern, especially the American, practice tends increasingly to omit them:

court-martial, still the usual form both in Britain and in America.
heir apparent, heir presumptive are the only forms in the U.S.A.; Britain likewise prefers the unhyphened forms, but permits *heir-apparent; heir-apparency* is British, the unhyphened form American. –
heir-at-law still predominates in both British and American English. –
price-current, which is merely predominant, not obligatory, is already obsolescent; only *price current* is seen in the United States.
sum-total is still the predominant form in Britain and still permissible in the U.S.A., where, however, *sum total* is much preferred.

Where the compound nouns treated in 2, *a* and *c* above are used as adjectives, they take hyphens: *barbed-wire entanglement, price-current publications, sum-total estimates*, etc.

3. *Noun and verb*

(*a*) Present participle + noun: no hyphen: *paying guest, standing orders*.

(*b*) Gerund + noun: no hyphen necessary, though often used:

boarding house and *dwelling house* – *walking stick* and *walking tour*.

(*c*) Noun + gerund of a transitive verb: in British English, the hyphen is obligatory, as in *labour-saving* and *steel-making* – and also for noun + agential noun from a transitive verb, thus *engine-driver*, *shock-absorber*, except for some long-established words, e.g. *bricklayer*; in American English, the hyphen is usually omitted, as in *laborsaving*, *metalworking*, *metalworker*.

4. *Verb and noun.* These compounds take a hyphen: *cure-all*, *save-all*, *know-nothing*.

5. *Verb and verb.* Such combinations are usually hyphenated, thus: *has-been*, *never-was*; *make-believe*. Compare also sub-group 8 below.

6. *Noun and adverb.* Such agential nouns deriving from verbs and bearing the suffix *-er* as precede an adverb have a hyphen between the two elements: *breaker-in* (of horses), *breaker-up* (of houses), *goer-by* (= *passer-by*), *hanger-on*, *listener-in*, *taker-down*, *-in*, *-off*, *-up*.

7. *Adverb and noun:* rare: usually hyphenated: *up-bow*.

8. *Verb and adverb; adverb and verb.* These combinations are, in British practice, usually hyphenated, as *break-through*, *go-between*, *lean-to*. In American practice, a one-syllabled verb and a short adverb are usually written solid as *blowout* (British *blow-out*), *breakup* (British *break-up*), *hangover* (British *hang-over*); an exception comes in such words as *flare-up*, *tie-up*, *cave-in*, where the hyphen separates final and initial vowel. Of the adverb-verb variation, a good example is *well-being* (good health; prosperity).

9. *Three-or-more-word nouns.* Whatever the special variety may be – and there are several – the usual practice is to hyphenate. Thus:

man-of-war, but *man about town*; *maid-of-all-work* (Americans omit the hyphens); *will-o'-the-wisp*. –
free-for-all (American colloquialism for a fight); *no-man's-land* (Americans write it as three words).
go-as-you-please (from the adjective); *forget-me-not*. –
give-and-take, *coming-and-going* (Americans write it as three words). –
ne'er-do-well; *never-never land*.

10. With (9) compare such English place-names as *Bradwell-juxta-Mare* and *Weston-super-Mare*; *Burton-on-Trent* and *Newcastle-upon-Tyne*. The last, however, is often written *Newcastle on Tyne*,

except when it is an adjective, as in *'Newcastle-on-Tyne* people are sturdily independent'.

III: COMPOUND PRONOUNS

1. Most compound pronouns are written solid, thus: *anybody* and its synonym *anyone* ('*any one* thing' is adjectival); *anything*; *something*; *somebody*; *someone* – the form recommended – or *some one*, but not *some-one*; *everybody, everyone*; *nobody*; *no one* – the form recommended – or *no-one*, but not the manifestly ludicrous *noone*.

2. With *else*, the forms that seem to be the most sensible are *anybody*, or *anyone*, *else*; *anything else, something else, everything else, nothing else; somebody*, or *everybody*, or *nobody*, *else*; *everyone else*; *no-one else*.

3. *Myself, thyself, himself, herself, ourselves, yourselves, themselves* are pronouns: *my self, our selves*, etc., are adjective-noun formations.

4. There are several literary and philosophical subtleties that cannot be ignored, all the more that the same remarks apply to their adjectival as to their substantival functions; strictly they are nouns, which can be used attributively. Thus –

Most of us are so egocentric that our fundamental attitude, very rarely acknowledged to others and seldom admitted even to ourselves, is express- ible in the psychological dictum, The world contains only two groups of persons: *I*, at the centre; *they*, all the others. This relationship constitutes the *I-they* of life; ours is the *I-they* attitude.

Yet some fortunates experience a warmer and less selfish emotion, the *you-I*, or the *you-and-I*, of reciprocated love; the *he-she* factor of well- being.

The *he-you-I*, or the *he-you-and-I*, nexus. The *they-you-we*, or the *they (-and)-you-and-we*, set of social circumstances.

IV: COMPOUND ADJECTIVES

Introductory

To the few cursory remarks passed in the sections MISCELLANEOUS (I, 1, 2, 4, 5, 6, 7, 10, 11) and COMPOUND NOUNS (II, 1, *f, g*; 2, *c*) much has to be added.

'Most compound adjectives consisting of two or more words and preceding the noun are hyphened' (Webster): 'a well-known man' but 'a man well known'. 'All genuine Compound Adjectives are hyphen- ated' (Skelton) – a statement more nearly true of British than of American English, the latter, as we have seen, tending much more than British English tends, to solid or continuous compounds. In all English whatsoever we nevertheless find that the majority of compound adjectives are, in the fact, hyphenated. To attempt to reduce an exacerbatingly obscure situation to something like clarity, I have arranged the material on principles of accidence – principles here according very closely with the recommendations suggested by good sense and hard-headed logic.

1. *Adjective and 'straight' adjective.* In these compounds, the first modifies the second, thus *dark-blue, red-hot, steamy-close, worldly-wise.*

1*a.* Proper Name adjective + Proper Name adjective, with one or both of the adjectives consisting of two or more words, are separated by a long hyphen (or short dash) instead of by the usual hyphen. Thus: 'the Chicago–New York train'; 'the Old World–New World dualism of his philosophy'; 'Anglo-Saxon–Norman French social customs, like the Anglo-Saxon–Anglo-French linguistic relationship, are very intricate and complicated'. (With thanks to Webster.)

2. *Adjective and present participle.* These likewise take a hyphen, as in *bad-looking, good-looking, fair-seeming, sweet-tasting.*

3. *Adjective and past participle,* as in *dark-hued* and especially in all compounds of *better* and *best,* and of *worse, worst,* as *better-placed, best-placed, worse-placed, worst-placed.*

4. *Adjective and noun,* as in *first-class, first-rate, secondary-school* (education).

5. *Adjective and noun* + '*-ed*', as in *able-bodied, double-faced.*

6. *Noun and adjective,* as in *pitch-black, snow-blind.*

7. *Noun and certain adjectives* (proof, tight; secure, sure) and *participial adjectives* (born, bred). British usage has tended to hyphenate all these, but is fast relaxing in some instances; American practice tends, with a few exceptions, to make all of them solid. Thus: *baseborn,* English, and *baseborn,* American; *base-bred,* English – *basebred,* American; English *free-born,* American *freeborn*; English *high-born, -bred*; American *highborn, highbred*; *airtight,* American and now British; *watertight,* now both; British *air-proof,* American *airproof*; British *fool-proof,* yielding gradually to American *foolproof;* and *waterproof,* common to both (British, originally hyphenated).

8. *Adjective and verb.* This very small and problematic subgroup consists of such words as *quick-fire* and *sure-fire*: quick to fire, hence synonymous with *quick-firing*; sure to fire, hence sure, certain, dependable.

9. *Noun and noun.* Compound fractions and compound numerals are, in British practice, always hyphenated; in American, compound

fractions only when they are used as adjectives. Thus: *thirty-two*, and *thirty-two degrees – three hundred and ninety-five* (with or without ensuing noun); *two-thirds* (British) or *two thirds* (American; English uses both forms indifferently) *of those present, a three-quarters majority;* *one-half* but *a half – half a pound*, but *a half-pound*; *one-and-a-half* (British) or *one and a half* (British and American noun) – *one-and-a-half* (British adjective), *one-and-one-half* (American adjective). Compare *half-holiday* (American: *half holiday*), *half-term, half-breed, half-caste, quarter-caste.*

10. When a compound adjective consists of a Proper Name composed of two or even three words, no hyphen is required. Thus: 'He resembled an *Old Testament* prophet' – 'Some of these *Middle English* words are very deceptive' – '*United States* immigratory regulations' – 'In *Medieval Ecclesiastical Greek* you will find . . .'.

11. *Noun and present participle*, as in 'a *stem-winding* watch'. Of this type, most examples are of noun + a present participle governing that noun, as in '*life-giving* water' or '*life-preserving* food' – *labour-saving* (American *laborsaving*).

12. *Noun and past participle*, as in *fear-crazed* and *terror-stricken* – *air-cooled* and *air-dried* and *air-minded* – *heart-broken* and *home-made*. This group forms a notable and populous class of compound adjectives.

13. *Noun + noun + '-ed'*, as in 'a *bull-necked* man' and 'a *sabre-toothed* tiger'.

14. *Past participle and adverb not in '-ly'*, as in '*burnt-out* farmhouse' and '*broken-down* motorcar'.

15. *Adverb and present participle*, a very common type: *far-reaching, far-seeing, hard-working, never-ending*.

16. *Adverb and past participle*, another populous set of compounds: 'a *far-flung* empire' – 'a *long-endured* torment' – 'a *slow-paced* movement' – 'a *worn-out* chassis'.

Note that, as for 14 and 15, an adverb in *-ly* never takes a hyphen, whether before or after a participle, present or past: 'a badly needed library' – 'a slowly pacing horse' – 'Your requests, brilliantly phrased though they are, have had to be shelved'.

17. Compounds with *ill*, adverb, and *well*, adverb, merit a separate paragraph.

With present participle: *ill-looking, well-meaning*.

With past participle: *ill-contrived*; *well-born, well-known, well-meant*, etc.,

exemplify the usual practice and are to be recommended for use before nouns ('a *well-known* person') and in such constructions as '*Well-meant*, it yet sounded insulting'; but in a complement, these compounds should be separate, thus: 'He was well known' – 'It was well meant'.

With noun + -*ed:* 'an ill-conditioned and ill-natured fellow' – 'a well-intentioned family of feckless bohemians'.

With a compound following *ill* or *well*, the hyphenation follows these lines: 'a well brought up boy' (my preference) or 'a well brought-up boy' (Skelton's) – 'an ill thought out scheme' (mine) or 'an ill thought-out scheme' (Skelton's).

18. *Adverbial prefixes in compound adjectives*, as, for instance, *mis-shapen:* see IX: PREFIXES.

19. *Prepositional phrases used as adjectives* are usually hyphenated: 'his *mother-in-law* obsession' – 'a *door-to-door* canvass' – 'a *house-to-house* search – 'a *face-to-face* (or, *tête-à-tête*) interview' – 'a *late-to-bed* sort of fellow' – 'an *up-to-date* encyclopedia' – 'a *sotto-voce* remark' – 'a *stick-in-the-mud* old fogey'. The first element can therefore be a noun, an adjective, a verb, an adverb, a preposition; and the nouns, where they exist, are likewise hyphenated: 'a *stick-in-the-mud*' – 'our *tête-à-tête*'.

20. Phrases that, used attributively, are hyphenated in order to avoid ambiguity: '*Black-and-white* contrasts inevitably lead to exaggeration' – 'This *cross-country* man' (not 'cross-countryman, nor 'cross countryman') – '*hard-and-fast* rules are seldom advisable'.

21. Adjectival phrases of three or more elements are usually hyphenated: 'a *happy-go-lucky* boy' – 'a *go-as-you-please* youth' – 'He wore an *I-shouldn't-care-to-know-you* air'.

V: COMPOUND VERBS

1. Where the first element of the compound is a prefix, the verb is usually written solid: compare I: MISCELLANEOUS, paragraphs 8 and 9, for *pre-* and *re-*, and para. 6 for *co-*: these three prefixes, in the circumstances there defined, constitute the only instances of hyphenation in prefix + verb compounds, except that British (not American) English writes *mis-shape*.

2. Such verbs as combine an adjective and a noun usually take a hyphen, as in 'to *cold-douche* or *cold-shoulder* someone'. 'Don't "*poor-wretch*" me!', with which compare 'I'd like to hear him "*silly-old-man*" that noble fellow, his grandfather'.

3. Intimately allied to (2) is that set of compound verbs in which the adjective is either proleptic or instrumental, thus –

Proleptic: 'to *cold-hammer* metal' = to hammer it until it cools. Instrumental: 'to *dry-clean*, or *French-clean*, a suit of clothes' = to clean it, not with water but with spirits; 'to *dry-dock* a ship' = to place it, for repairs, in a dry dock.

(Based upon Webster.)

4. To avoid ambiguity, it is occasionally necessary to hyphenate where otherwise one would not do so. For instance:

He *lies-in* in the morning
She will *go-on* [make a fuss] in the street.

These temporary hyphens are to be used only when necessary; some writers imagine ambiguities. On the other hand, never omit one if it removes an ambiguity or eases the flow of the sentence.

VI: COMPOUND ADVERBS

1. Adverbs in *-ly* from such hyphenated adjectives as *double-faced*, *hard-headed*, i.e. compound adjectives formed of adjective + noun + *-ed*, are hyphenated: *double-facedly*, *hard-headedly*, *swollen-headedly*. Some of the adverbs of this type will be avoided by stylists because of their cacophony.

2. Most adverbs composed of two or more words are hyphenated, thus: 'They collided *head-on*' – 'The case is *well-nigh* hopeless' (although *well nigh* would be unambiguous) – 'He perorated *Disraeli-fashion*' – 'He acted *queer-like*' (an illiterate colloqiualism).

(With thanks to Webster.)

VII: COMPOUND PREPOSITIONS

1. There are naturally few such prepositions, which arise either from slackness and an unnecessary elaboration or from a scrupulous subtlety and a necessary elaboration. As an example of the former, *in among* and *in between* appear to add nothing to *among* and *between*, as '*In between times* he does odd jobs' will make clear; of the latter, *from above* and *from below* do considerably modify both *from* and *above* or *below*. In *Mansion's English-French Dictionary* I find this neat example: '*Her curls came out from under her hat*, ses boucles ressortaient de sous son chapeau'.

2. Such prepositions do not need a hyphen, nor do the phrasal prepositions – *in respect of*, *with regard to*, *in consideration of*, and the like.

VIII: PREFIX COMPOUNDS

1. See I: MISCELLANEOUS, paragraphs 3–11 (pp. 137–8).

2. All that remains to be said is that few prefixes are hyphen-separated from the stem. The following may be noted:

(a) *English* (*fundamentally: Germanic*) *prefixes:*

a-, in such words as *a-fishing* and *a-hunting* – but *abed, ashore, asleep:*

by-, as in *by-law* (American *bylaw*), *by-form, by-pass, by-play* (American *byplay*), *by-product* – but *bystander.*

down compounds are mostly written solid, but British English usually hyphenates *down-draught, down-grade, down-stroke,* and inconsistently *down-fallen.*

mid-day (American and increasingly in British English: *midday:* on the analogy of *midnight*).

mis- compounds are written always solid in American English, and in British English usually solid, as in *misbehave, misdo, misdoubt, misknow,* with a few such exceptions as *mis-shapen, mis-speak, mis-spell.*

off-chance, off-licence, off-lying, off-play (cf. *off-drive*), *off-print* or *offprint* – but *offscouring, offset, offshoot, offspring,* etc.

on-coming (American – and why not British? – *oncoming*), *on-licence, on-play* (and *on-drive*) – but *oncome, ongoing, onrush, onset.*

over, literal (as in *overcoat, overhang*), takes no hyphen; *over,* excessively, often does, as in *over-act* (now usually *overact*), *over-confident, over-daring, over-delicacy, over-particular, over-scrupulous.*

to-day, to-night, to-morrow, fast becoming continuous words in British, as they have long been in American, practice.

under-bred, under-estimate, under-proof, are fast yielding to the more sensible *underbred, underestimate, underproof,* long customary in America. Note that sometimes the hyphen is necessary, as in 'He understudied the leading actor, but he under-studied "the book of words" and therefore never got another chance'.

up compounds are usually continuous, the chief exceptions being *up-bank, up-country* (American *upcountry*), *up-grade* (American *upgrade*), *up-put, -putter, -putting, up-stream* (American *upstream*), *up-stroke* (American *upstroke*), *up-*

town (American *uptown*), *up-wind* (American *upwind*).

(*b*) *Non-Germanic prefixes.* (1) *Latin*

ante, before, in front of: hyphenated only before Proper Names and Proper Adjectives, as in *ante-Classical.*

co, See 1: MISCELLANEOUS, para. 6 (p. 137).

counter-battery (American *counterbattery*), *counter-offer*; but *counterclaim* and, especially in American English, most other *counter* compounds are written solid. In British English, there is one quasi-rule: *counter* being often apprehended as holding the pronunciation *counta*, *counter* usually takes a hyphen before a stem or main word beginning with a vowel, as in *counter-attraction.*

de, from, down from, away: hyphenated only where the combination would cause either a phonetic awkwardness or a semantic absurdity: *de-ice.*

ex, out of, from; (hence) formerly: *ex-convict*, *ex-officer*, *ex-president.* Before compounds, it is sensible to italicize *ex* and omit the hyphen, as in '*ex* Lord (-) Mayor' and '*ex* assistant-secretary', as Skelton has recommended.

extra, outside of, beyond. There is no need to hyphenate such literal compounds as *extraterrestrial*, *extraterritorial.* But colloquialisms, where *extra* connotes 'additionally' or 'unusually', do need a hyphen, as *extra-nice.*

infra, on the under side, below: both British and American English hyphenates before a vowel, as in *infra-axillary*, *infra-orbital, infra-umbilical;* and British only, *infra-red.*

non, not. See 1: MISCELLANEOUS, para. 11 (p. 138).

post, behind, after: hyphen only before Proper Names and Adjectives, as in *post-Classical:* compare *ante* (above). The hyphen is unnecessary in such words as *postdate*; *post-war* is giving way to *postwar* (the American form).

pre, before: hyphenate only before Proper Names and Adjectives; elsewhere only if the omission of the hyphen would cause extreme awkwardness or a rank absurdity, as in 'a *pre-engineering* course'.

pro, in front of; in place of. Same remarks as for *pre*: e.g., *pro-Ally, pro-infinitive.*

(*quasi*, as if. This example of an element rather than a prefix-compound takes a hyphen before Proper Names and Adjectives, as in *quasi-American*, and usually before a vowel, as in *quasi-ancient.* Sometimes – especially in American practice – *quasi* and the word following are written separately, as in *quasi member* (of, e.g., a committee).)

re. See I: MISCELLANEOUS, para. 9 (p. 138).

sub, under; (hence) subordinate, inferior: hyphen before Proper Names and Adjectives; elsewhere, only before nouns, as *sub-committee, sub-group*; Americans, however, write *subcommittee, subgroup* (now fairly common in British English also).

super, over or above: in American practice, it never takes a hyphen; in British, very rarely, as decreasingly in *supersaturated*. The French derivative *sur* is hyphenated in *sur-invest* and *sur-match*.

supra, above: apparently never hyphenated except before a Proper Name or a vowel, as in *supra-angular, supra-auricular, supra-axillary, supra-orbital* (American: solid).

ultra, beyond: same remarks as for *supra: ultra-academic, ultra-Byronic*. American *ultraviolet*, British *ultra-violet*.

vice, instead of: usually hyphenated, as in *vice-admiral, vice-chancellor, vice-consul, vice-president*; but *viceregent, viceregal, vicereine, viceroy*. Write *vice versa* as two words.

2. *Greek prefixes and elements.* These are very numerous, but the following perhaps merit a particular mention:

anti, against: hyphenated before Proper Names and Adjectives, but before very few other words – (sometimes) *anti-corrosive, anti-freeze* (American: solid), *anti-gray (grey)-hair vitamin, anti-icer, anti-personnel* (American: solid).

electro-: in British practice, usually hyphenated, as in *electro-capillary, -chemical, -coating, -copper, -deposit, -magnet, -negative, -plate*, etc.; in American, never.

oxy-, sharp, acute: British usage hyphenates before a vowel, as in *oxy-acetylene;* American, never.

pseudo-, false: British usage hyphenates before Proper Nouns and Adjectives (*pseudo-Christian*), before other words beginning with a vowel (*pseudo-archaic*) and before certain other words (*pseudo-bacillus*) especially if non-Greek or, at best, non-Latin (*pseudo-dyke*); American usage, except for Proper Names, never hyphenates, but writes the words either solid (*pseudoacademic*) or – a practice virtually unknown in British English – as two distinct words (*pseudo acceptance, pseudo signature*).

IX: NEGATIVES OF COMPOUND WORDS – MCSTLY ADJECTIVES AND ADVERBS

Let us take *co-operative(ly)* and *co-ordinated*. Theoretically, we should write *un-co-operative(ly)* and *un-co-ordinated*; practically, write *unco-operative(ly)* and *unco-ordinated*. Note that if the unfortunately obsolescent *coöperative* and *coördinated* had been retained, we could have written *uncoöperative(ly)* and *uncoördinated*, which look odd – but only because we did not have the opportunity to get used to them.

As for *non* before a compound: British usage hyphenates, American does not hyphenate (*nonundergraduate*).

X: HYPHENS AND CAPITALS

Obviously two or more Proper Names remain unaffected by hyphenation, as in 'the Berlin-Rome-Tokio axis'. But what happens when the element or elements other than the first normally bear no capital? The usual practice is exemplified in

Her nickname was Ever-constant, occasionally Forget-me-not.

But I strongly recommend

Her nickname was Ever-Constant, occasionally Forget-Me-Not.

Articles and prepositions, however, have a small initial letter when they occur in the second or any later position, thus:

That notable Red Indian chief, Fine-Boatman-in-the-Rapids, died in 1880

At this period her friends alluded to her as Love-in-a-Mist.

THE VIRGULE (OR VIRGIL) OR THE OBLIQUE

The *oblique*, short for *oblique stroke* or *line*, is written /, originally the French way of writing or printing a comma. Hence the French name for a comma: *virgule*, from Latin *virgula* (strictly *uirgula*), a small rod, diminutive of *virga* (strictly *uirga*), a rod. This oblique stroke / – a stroke written obliquely in order to stand out more clearly, more separatively – was the earliest form, both of the comma and also of the division of a word at the end of a line, a division now indicated by a hyphen.

When used in such combinations as *and/or*, the *oblique* or the *virgule* (occasionally anglicized as *virgil* – a form apparently unknown in the United States) tells the reader that, to interpret the meaning, he may read and understand either of the words thus separated. The sign occurs also in philology, either in the form '*uirga/uerga*, whence *uirgula/uergula*' or in the form 'L. *Bacchus*/Gr. *Bakkhos*/Lydian *Bakis*': the former serves to indicate a variant, the latter to state the etymology.

In abbreviations the oblique is employed to separate the two elements of a compound, as in *c/o*, care of, and *i/c*, in charge, and *u/m*, undermentioned, and *A/C 2* (preferable to *A/C.2* and varying *A.C.2*) or to show that letters have been omitted from within a single word, as in *a/c*, account.

Then there is the commercial use for prices, as in *5s/6d* (preferable to *5s./6d.*) or, wherever the context permits, *5/6*; better still, perhaps, is 5s/6d: a use corresponding very closely to that made of the oblique in mathematics – to indicate fractions, whether simply, as *1/3*, one-third, and *2/7*, two-sevenths, or less simply, *1/13″*, one-thirteenth of an inch, and *1/4 lb*, one-quarter of a pound avoirdupois.

Where the virgule or oblique can be used to very great advantage is in such contexts as these:

London/Aden/Karachi/Colombo

and better still in:

London/New York/San Francisco/Honolulu/Perth or Port Darwin.

One rejoices to see that this piece of good sense is gaining over the inadequacy of:

London–New York–San Francisco–Honolulu–Perth or Port Darwin.

A still better example occurs in this type:

The bus took the rather odd route indicated by the stages London/ Great Missenden, Bucks./Sutton Courtenay, Berks./Chipping Campden/ Bristol/Weston-super-Mare

which is vastly superior to:

. . . London–Great Missenden (Bucks.)–Sutton Courtenay (Berks.)– Chipping Campden–Bristol–Weston-super-Mare;

and superior, though less superior, to:

. . . London–Great Missenden, Bucks.–Sutton Courtenay, Berks.– Chipping Campden–Bristol–Weston-super-Mare.

Some ingenious person, if I did not mention it, would be sure to suggest the following typographical device:

. . . London   Great Missenden, Bucks.   Sutton Courtenay, Berks. Chipping Campden   Bristol   Weston-super-Mare

or the 'London   Great Missenden (Bucks.)   Sutton Courtenay (Berks.)' variation. But the typeless intervals will, if they are sufficiently long to differentiate clearly between the elements, inevitably look very odd.

THE BRACE OR VINCULUM

The *brace*, that which braces or draws together, and *vinculum*, a bond – that which binds (from Latin *vincire*, strictly *uincire*, to bind), are often used as synonyms for the curved, upright line { or }. Strictly, however, this mark is called a brace and is used as in:

$$\left.\begin{array}{l} bad \\ good \\ evil \end{array}\right\}\text{Teutonic}$$

$$\left.\begin{array}{l} excellent \\ favourable \end{array}\right\}\text{Latin}$$

Written out, the words would form the sentence '*Bad*, *good*, *evil* are Teutonic; *excellent* and *favourable*, Latin'. In reverse:

$$\text{Teutonic}\left\{\begin{array}{l} bad \\ good \\ evil \end{array}\right.$$

In both arrangements, one notices, there is no ostensible punctuation. Nevertheless the brace, in addition to ensuring clarity and forming a visual aid, includes in its function a virtual punctuation.

The *vinculum* is now restricted to mean that line over two algebraic symbols which is equivalent to a pair of parentheses enclosing them, as Webster shows thus: '$a - \overline{b - c} = a - (b - c)$'. The symbols may number more than two, and the 'bound' portion may instead consist of figures.

Both the *brace* { or, of course, } and the *vinculum* are occasionally called a *bracket*, which is suitable enough for the former, highly unsuitable for the latter. And *brackets*, by the way, are sometimes used for square parentheses [......] – a usage to be deprecated; to be still more strongly condemned is *in brackets* for 'in parentheses'.

Chapter 18

THE APOSTROPHE

THE *apostrophe*, indicated by ', has been adopted from the French, which took it from Latin *apostrophus*, itself from Greek ἡ ἀπόστροφος προσῳδία, 'he *apostrophos* prosōdia', the accent of turning away (*apostrephein*, to turn away) – that is, of elision or omission. There has been some confusion with *apostrophe* (from Gr. ἀποστροφή, *apostrophē*) – that rhetorical figure which consists of an exclamatory address to some person or thing.

§ 1: Strictly Irrelevant*

It serves to close a quotation, as in:

'He was a strange fellow'.

When double quotation marks are employed, the quotation closes with a pair of apostrophes – more strictly, with a pair of quotation marks, thus:

"He was a strange fellow".

§ 2: Omission

An apostrophe indicates the omission either of a letter, or letters, or of a figure, or figures, whether initially or medially or finally.

Initially: *'Fraid* I cannot manage it (*afraid*).
In *'39*, as you remember, war broke out (*1939*).

Medially: The man is a ne'er-do-well (*never*).
I fear I can't manage it (*cannot*).

Finally: In a muzzy voice he muttered, 'My house was *burn'* down lust night' (*burnt*).
It *'ll* do, he *'d* say. (It *will* do, he *would* say.)

---

* Irrelevant, because only in shape does a final quotation mark resemble a final apostrophe. French, for instance, uses « . . . . » to indicate quotation.

A special instance occurs in such a surname as *'Espinasse*, used by a French family that came to Britain ca. 1688 and has distinguished itself in Ireland and England: *'Espinasse* is short for *de l'Espinasse*, earlier *Espinassey*; the original family name was written *Espinassey de l'Espinassey*: the apostrophe may therefore be regarded as indicating the omission of *de l* (= *l'*). In one or two other names, this initial apostrophe represents either *l'* or *de*.

§ 3: Plurals of Letters, Figures, Symbols

Several examples will suffice:

(1) His name contains two *l*'s and his regimental number six 8's.
(2) Too many *I*'s render a letter egotistical.
(3) Such symbols as β's and γ's are beloved of schoolmasters and scientists.

In the third, the beta's and gamma's could be and often are written 'βs and γs'.

(4) The staff has two *Ph.D.*'s, three *B.Litt.*'s, six *M.A.*'s and, strange to relate, two former *M.P.*'s.

In (4) the apostrophe is gradually yielding to the full stop; thus:

Two *Ph.D.*s, three *B.Litt.*s, six *M.A.*s, two *M.P.*s.

This use of period for apostrophe may be more logical, but it is sometimes a little confusing. (I prefer the apostrophe.)

Formerly the apostrophe was often used in the plural to indicate the omission of *e*, as in *folio's* for *folioes*; this practice has fallen into disuse. It lingers – rightly lingers – for words with plural in *s*, not *-es*, where the *s* would, without an apostrophe, create an ambiguity or other awkwardness, as in

(1) The class includes three Louis's and two Lewises.
(2) He could not walk that distance – 873 *li*'s or Chinese miles.
(3) Grandpa's and grandma's abounded.
(4) The *thine*'s of archaic English.

Note that in (2) and (4) *li* and *thine* are italicized because the words are regarded very much as words; in (3) modern writers seem to prefer 'Grandpas and grandmas' – a tendency that, since it has not yet become usage, might profitably be resisted.

§ 4: The Possessive

For the genitive or possessive case – a *boy's* ambition, the *girls'* school, *Moses'* fate, *men's* lot, *conscience'* sake – the apostrophe 'originally marked merely the omission of *e* in writing, as in *fox's*, *James's* . . . ; it was gradually . . . extended to all possessives, even where *e* had not previously been written, as in *man's*, *children's*, *conscience'* sake. This was not yet established in 1725' (*The Oxford English Dictionary*).

I: UNCHANGEABLES

Such nouns as *sheep*, *deer*, *grouse*, the same in the plural as in the singular, always take *'s*, as in

A wolf in *sheep's* clothing.–Wolves in *sheep's* clothing.

For such nouns as *glanders*, *measles*, *mumps*, *corps*, *innings*, see the section 'Nouns in -*s*'.

II: WORDS CHANGED MEDIALLY AND FINALLY

Such nouns as *man – men*, *woman – women*, *foot – feet*, *tooth – teeth*, *goose – geese*, *louse – lice*, *mouse – mice*, always take *'s*, thus:

One *man's* rations cannot satisfy two *men's* appetites
A *goose's* gander, *geese's* ganders
A *mouse's* paradise, *mice's* titbits.

Such nouns as *brother – brethren*, *child – children*, *ox – oxen*, *cow – kine*, *sow – swine*, undergoing a change partly medial and partly final, and such as undergo only a final change, *die – dice* and *penny – pence*, likewise take always *'s*.

The *brethren's* dearest wish is to satisfy the *children's* needs, not merely one *child's* needs.
The *cow's* or the *ox's*, the *kine's* or the *oxen's* fodder. (*Kine* is archaic.)
A *threepence's* value is thrice one *penny's*.

The rare nouns with 'foreign' plurals, e.g. *stigma – stigmata*, *automaton – automata*, *formula – formulae*, *stimulus – stimuli*, where they are used in the possessive at all, take always *'s*, thus

One *automaton's* emotions, like three *automata's*, are precisely nil.
stimulus's, *stimuli's*.

III: ORDINARY NOUNS – THAT IS, ALL THOSE NOUNS
WHICH ADD *s* OR *es* TO FORM THE PLURAL

The golden rule for the formation of the genitive – the rule governing all nouns except those in groups I, II and IV, V, VI – is very simple. Add *'s* to the singular and merely the apostrophe to the plural, as in:

a *boy's* coat – four *boys'* tickets
a *ship's* captain – two *ships'* crews
a *fish's* scales – the *fishes'* speed upstream is remarkable
Keats's poems.

This rule accounts for the vast majority of English nouns.

IV: NOUNS ENDING IN *-nce*

Such nouns as *conscience* and *patience* take, in the singular, only the apostrophe:

for *conscience'* sake – for *patience'* sake.

If, however, the *-(e)nce* is not preceded by a sound approximating to 'sh' (*conshence, pashence*) – if the word therefore belongs to the *silence* or, with a different vowel, the *endurance* type – the genitive usually takes *'s*, as in

at *endurance's* end – in *Silence's* chill vacuum.

V: PROPER NAMES IN *-s*

There used to be, to a large extent there still is, a tendency to add merely an apostrophe to all ancient Proper Nouns, especially Hebrew, Greek, Latin, thus:

Boaz' wife, *Thucydides'* History, *Hercules'* story, *Horatius'* Odes:

nowadays, however, most people write *Boaz's*, *Thucydides's*, *Hercules's*, *Horatius's*, unless, avoiding cacophony, they prefer *of Boaz*, *of Thucydides*, etc. If the ugly plurals *Boazes, Thucydideses, Herculeses, Horatiuses* be risked, their genitives are formed in the usual way – by adding the simple apostrophe.

For such Proper Nouns as Mo*ses*, Xer*xes*, Croe*sus*, see: –

VI: THE *s-s* TYPE

Most words of this type are those which end in *-ces* (or *-cess*) or *-cis*, *-sces* or *-scess*, *-ses* (or *-sess*) or *-sis*, *-sas*(s) or *-sos*(s) or *-sus*(s); *-xes* or *-xis*; *-zes* or *-zis*. In the singular, these take only the apostrophe:

Xerxes' army – an *abscess'* description – *Ulysses'*, that is *Odysseus'*, story – *Jesus'* dreadful sufferings – *Berossos'* great work on Babylonian science – *Moses'* prophecy – a *princess'* birthday.

Note that all these nouns, but particularly *princess*, are, in modern usage, tending (or, at the least, beginning to tend) to add *'s*, as in

the *Princess's* unexpected accession to the throne.

Stylists will continue to prefer the *of Odysseus* form of genitive to all such genitival cacophonies – except *princess's*, which has become so very widely accepted as to be usage. Webster's set of rules for Classical nouns is, in its way, admirable – but arbitrary and no longer generally applicable.

This shift to or, at the least, towards simplicity and regularity is further exemplified in the changed attitude to nouns ending in *-ess*. Whereas formerly it was usual to write:

a *shepherdess'* crook, a *hostess'* privilege:

now we prefer:

a *shepherdess's* crook, a *hostess's* privilege.

The genitive plural has always been *shepherdesses'*, *hostesses'*, etc.

VII: ABBREVIATIONS

Abbreviations follow the general rule for the genitive singular:

James *I's*; the General Electrical *Co.'s* balance-sheet.

Such combinations belong in part to: –

VIII: THE GROUP GENITIVE

A few examples will exemplify the principle that only the last member of a noun group takes the apostrophe:

William and *Mary's* reign.
King Charles the First of *England's* strange death.
Jack, Tom and *Mary's* uncle. (Brothers and sister.)
Arthur Wellesley, Duke of Wellington, the Field *Marshal's* victory at Waterloo.

Where only one person, animal, thing, etc., is in the genitive, there are no exceptions; where two or more distinct persons, animals, etc., are in the genitive, the group genitive applies only where there is joint possession, responsibility, relationship, as in 'William and *Mary's* reign' and 'Jack, Tom and *Mary's* uncle'. If two separate possessions or other relationships are concerned, each noun must clearly be shown in the genitive, thus:

Great political difficulties characterized both William the *First's* and Mary *Tudor's* reign (bettei: reigns).
Jack's, Tom's and Mary's uncle (better: uncles) could not come to the prize-giving.

Where pronouns are concerned, we always use the possessive.

Your and *my* contract. (You and I are the signatories.)
Your and *my* contracts. (Two or more different contracts.)
His, your and *my* contract. (One contract, affecting three persons.)
His, your and *my* contracts. (Different contracts.)
John's and *your* ⎫
Your and *John's*⎭ contract. (Mutual.)
John's and *your* ⎫
Your and *John's*⎭ contracts. (Different.)

Where the contracts are different, one can vary the structure by writing, for instance:

His contract, and *yours*, and *mine*
Your contract and *John's*.

IX: ONE OR TWO ANOMALIES

Such formations as 'an idea *of* my *father's*' belong, not to a discussion of the apostrophe but to a treatise on syntax. For an admirable treatment of the genitive or possessive case, see pp. 70–88 of George O. Curme's book on English syntax; for a short account, my *Usage and Abusage* at pp. 128–133.

X: MODERN GOOD SENSE

'There is a laudable tendency in modern usage to omit the apostrophe, especially in plural nouns, where the nouns are adjectival without any real possessive sense [and where, in fact, the sense is not 'of' + noun but 'for' + noun]: "Womens Institute", "Boys School", "Students Union", "Miners Federation" ' (G. H. Vallins, *Good English: How to Write It*, Library Edition, 1952).

That tendency merely follows the pattern established by the omission of the apostrophe from the end of place-names, e.g. *St Albans*, from *ecclesia sancti Albani*, the church of St Alban; *St Andrews*, probably from a monastery; *St Bees*, (the church of) St Bega; *St Briavels*, *castellum* or fort of St Briavel; *St Helens*, from a church dedicated to St Helen; *St Neots*, probably from *villa sancti Neoti*; *St Pauls*, from *monasterium sancti Pauli*; and so forth.* But the capital of Newfoundland is written *St John's* (? St John's Port), as also is *St John's*, a county and a city in the Province of Quebec, Canada. *St Pauls* is still, more often than not, written *St Paul's*, in common with most other churches (*St Margaret's*, *St Martin's-in-the-Field*, etc.) and with most colleges that have a 'possessive' name. In such names as *Regent's Park*, *Earl's Court*, *King's Road*, the apostrophe is gradually disappearing: let it go, for such is the direction taken by usage, which seldom (? ever) errs in these matters.

* With thanks to Ekwall's *Concise Dictionary of English Place-Names.*

Chapter 19

TITLES OF BOOKS, PERIODICALS, CHAPTERS, ARTICLES

LET EXAMPLES point the precepts:

His letter in *The Times*, like that in *The Daily Telegraph*, concerned *A Concise Gazetteer*, by Sir William Geographicus. Now, Geographicus's *Concise Gazetteer* is as terse and accurate as the *Daily Telegraph* and *Times* letters.

His letter in 'The Times', like that in 'The Daily Telegraph', concerned 'A Concise Gazetteer', by Sir William Geographicus.

The Ghost at The Times or *The Ghost at 'The Times'*.*

The Man-Eaters of Borneo!, which seems to be a title doubly odd, might almost have been called *A Gastronomic 'Sour Grapes'* or *From the Modern to the Primitive*.

In Book I, 'The Essence of Religion', of this vast *Encyclopaedia of Religion and Myth*, the most readable portion is Chapter 8, 'The Merging of Myth and Religion?', which is both profound and witty. *An Encyclopaedia*, edited by Sir Thoresby Tinker, contains four other fascinating chapters, 'The Magi and Magic', 'Zoroaster and Confucius', 'The Wonder-Workers' and 'Science and the Miracles', all but one occurring in Book II, 'The Intermediate Stage', the exception being 'Science and the Miracles', which naturally appears in the third and final Book, 'The Modern Period'.

If one wished to differentiate more precisely between the entire work and its parts, one could have done it thus:

AN ENCYCLOPAEDIA OF RELIGION AND MYTH falls into three Books, of which the last is *The Modern Period*, with at least one memorable chapter, 'Science and the Miracles'.

Where a title begins with *A* or *The*, do not, except in the instances treated in the two paragraphs ensuing, omit *A*, *The*: for one thing, *A* is more modest than *The*, and the author, forbidden to acquire or retain capital, might perhaps be allowed to retain his modesty. Both

---

* In general it is better to 'quote' than to italicize special words in titles: 'quoted', they stand out more clearly. Where a title is already in italics, one cannot strictly italicize a word within that title; the usual device is to put the word or words into capitals, as in *The Ghost at* THE TIMES, but when the capitals occur at the end of the title, they look rather odd.

initial *a* and initial *the* should be capitalled and either italicized or, if the quotation mode (an inferior mode) is being used, placed after the opening inverted comma or commas. Do not fall into the ineptitude of 'a reporter on *the Times*' or 'on the *"Times"* '.

The only exceptionless exception occurs when the title is used attributively, as in 'I saw that *Times* correspondent at Cowes the other day'.

Where a possessive adjective (*my, your, his, their,* etc.) or a descriptive adjective (*careful, well-written, admirable,* etc.) precedes a title beginning with *A* or *The,* the usual practice is to omit *A* or *The,* as in

His *Dictionary of the Arts* is a valuable piece of work.
The admirable *Dictionary of Modern English Usage* by H. W. Fowler is a classic.

But an author referring to his own work may, as we have seen, prefer to say

My little *The Art of Concealing Art* has long been out of print.
My *A Guide to Modern Bacteriology* will appear next year.

Then there is this: How distinguish between *A –* or *The – Manual of Beekeeping* and the terse *Manual of Beekeeping*? Occasionally there may be no need to distinguish; whenever there is – distinguish!

'What words in book and other such titles – apart from the initial word, of course – are written small?' is a question frequently asked. The answer is:

a, an, and *the*
all conjunctions (*and, but,* even the longer *because,* etc.)
all prepositions (*of, to, for, from, at,* etc.):

my own practice is, in the titles of books, articles, etc., to capital every word other than those. The rather frequent habit of putting *is, are, was, were, will, shall, would, should, could, can, may, might, must, ought,* into lower-case lacks both sense and consistency. If '*She Fell Ill* is a good story', why not '*She Is Ill* is a good story'?

To say that 'all important words' – including the initial word – 'should be capitalled' is to beg the question, for the author may differ from the publisher, the printer from both, and all three from the critics, on the relative importance or insignificance of the various elements of a title, especially of such a magazine article as '*Did She Fall or Was She Pushed?*' : the *Ethics of Crime Fiction* or '*Save Me or*

I Perish!' She Cried to the Villain: A Study in the Language of Melodrama.

There is a neat way of side-stepping these tiny yet nagging problems: write all titles, whether of books or periodicals, whether of chapters or essays or articles or poems – write all titles entirely in capitals; that is, uniformly in small capitals, not in large and small capitals, a method leaving the problem untouched. Thus:

THE GHOST AT 'THE TIMES'.

Librarians in many countries adopt the following rational system:

Russell, Bernard. Philosophy of pacifism, the. 1916.
or   „   „   . *Philosophy of pacifism, the.* 1916.

There, *a(n)* and *the* are, as in all library-cataloguing, treated as lying outside the core of the title, and only the first word is capitalled. For books, periodicals, etc., the use of small capitals is preferable, as also is the system exemplified in *The Philosophy of Pacifism*.

There are, in consecutive writing, four ways to indicate titles:

(1) The Philosophy of Pacifism
(2) 'The Philosophy of Pacifism'
(3) *The Philosophy of Pacifism*
(4) THE PHILOSOPHY OF PACIFISM

Let us examine these, in relation to manuscript, typescript, print, both for the titles themselves on the title-page of a book (or on the spine or the jacket) or at the head of an article, an essay, a poem, etc., and in references to those titles.

Nos. (1) and (2) are to be avoided, for they do not set off a title clearly enough; only if the title is comparatively unimportant, is (1) adequate; (2) is almost inept, for it is neither completely fluid nor sufficiently separative; (4) should be used only where (3) occurs in the same reference; (3) – underlined in handwriting and in typewriting – is, on every count, the best of all.

Punctuation within a title is identical with punctuation within any other coherent and unitive group of words: and terminal punctuation of titles is more aptly treated in Chapter 22, Concert of Punctuation and Its Allies. Moreover, the examples given at the beginning of the present chapter imply most of the precepts involved.

Chapter 20

INDENTION AND PARAGRAPHING

§ 1: Indention

INDENTION* OR indenting is the act of starting a line or indeed a set of lines a little way in from the margin of the text; hence an indention is also the space thus left free of handwritten or type-written or printed matter – in printing, the space left at the beginning of a paragraph is quite often that occupied by an em-quad.† In this work, as the type measure is 25 ems the paragraph indention is $1\frac{1}{2}$ ems. When a book has a measure of 30 ems or over, the indent is usually 2 cms. Paragraph indention, by the way, arises from that habit of early printers, following the practice of scribes, which consists in leaving a blank space for the insertion of a large initial by the illuminator.

Obviously there is indention other than that which indicates the beginning of a new paragraph. Consider the following mixture of prose and verse:

Milton is recognized as the greatest British epic poet and one of the three or four greatest of all epic poets.

His finest poem is *Paradise Lost*, although one would hardly deduce that fact from the following:

Say first – for Heaven hides nothing from thy view,
Nor the deep tract of Hell – say first what cause
Moved our grand Parents, in that happy state,
Favoured of Heaven so highly, to fall off
From their Creator – and transgress his will
For one restraint, lords of the world besides.

Who first seduced them to that foul revolt?
The infernal Serpent; he it was whose guile,
Stirred up with envy and revenge, deceived
The mother of mankind. . . . . .

---

* From *indent*, literally to make a tooth-like incision at the edge, from *dens* (genitive *dentis*), a tooth; instead of *indentation*.

Paragraph: French *paragraphe*: Late Latin *paragraphus*: Greek παράγραφος, *paragraphos*, a line, a stroke, drawn at the side: *paragraphein*, to write (*graphein*) beside (*para*).

† A *quad* (short for quadrat) is a piece of metal used by printers for spacing; an em quad has 'length' equal to the 'width' of the letter *m*.

165

That, admittedly, is no fair test. For one dull, plodding passage there are two neither dull nor plodding, and at least one magnificent scene or incident in every Book.

There we have a passage, itself indented; a passage consisting of three prose paragraphs, beginning at 'Milton' – 'His' – 'That'. The second prose paragraph contains a quotation in verse: the entire quotation is indented in relation to the surrounding prose. Moreover, this verse quotation contains one complete paragraph and the beginning of another, and both of them are indicated, as prose paragraphs would be, by an indention.

Hanging, or *reverse, indention* is often used for short prose quotations and especially for brief examples, thus:

The preceding paragraphs have stated and proved what is meant by *indention*; merely implying the meaning of *paragraphing*, they have not told us the uses and purposes of paragraphs.

Here, all lines are indented except the first, which is left hanging – an arrangement the exact opposite of normal indention.

§ 2: Paragraphing

As the etymology of paragraph has at least hinted, the earliest equivalent of the space now indicating the beginning of a new paragraph (or indeed of any paragraph whatsoever) was a stroke, usually with a dot over it, serving especially to separate the speeches of the various characters in a stage-play or in a Platonic dialogue; the stroke was placed immediately to the left of the first line of every speech except the first. However short a speech might be, it did constitute a paragraph.

To some writers on punctuation, the paragraph seems to be extraneous; paragraphing, although it rarely affects punctuation itself, does affect the use of quotation marks; paragraphing may not, like quotation marks, rank as an ally, but it is certainly an accessory, both of the allies and of punctuation proper. It is therefore with pleasure that I again quote a short passage from an excellent book * undeservedly forgotten.

Concerning the principles which determine the division of subject-

---

* T. F. & M. F. A. Husband, *Punctuation: Its Principles and Practice*, 1905.

matter into paragraphs it is beyond our province . . . to speak; our present purposes are sufficiently served if we assume that in the treatment of a subject, be it narrative, descriptive, or expository, the paragraph properly contains a logical division of the whole. [But it contains nothing additional or extraneous to the matter forming that logical division.] It concentrates attention upon a particular element or aspect of the subject-matter, and elaborates it by grouping together ideas and facts that explain and support it. Taken as a whole, therefore, the paragraph gives a certain completeness of conception; running through all the sentences that go to make it up there is a common thread of discourse, round which are grouped relative considerations essential to the matter in hand. The various degrees of importance to be attached to these secondary elements are indicated by the prominence given to them, for, in order to convey his exact meaning to a reader, the writer must emphasize the weighty ideas and so arrange the subordinate ones that their degrees of relative importance may be clear.

The nature, like the place or relative value of a paragraph, can be very clearly seen in the following hierarchy:

the complete book
the chapter
the section (a stage often absent)
the paragraph
the sentence.

As Alexander Bain, philosopher and rhetorician, has remarked, a paragraph is a series of sentences – or perhaps only one sentence – informed and unified by a single purpose. 'Between one paragraph and another,' he says, 'there is a greater break in the subject than between one sentence and another. The internal arrangement comes under laws that are essentially the same as in a sentence, but on a greater scale.'

'The Paragraph laws,' he continues, 'are important, not only for their own sake, but also for their bearing on an entire composition. They are the general principles that must regulate the structure of sections, chapters, and books. . . . . . We may adapt an old homely maxim, and say, "Look to the Paragraphs, and the Discourse will take care of itself".'

Each paragraph corresponds to a topic, an aspect, an incident of the exposition or description or narrative. Once you have established the architectonics of a book, the natural chapter-order ensues; once you have established the ordonnance of a chapter or, as it may be, of a self-contained article or essay, you will find – indeed, you have already found – that particular order of treatment which is superior to all others. Hence the general rule:

By establishing the order in which you wish to make the points of your exposition or your argument, to set forth the incidents of your narrative, the aspects of your description, you simultaneously and inevitably establish the division into paragraphs, and the natural, because the best – the best, because the entirely natural – order of those paragraphs.*

That one general rule should suffice. There are, however, several particular rules helpful both to learners and to those who feel that perhaps they have learnt badly or insufficiently.

I. Whenever a paragraph looks as though it might easily become too long and even downright tedious, it is advisable to break it up into two or three parts (i.e., paragraphs). The transitions must be smooth: smoothness is not difficult to ensure, provided that the development of the thought or the flow of the narrative run uninterruptedly along the line of naturalness. One can, keeping the main purpose in view, further that purpose by some such conjunction as 'then' or 'therefore' or by some such conjunctival phrase as 'in these circumstances': for these will indicate the interdependence of the new set of paragraphs formed from one cumbrous paragraph, clarify the relationship and at the same time carry the theme forward; all to the benefit of the reader.

II. Do not write an article, an essay, a chapter, in a series of very short paragraphs; this trick, common in the so-called National Press, irritates the reader.

III. But to interpose, at long intervals, a one-sentence paragraph affords a resting-place for eye and mind. Compare the practice mentioned by the Husbands thus: 'Many writers introduce the subject of a chapter or an essay or an article, or sum its results, in a sentence-paragraph, thereby focussing attention on the main position'.

IV. If one develops a theme, paints a verbal picture, tells a story in a natural and therefore logical manner, one's paragraphs succeed one another so smoothly that conjunctions at the beginning of paragraphs will often be unnecessary. This, admittedly, is a matter of style; yet it does concern good paragraphing, which forms a minor element of all composition above the level of the moronic.

To sum up: the best way in which to learn the art of paragraphing is to assimilate it from the pages of the better novelists, essayists,

---

* Slightly adapted from *Usage and Abusage*. That section on paragraphing has furnished me also with the four minor rules that follow.

historians and biographers. Even this chapter is quite tolerably paragraphed. Webster has neatly summarized the principles involved when he defines the paragraph thus: 'A distinct section or subdivision of a discourse, chapter, or writing, whether of one or many sentences, that forms a rhetorical unit as dealing with a particular point of the subject, or as comprising the words of a distinct speaker, etc.' – as in all dialogue, whether formally in plays or informally in the conversation introduced into short story or novel or biography.*

In expository or instructive books, important paragraphs are, like those larger units, sections, often set off still more distinctly by the use of

'Centred' Headings

or of

Side Headings.

The latter are sometimes indented, and usually they are either italicized or printed in heavy type (Clarendon) or capitalled. All three means are available to the printer; to indicate heavy type, the handwriter has to use either a double underlining ========† or a wavy line ∿∿∿∿∿; a typist uses either ========† or ∪∪∪∪∪∪∪∪.

But take care not to overdo this sort of thing. All such devices are to be employed as sparingly as possible.

* For practical exemplification additional to the paragraphing of this very chapter, see Chapter 23, second 'half' (passages consisting of more than one paragraph).

† But unless a 'key' is given with such marking ========, this is usually interpreted as the marking of small capitals.

Chapter 21

VARIOUS MODES OF QUOTATION IN PROSE
AND VERSE; RELATIONSHIP OF
QUOTATION TO PARAGRAPHING

§ 1: Quotation in Reference to Paragraphing

EVERY QUOTATION, as we have seen (Chapter 15), begins and ends either with two quotation marks or inverted commas – "double quotes" – or with one such mark – 'single quotes'. If a quotation extends to an entire paragraph, the same marking applies.

When, however, the quotation consists of an entire passage of two or more paragraphs, there are two different practices with, of course, one feature in common: quotation mark(s) at beginning and end. One practice is to begin and end every paragraph with quotation mark(s); the other is to omit them from the end (but not from the beginning) of all but the last. The former is perhaps the safer, although the precaution does strike the economically minded and the unforgetful as being excessive.*

§ 2: The Various Modes of Quotation

I: MODES PRACTICABLE IN BOTH SCRIPT AND PRINT

(i) By far the commonest mode is the use of quotation marks, whether single or double. Both double and single quotation marks are correct; modern usage tends more and more to use the single. For general comment, see Chapter 15, Introductory and § 1, Strictly Quoted; for the alternation of single and double 'quotes', where there is an internal quotation, see § 8 of the same chapter.

'Thou shalt not kill.' (*Or:* "Thou . . .")
The commandment says, 'Thou shalt not kill'.
'Thou shalt not kill,' says the commandment.
'Do you,' he asked, 'like the word "phoney"?'

---

* I always use the second method.

(ii) Italic, which in print is indicated by a thinner, sloping type, and in handwriting and typewriting by underlining, is quite often employed.

Thou shalt not kill.
The commandment says, *Thou shalt not kill.*
Thou shalt not kill, says the commandment.
Do you, he asked, *like the word* phoney?
(Or: *Do you,* he asked, *like the word 'phoney'?*)

Compare Chapter 14, Italics, § 8.

(iii) Obviously applicable only within a sentence: the use of that initial capital which marks the beginning of every true quotation as distinct from a mere reference, without recourse to quotation marks or italics or a mere typographical device (as in iv, v, vi) – a mode to be used with great care, as can be seen from the opening paragraph of:

He said, You are hardly telling the truth, and, after an uncomfortable pause, he added, It cannot have escaped your notice that I'm being unusually polite.

You are being polite, I replied, because you know what would happen if you weren't.

Any internal quotation must be set off, either with 'quotes' or with italics, thus:

He said, You are a 'phoney' [or: *phoney*] and I don't trust you.

(iv) Without 'quotes' and without italics, a quotation can be indicated quite clearly by inserting a dash (–) both before and after, or merely before or merely after. The uses of these three varieties of the one method, the quotational dash, are differentiated thus:

Before and after, only when both are necessary to prevent ambiguity;
before, in dialogue;
after, to prevent quotation from merging with non-quotation.

A few examples will clarify a situation that, although not equivocal, is rather vague.

Don't do it, he said. – Why not? I asked. – Oh, please yourself. But you'll get hurt if you do. – Why, thanks! That's really considerate of you.

Don't do it.
– Why not?
– Oh, please yourself. But you'll get hurt if you do.
– Why, thanks! That's really considerate of you.

Suddenly he exclaimed, In your place I think I'd have acted rather differently. – I believe he would have, too, but I should have expected him to do so, he's so very different from me.

(v) Merely by indention, although after some indication that a speech or a quotation is to ensue. To render the quoted matter indisputably quoted, it may be necessary to continue the rest of the context with a line starting flush with the inner margin of the type area, thus:

> Gazing deliberately about him, he unhurriedly began:
> Ladies and gentlemen, unaccustomed as I am to public speaking,
> I shall come immediately – well, perhaps not quite immediately –
> to the point. Our lives are at stake. Clearly, we must do something
> about it. But what?

At this point, he again looked about him.
What, I ask, shall we do?
Yet another pause.

An indented passage is better indented from both margins than merely from the left-hand margin: double indention has been shown in the longer of the two spoken passages above; obviously it was not required for the shorter.

(vi) By inserting a double space before and after the spoken or quoted matter. This device, like the preceding one, renders quotation marks or italics unnecessary.

> Gazing deliberately about him, he unhurriedly began:
>
> Ladies and gentlemen, ...
> .... But what?

At this point, he again looked about him.

What, I ask, shall we do?

Yet another pause.

(vii) Whether initial capital only or quotation marks or italics are used, it is customary to introduce the speech or the quotation with a comma or a colon or, although now rarely, a colon-dash (: –), placed at the end of the preceding matter, thus:

> He said, 'I don't like it'.
> As the poet said, 'There comes a tide'.

He said: 'I don't like it'.
As the poet said: 'There comes a tide'.
But not: He said: – 'I don't like it'
    nor: As the poet said: – 'There comes a tide'.

Whether preceding a short speech or a short quotation, the colon-dash is rightly felt to be excessive. If used at all before speech or quotation – modern usage tends to discard it – the colon-dash should come only before a long passage.
    Compare:

He said, *I don't like it*
As the poet said, *There comes a tide*
He said: *I don't like it*
As the poet said: *There comes a tide*:

and you will perceive that before a very short speech or a very short quotation, even the colon seems just a little too solemn. The comma is the point most suitable before very short speeches and quotations: and by 'very short' I mean speeches and quotations of one sentence.
    But is it necessary that we should always punctuate the clause immediately preceding a speech or a quotation? Let us glance at the following examples:

He said 'I don't like it'
He said *I don't like it*
As the poet said 'There comes a tide'
As the poet said *There comes a tide*.

In the second pair, a point – preferably a comma – is certainly required; in the first pair, it is not required, – yet this omission has not yet become usage and perhaps it never will. I myself do believe that this omission, which already one sees used fairly often, will attain to the status of usage: and although, from sheer habit, I nearly always insert a comma immediately before a short speech or quotation and a colon (or occasionally a dash) before all others, I recommend the omission of the comma, as in

He said 'I don't like it'
He said *I don't like it*.

What, then, of the colon or dash before a speech or a quotation longer than one sentence? My recommendation is this: if the beginning of the speech or quotation falls into the same line as the 'introducer' (*says, replied, asked,* etc.) or at the very margin of the next line (that is, if there be no indention), use the colon or, if the context demands it, a dash; but if the speech or quotation – of more than one sentence, remember? – begins on a fresh and indented line, the colon or dash might well be omitted, especially if the matter be printed and the type be of a fount smaller (– almost never is it larger –) than that of the body of the book.

Certain writers go even further. They write such sentences as

'I don't like it' he said
I don't like it he said

'I can't' he said 'do it'
I can't he said *do it*

'Must I' he asked 'do it?'
Must I he asked *do it?*

This kind of thing is not general practice. It is less reprehensible than, at first, it strikes one as being, for it is based upon analogy. After all, we write

'Must I?' he asked
Must I? he asked

and not 'Must I?', he asked
Must I?, he asked.

But this particular sort of omission will not do, as we can see from examining a couple of examples, where neither quotation marks nor italics are used:

I can't he said do it
Must I he asked do it?

The commas in: 'I can't,' he said, 'do it'
I can't, he said, *do it*
I can't, he said, do it:

are syntactical, as they are, for instance, in:

As you know, 'A stitch in time saves nine'.

To sum up, we may rule that, whereas

He said 'I can't do it'
He said *I can't do it*

are permissible and, prejudice apart, commendable, and whereas

'I can't do it' he said

is, at first sight, a trifle odd, yet permissible, and whereas

I can't do it he said

is much odder and, all in all, to be avoided, such point-less sentences as

'I can't' he said 'do it'
I can't he said *do it*

are syntactically incorrect; and such a sentence as

I can't he said do it

is both syntactically incorrect and, even in that simple example, extremely ambiguous.

II: A MODE PRACTICABLE IN PRINT ONLY

In print there exists a mode impracticable on the typewriter and so inconvenient to the handwriter as to be never or virtually never used: the putting of all quoted matter (whether speech or reference-quotation) into noticeably smaller type, thus –

When this is done, neither quotation marks nor italics are required, and indention is present merely because every fresh paragraph is, as a rule, indented.

This typographical device, which possesses the virtue of great convenience and great distinctness, might be compared to the handwriter's very effective yet rarely employed device of using a different-coloured ink for the purpose of making a quotation stand out unmistakably.

Book III

ORCHESTRATION

Book III

ORCHESTRATION

Chapter 22

ALLIANCE OF PUNCTUATION AND QUOTATION. – PUNCTUATION AN ART, NOT A HAPHAZARDRY NOR YET A PERFUNCTORINESS

§ 1: Punctuation and Quotation

I N B O O K I I we have, in progressive stages, seen punctuation in the strict or narrow sense interacting with its allies and accessories. There is no need to labour the point, especially as we shall, in the next chapter, watch the full orchestra at work.

Yet there does remain a matter that we can only here treat satisfactorily: the interaction of quotation, in the fullest and every other sense, with punctuation; or, if you prefer, punctuation and its fellows co-operating with quotation.

Here we have a difficult subject: The position of points in relation to quoted matter – the conversation and speeches of persons real or imaginary, excerpts or other examples from literature, phrases and words set off between inverted commas or – much easier – in italics. Let me give a few instances of what I hold to be correct pointing and then comment on a few of the debatable matters.

(1) 'Modern British practice,' he said, 'appears to be more consistent and, in a sense, more ruthless than American.'

(2) He remarked, with a disarming smile, 'British practice is more consistent and ruthless than American'.

(3) 'Heaven,' he suggested, 'is an atmospheric word'; and after a reflective pause, 'and a beautiful one'.

(4) 'Heavens!' he exclaimed, 'He [or: 'he'] shouldn't be doing that, should he?' – 'I don't know,' replied Smith. 'Perhaps he shouldn't.'

(5) 'Among the words he mentioned as having an obscure origin were "boy" and "girl",' Jones recalled; 'Oh, yes! and also

179

"lad", "lass", "cat", "dog", "dodge", "jump", "bun" and "dun" (the verb); and I myself should like to add "wren", "chum", "pet", "culvert", "theodolite".' To this, I felt bound to add something. 'Well,' I suggested, 'what about "blouse", "cameo", "lounge", and such puzzles – these short words are the very deuce! – as "bob", "job", and "fag", "tag"?'

(6) 'If you do that' – 'What,' Jim shouted, 'makes you think I'm "windy" of you?' – 'I'll knock you into next week. And I don't mean "maybe",' I added.

(7) 'Did I hear you say "Why?"'

'You did,' he answered; 'and by that I implied "Why use such outmoded journalese as "eventuate" and "transpire" when all you intend is "happen"?'

'Well, you see, I *am* a journalist – oh! you didn't mutter "a *what?*" – writing for a newspaper whose readers enjoy that sort of tripe.'

(8) 'The bookworm told me that the title of the Ambrose Bierce book I was seeking is "Can Such Things Be?" and that the Thorne Smith "thriller" (apparently he wrote only *one* "thriller"!) is "Did She Fall?" – obviously elliptical (what's "elliptical"?), he told me, for "Did She Fall or Was She Pushed?"' said John a shade ruefully.

(9) 'I didn't describe the book as "bad". I described it less complimentarily: I said, "It stinks". Indeed I might adapt a cliché and say, "It stinks to high heaven and in the nostrils of all right-thinking persons". Now are you satisfied?'

(10) 'He looked the question "Barmy?" or, if you prefer American, "Nuts?" Did you hear me say "Nuts?"?' – 'Oh, I heard you all right, and what I say is "Nuts!" or, if you prefer, "Barmy!"'*

There we have British practice at its most modern and at its best – at its best, that is, if we accept certain complications that a scrupulous writer would, for the sake of his readers, avoid; avoid, not evade, for after all it's really simpler to walk beside a high, broken-glassed wall to the nearest door than to show how skilful and brave one is by ruining one's clothes, barking one's knees and cutting one's hands in scaling the thing.

Occasionally such examples as those numbered above are unavoidable, or perhaps, for some stylistic or intellectual reason, preferable. We shall assume that these numbered examples are justified.

* Several of those quotations show very clearly the superiority of italics to 'quotes' in complicated passages: italics preclude ambiguity and lessen the strain both on the reader and on the compositor and, by the way, also on the author. But that is not the question here.

American practice has been summarized by Webster thus:

'Quotation marks enclose any other punctuation marks of the passage quoted, as in the instance just given', that instance being 'The youth replies, "I will!"' '

That practice, as we have seen, is also British practice. Now for a difference: 'At the end of a quotation [even of a single word] the comma or the period should be included within the quotation marks; the colon, semicolon, question mark, or exclamation point [or, of course, the dash] should be placed inside or outside according as it belongs to the quoted matter or to the whole sentence: He asked, "Are you there?" Were you ever in a city called "Zenith"?' (End of quotation from *Webster's Dictionary*.) *

It is difficult to see why American practice should agree with the British practice, with logic, with good sense, in putting outside of the quotation marks indicating quoted matter all colons, semicolons, dashes, question and exclamation marks that don't belong to the quoted matter, yet should put inside the quotation marks even those commas and periods which don't belong to the quoted matter at all but which concern only the sentences as a whole.

A few examples will simplify the matter. Both British and American practice have:

He asked, first 'Are you there?' and then, 'What?'

He exclaimed, 'What a mess!' and then, 'What?'

He wished to know my opinion of 'some corner of a foreign field That is for ever England'; and then disagreed violently by shouting 'Fiddlesticks!'; we parted unfriendly.

He rose 'e'en at the dawn': that was his poetical way of intimating that he had dashed out of bed at nine in the morning.

But general American, only bad British, practice permits:

I cannot believe that he should say 'Fiddlesticks,' for it isn't in his character.

What he did, in fact, say was 'Fiddlededee.'

And both bad British and bad American practice are to be seen in:

(1) That's absolutely 'batty!'

(2) What do you mean by 'batty?'

---

* If we put those last two examples inside quotation marks, we obtain:

'. . . . . according as it belongs to the quoted matter or to the whole sentence: "He asked, 'Are you there?' " "Were you ever in a city called 'Zenith'?" '

(3) That's an odd word, 'batty;' and a very English piece of slang, 'at that:' but I suppose it's no odder than 'keen – ' which Americans use.

No. (3) is a particularly glaring example of bad interaction between quotation and punctuation.

See also Chapter 21, § 2, sub-section I, division vii (pp. 172–3): where certain points of punctuation between quoted words, phrases, passages, have been treated.

§ 2: Punctuation an Art, not a Haphazardry nor yet a Perfunctoriness

If we compare the punctuation of a good writer of today with that of a comparably good writer of ca. 1900, we notice that the older writer used a less various, less discriminatory, less subtle punctuation, which, by the way, was also less correct. The attitude towards punctuation has been changing throughout the present century, and changing for the better, in that writers and journalists, scholars and laymen, tend to punctuate according to the needs of the subject they happen to be treating and to resist both the usually too rigid 'house rules' of the printing firms * and the unimaginative, humdrum rules of Nesfield and his indoctrinated disciples.

But whereas the theory and the very concept of punctuation have much improved, the practice of punctuation, no less improved among good writers, has only a little improved among the rank and file of writers and journalists, scholars and schoolteachers. Nevertheless, the general attitude towards punctuation is now much more sensible than it was in (say) 1906, when the lessons inculcated in *The King's English* slowly began to take effect. Nowadays we rarely hear enunciated the deleterious and dangerous doctrine, 'Punctuation is a necessary evil'.

That punctuation is a necessity, even a child will admit: why else, in the fact, did it arise? and why else, in theory, should it have arisen? But to talk of punctuation as an evil is itself an evil – or, at the least, a piece of the crassest folly.

A teacher introducing punctuation to a class by saying, 'Well, chaps (*or* girls), we know that punctuation is a nuisance; but it has to

* There are several honourable exceptions – most notably, perhaps, the Oxford University Press.

be learnt, so let's make the best of a bad job', is implying an attitude
directly opposed to the one he should be encouraging them to adopt.
Rather should he approach the subject by hinting that the whole thing
is quite fun and that the ability to handle punctuation skilfully and
easily affords no less pleasure – and ultimately be incalculably more
useful – than the ability to bat or bowl well at cricket or to hit or
pitch well at baseball: that, indeed, the intelligent or, at worst, alert
exercise of any art inevitably brings pleasure, satisfaction, perhaps
even pride.

Punctuation is both an art and a craft; predominantly, however,
it is an art; a humble yet far from insignificant art, for it forms a means
to an end and is not in itself an end. The purpose it serves, the art it
subserves, is the art of good writing. As no good writer, whether of
prose or of verse, writes haphazardly, for haphazardly he cannot write
convincingly, effectively, beautifully, nor clearly; so no good writer
permits himself to be perfunctory, for by being perfunctory he insults
his readers. If a writer's punctuation is haphazard and perfunctory,
he positively misleads and irritates and negatively fails to please.

But no writer, be it only of a letter to the grocer, can afford to
become ambiguous and perhaps harmfully misunderstood, and thereby receive the wrong sort of cabbage, merely because he had not
learnt to punctuate adequately or could not see how useful – rather,
how necessary – it is to be able to punctuate well enough to obtain
what he wants instead of ignominiously omitting to insert that comma
which would have made all the difference.

The Fowlers have said that everyone should avoid depending on
his stops. Well, of course! But it could with still greater validity be
said that to eschew the astonishingly ample resources of punctuation,
to fail to profit by this storehouse of instruments that clarify and simplify, that variegate and enliven, that refine and subtilize, closely
resembles the action of a pig-headed fellow badly needing spectacles –
and refusing to wear them.

To the statement that punctuation * is an art, the philistine will
say, 'But I'm not interested in art!' But he is interested in craft – or,
if not in craft, at least in his livelihood. Not even a philistine can
afford to have it openly said of him, 'Oh, Black-market Smithereens
can't write a letter'; nor does it much help him to have it rumoured
among his competitors that his secretary not merely types his letters
but puts his half-formulated ideas into intelligible words and spells

* Here, as throughout this section, *punctuation* is to be understood as
'punctuation and its allies and accessories'.

and punctuates for him. If he himself doesn't need punctuation, his secretary certainly does: and the better she punctuates, the more favourable the impressions formed, by outsiders, of that boss who can afford to employ 'a real smasher'.

To punctuate intelligibly is a commercial and social 'basic unit' or 'minimum requirement'; to punctuate well, a social advantage; to punctuate very well, a social and intellectual distinction. More: good punctuation, in addition to preventing ambiguity and confusion, smoothes the path of the reader.

Chapter 23

FULL ORCHESTRA

To DESCRIBE and expound at greater length, to formulate more rules and make further regulations, would be very easy to do. And entirely unnecessary. The time has come to cease talking and begin working, not in short bursts but continuously for at least the duration of a paragraph; not merely using the wretchedly overworked full stop and the much-abused comma, but also enlisting the allies and utilizing the accessories.

First we shall deal with single, self-contained paragraphs, which, therefore, will at least require no paragraphing; then with consecutive passages of two or more paragraphs.

The examples have been so arranged that, with every 'opening' (a left-hand page and its complementary right-hand page) constituting a unit, we begin on the left (A) with a paragraph unstopped, uncapitalled, unitalicized, 'unquoted', pass in the next column (B) to a semi-literate or, at best, a very slipshod handling of the same paragraph; then in the third column (C – on the left of the right-hand page), this paragraph competently, unimaginatively, unsubtly pointed, capitalled, italicized, etc.; and finally, in the fourth column (D), an artistic or imaginative, a subtle and delicate treatment. In (II), Consecutive Passages, we deal with the same features, with the addition of paragraphing that ascends from null to stupid or careless, then to competent but dull, and ending with something rather more satisfying.

First, the single paragraphs or paragraph-equivalents.

(A) UNTOUCHED

(B) SEMI-LITERATE; OR CARELESS

(1) short sentences have many advantages over long ones they are simple clear and easily understood at the same time too they offer few opportunities for wordy and irrelevant digression for example prudence is the virtue of the senses it is the science of appearance it is the outmost action of the inward life

(1) Short sentences have many advantages over long ones, they are simple, clear and easily understood. At the same time too they offer few opportunities for wordy and irrelevant digression, for example: Prudence is the virtue of the senses, it is the science of appearances. It is the outmost action of the inward life.

(2) no sentence is to be condemned for mere length a really skilful writer can fill a page with one and not tire his reader though a succession of long sentences without the relief of short ones interspersed is almost sure to be forbidding but the tiro and even the good writer who is not prepared to take the trouble of reading aloud what he has written should confine himself to the easily manageable the tendency is to allow some part of a sentence to develop unnatural proportions or a half parenthetic insertion to separate too widely the essential parts the cure indispensable for every one who aims at a passable style and infallible for any one who has a good ear is reading aloud after writing

(2) No sentence is to be condemned for mere length – a really skilful writer can fill a page with one, and not tire his reader though a succession of long sentences without the relief of short ones interspersed, is almost sure to be forbidding, but the tiro and even the good writer who is not prepared to take the trouble of reading aloud what he has written, should confine himself to the easily manageable. The tendency is to allow some part of a sentence to develop unnatural proportions, or a half parenthetic insertion to separate too widely the essential parts; the cure indispensable for every one who aims at a passable style and infallible for any one who has a good ear, is reading aloud after writing.

(3) let us pass from those two wisely simple not so simple men the wits charles lamb and douglas jerrold to the sophisticated james abbott mcneill whistler 1834 1903 and oscar wilde 1856 1900 here I draw upon walter jerrolds a book of famous wits 1912 whistler however was not a frequent punster he was a frequent wit but we

(3) Let us pass from those two wisely simple, not so simple men, the wits, Charles Lamb and Douglas Jerrold, to the sophisticated James Abbott McNeill Whistler, 1834–1903, and Oscar Wilde, 1856–1900. Here I draw upon Walter Jerrold's *Book of Famous Wits*, 1912. Whistler however was not a frequent punster, he was a frequent wit.

(C) AVERAGE; OR MERELY COMPETENT

(1) Short sentences have many advantages over long ones. They are simple, clear, and easily understood; at the same time too they offer few opportunities for wordy and irrelevant digression. For example: – Prudence is the virtue of the senses. It is the science of appearances. It is the outmost action of the inward life.*

(2) No sentence is to be condemned for mere length; a really skilful writer can fill a page with one and not tire his reader, though a succession of long sentences without the relief of short ones interspersed is almost sure to be forbidding. But the tiro, and even the good writer who is not prepared to take the trouble of reading aloud what he has written, should confine himself to the easily manageable. The tendency is to allow some part of a sentence to develop unnatural proportions, or a half parenthetic insertion to separate too widely the essential parts. The cure, indispensable for every one who aims at a passable style, and infallible for any one who has a good ear, is reading aloud after writing.†

(3) Let us pass from those two wisely-simple, not-so-simple men, the wits, Charles Lamb and Douglas Jerrold, to the sophisticated James Abbott McNeill Whistler (1834–1903) and Oscar Wilde (1856–1900). Here I draw upon Walter Jerrold's *Book of Famous Wits*, 1912. Whistler, however, was not a frequent punster – he was a fre-

(D) PUNCTUATION AN ART

(1) Short sentences have many advantages over long ones: they are simple, clear, and easily understood; at the same time too, they offer few opportunities for wordy and irrelevant digression. For example: Prudence is the virtue of the senses; it is the science of appearances; it is the outmost action of the inward life.

(2) No sentence is to be condemned for mere length. A really skilful writer can fill a page with one and not tire his reader, though a succession of long sentences without the relief of short ones interspersed is almost sure to be forbidding. But the tiro – and even the good writer who is not prepared to take the trouble of reading aloud what he has written – should confine himself to the easily manageable. The tendency is to allow some part of a sentence to develop unnatural proportions, or a half-parenthetic insertion to separate too widely the essential parts. The cure, indispensable for everyone who aims at a passable style, and infallible for anyone with a good ear, is reading aloud after writing.

(3) Let us pass from those two wisely simple, not so simple men, the wits Charles Lamb and Douglas Jerrold, to the sophisticated James Abbott McNeill Whistler (1854–1903) and Oscar Wilde (1856–1900). Here I draw upon Walter Jerrold's *A Book of Famous Wits*, 1912. Whistler, however, was not a frequent punster; he

---

* T. F. & M. F. A. Husband, *Punctuation: Its Principles and Practice*; quotation from R. W. Emerson.

† *The King's English*. The punctuation, obviously, is very good. But, written in 1905 or 1906, it exhibits several traits no longer accordant with post-1940 practice.

(A) UNTOUCHED	(B) SEMI-LITERATE; OR CARELESS
may record that whistler having made some happy remark wilde showed his appreciation by saying i wish i had said that whistler you will oscar you will said whistler dryly. . . . . . one of wildes retaliations may perhaps be recognized in his remark that whistler with all his faults was never guilty of writing a line of poetry	But we may record that Whistler, having made some happy remark, Wilde showed his appreciation by saying: – I wish I had said that, Whistler. You will, Oscar, you will, said Whistler dryly. . . . . . One of Wilde's retaliations may perhaps be recognized in his remark that Whistler with all his faults was never guilty of writing a line of poetry.
(4) to a very thin man who had been boring him douglas jerrold said sir you are like a pin but without either its head or its point not so sharp as a pin in fact.	(4) To a very thin man who had been boring him, Douglas Jerrold said: Sir, you are like a pin but without either its head or its point. Not so sharp as a pin in fact.
(5) certain english words have a fascinating etymology he said among these are ambassador cockney heathen pagan satellite worm zany all of which you will find treated with respect and with a sense of historical romance by websters new international dictionary by the oxford english dictionary and by ernest weekley in his concise etymological dictionary of modern english	(5) 'Certain English words have a fascinating etymology,' he said; 'among these are 'ambassador,' 'cockney,' 'heathen,' 'pagan,' 'satellite,' 'worm,' 'zany,' all of which you will find treated with respect and with a sense of historical romance by 'Websters New International Dictionary,' by the 'Oxford English Dictionary,' and by Ernest Weekley in his Concise Etymological Dictionary of Modern English.'
(6) rhodope . . . . . . let me pause and consider a little if you please i begin to suspect that as gods formerly did you have been turning men into beasts and beasts into men but aesop you should never say the thing that is untrue aesop we say and do and look no other all our lives rhodope do we never know better aesop yes when we cease to please and to wish it when death is settling the features and the cerements are ready to render them	(6) Rhodope . . . . . . Let me pause and consider a little. If you please, I begin to suspect that as gods formerly did you have been turning men into beasts and beasts into men, but, Aesop, you should never say the thing that is untrue. Aesop. We say and do and look, no other, all our lives. Rhodope. Do we never know better? Aesop. Yes, when we cease to please and to wish it, when death is settling

(C) AVERAGE; OR MERELY COMPETENT

quent wit. But we may record that, Whistler 'having made some happy remark, Wilde showed his appreciation by saying: "I wish I had said that, Whistler." "You will, Oscar, you will," said Whistler dryly. . . . . . One of Wilde's retaliations may, perhaps, be recognized in his remark that "Whistler, with all his faults, was never guilty of writing a line of poetry".'

(4) To a very thin man, who had been boring him, Douglas Jerrold said: 'Sir, you are like a pin; but without either its head or its point.' (Not so sharp as a pin, in fact.)

(5) 'Certain English words have a fascinating etymology,' he said; 'among these are 'ambassador', 'cockney', 'heathen', 'pagan', 'satellite', 'worm', 'zany', all of which you will find treated with respect and with a sense of historical romance by *Webster's New International Dictionary*, by the *Oxford English Dictionary*, and by Ernest Weekley in his *Concise Etymological Dictionary of Modern English*.

(6) *Rhodope* . . . . . Let me pause, and consider a little, if you please. I begin to suspect that as gods formerly did, you have been turning men into beasts and beasts into men. But, Aesop, you should never say the thing that is untrue.
Aesop. We say and do and look no other, all our lives.
Rhodope. Do we never know better?
Aesop. Yes! When we cease to please, and to wish it. When death is

(D) PUNCTUATION AN ART

was a frequent wit. But we may record that, Whistler 'having made some happy remark, Wilde showed his appreciation by saying, "I wish I had said that, Whistler". "You will, Oscar; you will," said Whistler dryly. . . . . . One of Wilde's retaliations may perhaps be recognized in his remark that "Whistler, with all his faults, was never guilty of writing a line of poetry".'

(4) To a very thin man, who had been boring him, Douglas Jerrold said, 'Sir, you are like a pin, but without either its head or its point'. (Not so sharp as a pin, in fact.)

(5) 'Certain English words have a fascinating etymology,' he said. 'Among these are *ambassador, cockney, heathen, pagan, satellite, worm, zany*: all of which you will find treated with respect and with a sense of historical romance by *Webster's New International Dictionary*, by *The Oxford English Dictionary* and by Ernest Weekley in his *Concise* [or: *A Concise*] *Etymological Dictionary of Modern English*.

(6) *Rhodope* . . . . . Let me pause and consider a little, if you please. I begin to suspect that, as the gods formerly did, you have been turning men into beasts, and beasts into men. But, Aesop, you should never say the thing that is untrue.
Aesop. We say and do and look no other all our lives.
Rhodope. Do we never know better?
Aesop. Yes; when we cease to please, and to wish it; when death is settling

Both (3) and (4) have been taken, with only clarificatory alteration, from the article on P U N S in *Usage and Abusage: A Guide to Good English*.

(A) UNTOUCHED	(B) SEMI-LITERATE; OR CARELESS
unchangeable rhodope alas alas aesop breathe rhodope breathe again those painless sighs they belong to thy vernal season	the features and the cerements are ready to render them unchangeable. Rhodope. Alas, alas. Aesop. Breathe, Rhodope, breathe again those painless sighs, they belong to thy vernal season.

We now pass to consecutive passages of two or more paragraphs; to these consecutive passages example no. (6) above forms a very convenient transition – almost a 'keyed' transition.

II (1) in some fruits of solitude 1693 william penn on the comfort of friends wrote thus they that love beyond the world cannot be separated by it death cannot kill what never dies nor can spirits ever be divided that love and live in the same divine principle the root and record of their friendship if absence be not death neither is theirs death is but crossing the world as friends do the seas they live in one another still for they must needs be present that love and live in that which is omnipresent in this divine glass they see face to face and their converse is free as well as pure this is the comfort of friends that though they may be said to die yet their friendship and society are in the best sense ever preserved because immortal.

II (1) In some 'Fruits of Solitude,' 1693, William Penn, on the comfort of friends, wrote thus: – They that love beyond the world cannot be separated by it. Death cannot kill what never dies, nor can spirits ever be divided that love and live in the same divine principle, the root and record of their friendship. If absence be not death neither is theirs; death is but crossing the world as friends do the seas; they live in one another still, for they must needs be present that love and live in that which is omnipresent in this divine glass. They see face to face and their converse is free as well as pure. This is the comfort of friends that though they may be said to die, yet their friendship and society are in the best sense ever preserved because immortal.

Note. In form this is a very easy passage to punctuate correctly, but in sense, lucidly though Penn writes, rather less easy. Two or three of the mistakes made in the next column are venial; one of them, indeed, is entirely natural.

(C) AVERAGE; OR MERELY COMPETENT

settling the features and the cerements are ready to render them unchangeable.
Rhodope. Alas, alas!
Aesop. Breathe, Rhodope, breathe again those painless sighs. They belong to thy vernal season.

(D) PUNCTUATION AN ART

the features, and the cerements are ready to render them unchangeable.
Rhodope. Alas! Alas!
Aesop. Breathe, Rhodope! breathe again those painless sighs: they belong to thy vernal season.–
W. S. LANDOR.

Note. For the speakers' names, especially if abbreviations are being used, small capitals are by many preferred to italics.

II (1) In *Some Fruits of Solitude* (1693), William Penn, on 'The Comfort of Friends', wrote thus: –
'They that love beyond the world, cannot be separated by it.'
'Death cannot kill what never dies. Nor can spirits ever be divided that love and live in the same divine principle, the root and record of their friendship.'
'If absence be not death, neither is theirs.'
'Death is but crossing the world, as friends do the seas. They live in one another, still; for they must needs be present that love and live in that which is omnipresent.'
'In this divine glass, they see face to face, and their converse is free as well as pure.'
'This is the comfort of friends, that, though they may be said to die, yet their friendship and society are, in the best sense, ever preserved, because immortal.'

II (1) In *Some Fruits of Solitude* (1693) William Penn, on 'The Comfort of Friends', wrote thus:
'They that love beyond the world cannot be separated by it.'
'Death cannot kill what never dies.'
'Nor can spirits ever be divided, that love and live in the same divine principle, the root and record of their friendship.'
'If absence be not death, neither is theirs.'
'Death is but crossing the world, as friends do the seas; they live in one another still.'
'For they must needs be present, who love and live in that which is omnipresent.'
'In this divine glass they see face to face; and their converse is free, as well as pure.'
'This is the comfort of friends, that though they may be said to die, yet their friendship and society are, in the best sense, ever preserved, because immortal.'

Note. Judged by the meaning alone, the passage could feasibly have been thus paragraphed: yet no one with a good ear or a sense of rhythm or even with a sense of balance and proportion would thus have paragraphed it.

Note. The quotation marks would be unnecessary if the entire quotation from Penn were printed in a type smaller than that of the introductory words. – A modern stylist might perhaps punctuate the seventh aphorism thus:

(A) UNTOUCHED	(B) SEMI-LITERATE; OR CARELESS

II (2) some people say it is a very easy thing to get up of a cold morning you have only they tell you to take the resolution and the thing is done this may be very true just as a boy at school has only to take a flogging and the thing is over but we have not at all made up our minds upon it and we find it a very pleasant exercise to discuss the matter candidly before we get up this at least is not idling though it may be lying it affords an excellent answer to those who ask how lying in bed can be indulged in by a reasoning being a rational creature how why with the argument calmly at work in ones head and the clothes over ones shoulder oh it is a fine way of spending a sensible impartial half hour if these people would be more charitable they would get on with their argument better but they are apt to reason so ill and to assert so dogmatically that one could wish to have them stand round ones bed of a bitter morning and lie before their faces they ought to hear both sides of the bed the inside and out if they cannot entertain themselves with their own thoughts for half an hour or so it is not the fault of those who can candid inquiries into ones decumbency besides the greater or less privileges to be allowed a man in proportion to his ability of keeping early hours the work given his faculties etc

II (2) Some people say, it is a very easy thing to get up of a cold morning; you have only (they tell you) to take the resolution and the thing is done. This may be very true, just as a boy at school has only to take a flogging and the thing is over. But we have not at all made up our minds upon it and we find it a very pleasant exercise to discuss the matter, candidly, before we get up. At least this is not idling though it may be lying. It affords an excellent answer to those who ask how lying in bed can be indulged in by a reasoning being – a rational creature. How? Why with the argument calmly at work in one's head and the clothes over one's shoulder. Oh! it is a fine way of spending a sensible impartial half hour. If these people would be more charitable they would get on with their argument better, but they are apt to reason so ill and to assert so dogmatically that one could wish to have them stand round one's bed of a bitter morning and lie before their faces.

They ought to hear both sides of the bed, the inside and the out; if they cannot entertain themselves with their own thoughts for half an hour or so it is not the fault of those who can.

Candid inquiries into one's decumbency, besides the greater or less privileges to be allowed a man in pro-

(C) AVERAGE; OR MERELY COMPETENT

(D) PUNCTUATION AN ART

'In this divine glass they see face to face: and their converse is free, as well as pure'; but only in order to differentiate this semicolon from that in the fifth aphorism. Penn's is a vigorous yet delicate, logical yet euphonious punctuation.

II (2) Some people say it is a very easy thing to get up of a cold morning. You have only, they tell you, to take the resolution; and the thing is done. This may be very true; just as a boy at school has only to take a flogging, and the thing is over. But we have not at all made up our minds upon it: and we find it a very pleasant exercise to discuss the matter, candidly, before we get up. This, at least, is not idling, though it may be lying. It affords an excellent answer to those who ask how lying in bed can be indulged in by a reasoning being, – a rational creature. How? Why, with the argument calmly at work in one's head, and the clothes over one's shoulder. Oh – it is a fine way of spending a sensible, impartial half-hour.

If these people would be more charitable they would get on with their argument better. But they are apt to reason so ill, and to assert so dogmatically, that one could wish to have them stand round one's bed, of a bitter morning, and *lie* before their faces. They ought to hear both sides of the bed, the inside and out. If they cannot entertain themselves with their own thoughts for half-an-hour or so, it is not the fault of those who can.

Candid inquiries into one's decumbency, besides the greater or less privileges to be allowed a man in pro-

II (2) Some people say it is a very easy thing to get up of a cold morning. You have only, they tell you, to take the resolution, and the thing is done. This may be very true; just as a boy at school has only to take a flogging, and the thing is over. But we have not at all made up our minds upon it: and we find it a very pleasant exercise to discuss the matter, candidly*, before we get up. This, at least, is not idling, though it may be lying. It affords an excellent answer to those who ask how lying in bed can be indulged in by a reasoning being – a rational creature. How? Why, with the argument calmly at work in one's head and the clothes over one's shoulder. Oh! it is a fine way of spending a sensible, impartial half-hour.

If these people would be more charitable, they would get on with their argument better. But they are apt to reason so ill, and to assert so dogmatically, that one could wish to have them stand round one's bed, of a bitter morning – and *lie* before their faces. They ought to hear both sides of the bed, the inside and out. If they cannot entertain themselves with their own thoughts for half an hour or so, it is not the fault of those who can.

Candid inquiries into one's decumbency, besides the greater or less privilege to be allowed a man in pro-

---

* Leigh Hunt is emphasizing 'candidly' – and therefore creates a pause before and after by setting the word off within a pair of commas.

(A) UNTOUCHED	(B) SEMI-LITERATE; OR CARELESS
will at least concede their due merits to such representations as the following	portion to his ability of keeping early hours, the work given to his faculties etc., will at least concede their due merits to such representations as the following.

II (3) no matter how advanced the essay writing the secret lies in the etymology of essay of which francis bacon 1597 remarked the word is late but the thing is ancient Bacon adopted it from the essais of montaigne the worlds greatest essayist the french essai comes from the late latin exagium a balance compare the classical latin examen a weighing and exigere one of the two basic senses of exigere is to complete a weighing an essay is a weighing a weighing up followed by a declaration of the weight the weight of whatever matter or subject or topic is under consideration but you not your teacher nor your examiner do the weighing and declare the weight in the opening paragraph you put the article into the scale in the body of the essay you weigh it carefully at the end you declare the weight and set the article aside an essay is your personal weighing of the subject your examination of the subject is partial and selective the choice of the aspects being your not someone elses choice you might weigh incorrectly the error is far less important than the activity you do the weighing yourself not supervise some third party you express freely whatever you have to say

II (3) No matter how advanced the essay writing the secret lies in the etymology of *essay*, of which Francis Bacon, 1597, remarked, 'The word is late but the thing is ancient.' Bacon adopted it from the *essais* of Montaigne, the world's greatest essayist. The French *essai* comes from the late Latin *exagium*, a balance – compare the classical Latin *examen*, a weighing, and *exigere*. One of the two basic senses of *exigere* is to complete with derivative to weigh via to complete a weighing.

An *essay* is a weighing – a weighing-up, followed by a declaration of the weight – the weight of whatever matter or subject or topic is under consideration. But you, not your teacher, nor your examiner, you do the weighing and declare the weight. In the opening paragraph you put the article in the scale, in the body of the essay you weigh it carefully, at the end you declare the weight and set the article aside. An essay is your personal weighing of the subject.

Your examination of the subject is partial and selective, the choice of the aspects being your, not someone else's choice. You might weigh incorrectly. The error is far less important than the activity. You do the weighing

(C) AVERAGE; OR MERELY COMPETENT

portion to his ability of keeping early hours, the work given his faculties, etc., will at least concede their due merits to such representations as the following . . . . . . – LEIGH HUNT.

Note. This is a delightful essay, but its punctuation is a shade monotonous. In the next column, the punctuation has also been modernized. The total number of changes is very small; the changes themselves, slight.

II (3) No matter how advanced the essay writing, the secret lies in the etymology of *essay*, of which Francis Bacon (1597) remarked, 'The word is late, but the thing is ancient'. Bacon adopted it from the *Essais* of Montaigne, the world's greatest essayist. The French *essai* comes from the Late Latin *exagium*, a balance. Compare Classical Latin *examen*, a weighing, and *exigere*: one of the two basic senses of *exigere* is 'to complete', with derivative 'to weigh', via 'to complete a weighing'. An essay is a weighing – a weighing up, followed by a declaration of the weight – the weight of whatever matter or subject or topic is under consideration.

But you, not your teacher nor your examiner, you do the weighing and declare the weight.

In the opening paragraph you put the article into the scale – in the body of the essay you weigh it carefully – at the end you declare the weight and set the article aside. An essay is your personal weighing of the subject.

Your examination of the subject is partial and selective, the choice of the aspects being your – not someone else's – choice. You might weigh incorrectly; the error is far less important than the activity. You do the

(D) PUNCTUATION AN ART

portion to his ability of keeping early hours, the work given his faculties, etc., will at least concede their due merits to such representations as the following.

II (3) No matter how advanced the essay-writing, the secret lies in the etymology of *essay* – of which Francis Bacon (1597) remarked, 'The word is late, but the thing is ancient'; Bacon adopted it from the *Essais* of Montaigne, the world's greatest essayist. The French *essai* comes from the Late Latin *exagium*, a balance: compare Classical Latin *examen*, a weighing, and *exigere*; one of the two basic senses of *exigere* is 'to complete', with derivative 'to weigh', via 'to complete a weighing'.

An essay is a weighing: a weighing-up, followed by a declaration of weight. The weight of whatever matter or subject or topic is under consideration.

But you – not your teacher, nor your examiner – *you* do the weighing and declare the weight. In the opening paragraph*, you put the article into the scale; in the body of the essay*, you weigh it carefully; at the end*, you declare the weight and set the article aside.

An essay is your personal weighing of the subject. Your *examination* of the subject is partial and selective, the choice of the aspects being your†, not someone else's choice. You might weigh incorrectly; the error is far less important than the activity. You do

(A) UNTOUCHED

(B) SEMI-LITERATE; OR
CARELESS

yourself, not supervise some third party; you express freely whatever you have to say.

your own response to a subject be that response intellectual aesthetic emotional is what the reader expects if he didnt he would go to an encyclopaedia or some other source you will be personal even about the esoteric aspect of cubism no less than about the happiest day of my life naturally however you will quantitatively be less personal about shinto than unless you are a japanese upon rock gardens more personal upon what I hope to do in life than upon municipal libraries each subject dictates or at the least suggests the degree of personalness you will express but no rules can be laid down upon the subject you will develop a flair in these matters a flair consisting of good taste social tact reticence and so forth of the principles of essay writing you already know sufficient anything further you may wish or be obliged to learn you will be wise to assimilate rather than to swot your teacher and if you go to a university your tutor will instruct you indirectly by criticizing your essays also you will learn as you go from the mere act of writing essays

Your own response to a subject (be that response intellectual, aesthetic, emotional) is what the reader expects. If he didn't he would go to an encyclopaedia, or some other source. You will be personal even about the esoteric aspect of cubism no less than about *The Happiest Day of My Life.* Naturally however you will quantitatively be less personal about Shinto than – unless you are a Japanese – upon rock gardens, more personal upon *What I Hope to Do in Life* than upon municipal libraries; each subject dictates or at the least suggests the degree of *personalness* you will express; but no rules can be laid down upon the subject.

You will develop a flair in these matters; a flair consisting of good taste, social tact, reticence, and so forth.

Of the principles of essay writing you already know sufficient, anything further you may wish or be obliged to learn you will be wise to assimilate rather than to *swot.* Your teacher and (if you go to a university) your tutor will instruct you indirectly by criticizing your essays; also you will *learn as you go* from the mere act of writing essays.

(c) AVERAGE; OR MERELY COMPETENT

weighing yourself, not supervise some third party. You express freely whatever you have to say.

Your own response to a subject – be that response intellectual, aesthetic, emotional – is what the reader expects. If he didn't, he would go to an encyclopaedia, or some other source. You will be personal even about the esoteric significance of cubism, no less than about *The Happiest Day of My Life*. Naturally, however, you will quantitatively be less personal upon Shinto than – unless you are a Japanese – upon rock gardens; more personal upon *What I Hope to Do in Life* than upon municipal libraries.

Each subject dictates or, at the least, suggests the degree of *personalness* you will express, but no rules can be laid down upon the subject. You will develop a flair in these matters; a flair consisting of good taste, social tact, reticence and so forth.

Of the principles of essay writing, you already know sufficient; anything further you may wish or be obliged to learn, you will be wise to assimilate rather than to *swot*. Your teacher and – if you go to a university – your tutor will instruct you indirectly by criticizing your essays; also you will *learn* as *you go* from the mere act of writing essays.

(d) PUNCTUATION AN ART

the weighing yourself, not supervise some third party. You express freely whatever *you* have to say.

Note: The commas at *, *, * are deliberate: the context demands the weight of a pause. Compare the comma at †.

Your own response to a subject, be that response intellectual, aesthetic, emotional, is what the reader expects; if he didn't, he would go to an encyclopaedia or some other source. You will be personal even about the esoteric significance of cubism, no less than about 'The Happiest Day of My Life'. Naturally, however, you will quantitatively be less personal upon Shinto than, unless you are a Japanese, upon rock-gardens; more personal upon 'What I Hope to Do in Life' than upon municipal libraries. Each subject dictates or, at the least, suggests the degree of 'personalness' you will express; but no rules can be laid down upon the subject. You will develop a flair in these matters: a flair consisting of good taste, social tact, reticence and so forth.

Of the principles of essay-writing you already know sufficient. Anything further you may wish or be obliged to learn, you will be wise to assimilate rather than to 'swot'. Your teacher and, if you go to a university, your tutor will instruct you indirectly – by criticizing your essays. Also, you will 'learn as you go', from the mere act of writing essays.

Note: This passage comes from 'Composition, III' in Book III of *English: A Course for Human Beings*. The punctuation there is superior to that in the preceding column, but I

(A) UNTOUCHED	(B) SEMI-LITERATE; OR CARELESS
II (4) well well well what are you do-ing here you old rascal oh nothing much just looking around for what you can pick up i suppose tut tut dont make me out to be a thief im only an opportunist after all you know but a very unusual sort of opportunist you don't merely grasp such opportunities as offer themselves to your remarkably observant eyes charles you do a great deal or so at least i suspect to create the opportunities why robert the con-versation is taking a strange turn you began by almost insulting me now you are paying me what is in effect a com-pliment indeed in its way a very high compliment darn it thats not quite correct i mean about the compliment for although i admire your versatility your resourcefulness your adaptability don't pile it on too thick old man dont interrupt as i was saying i admire these qualities others i deplore but you are quite right we seem to be dropping into a fin de siecle persiflage and hatred of being earnest however i wanted to ask you for sorry old chap must tear myself away my bus you know	II (4) Well, well, well, what are you doing here, you old rascal? Oh, noth-ing much. Just looking around for what you can pick up, I suppose. Tut, tut, don't make me out to be a thief, I'm only an opportunist after all, you know. But a very unusual sort of op-portunist. You don't merely grasp such opportunities as offer themselves to your remarkably observant eyes, Charles. You do a great deal or so at least I suspect to create the oppor-tunities. Why, Robert, the conversa-tion is taking a strange turn – you be-gan by almost insulting me, now you are paying me what is in effect a com-pliment, indeed in its way a very high compliment. Darn it! That's not quite correct, I mean about the compliment, for although I admire your versatility, your resourcefulness, your adapt-ability — Don't pile it on too thick, old man — Don't interrupt! As I was saying, I admire these qualities, others I deplore; but you are quite right, we seem to be dropping into a 'fin de siecle' persiflage and hatred of being earnest. However, I wanted to ask you for — Sorry, old chap. Must tear my-self away. My bus, you know.
II (5) luckily business letters do not require the use of the third person for most of them are bad enough as it is avoid favour for letter be in receipt of for have received as in i am in receipt of your favour your good self or selves	II (5) Luckily business letters do not require the use of the third person, for most of them are bad enough, as it is. Avoid 'favour' for 'letter,' 'be in re-ceipt of' for 'have received,' as in 'I am in receipt of your favour,' 'your

(C) AVERAGE; OR MERELY COMPETENT

(D) PUNCTUATION AN ART

am not satisfied with it: hence the slightly improved version set forth in the column above this note.

II (4) Well, well, well! what are you doing here, you old rascal? — Oh, nothing much. — Just looking around for what you can pick up, I suppose. — Tut, tut! Don't make me out to be a thief! I'm only an opportunist, after all, you know. — But a very unusual sort of opportunist. You don't merely grasp such opportunities as offer themselves to your remarkably observant eyes, Charles; you do a great deal, or so at least I suspect, to create the opportunities. — Why, Robert! the conversation is taking a strange turn. You began by almost insulting me; now you are paying me what is, in effect, a compliment, indeed in its way a very high compliment. — Darn it! That's not quite correct – I mean about the compliment – for although I admire your versatility, your resourcefulness, your adaptability —. Don't pile it on too thick, old man! — Don't interrupt! As I was saying, I admire these qualities; others I deplore. But you are quite right, we seem to be dropping into a 'fin de siecle' persiflage and hatred of being earnest. However, I wanted to ask you for —. Sorry, old chap! Must tear myself away. My bus, you know.

II (4) Well, well, well! What are *you* doing here, you old rascal?

Oh, nothing much.

Just looking around for what you can pick up, I suppose?

Tut, tut! Don't make me out to be a thief. I'm only an opportunist, after all, you know.

But a very unusual sort of opportunist: you don't merely grasp such opportunities as offer themselves to your remarkably observant eyes, Charles; you do a great deal – or so, at least, I suspect – to create the opportunities.

Why, *Robert!* The conversation is taking a strange turn. You began by almost insulting me; now you are paying me what is, in effect, a compliment – indeed, in its way, a very high compliment.

Darn it! That's not quite correct – I mean about the compliment – for although I admire your versatility, your resourcefulness, your adaptability —

Don't pile it on *too* thick, old man! Don't interrupt! As I was saying, I admire these qualities; others I deplore. But you are quite right: we seem to be dropping into a *fin de siècle* persiflage and hatred of being earnest. However, I wanted to ask you for —

Sorry, old chap! Must tear myself away – my bus, you know.

II (5) Luckily business letters do not require the use of the third person, for most of them are bad enough as it is. Avoid *favour* for 'letter' – *be in receipt of* for 'have received', as in 'I am in receipt of your favour' – *your good self*

II (5) Luckily business letters do not require the use of the third person, for most of them are bad enough as it is. Avoid *favour* for 'letter', *be in receipt of* for 'have received' (as in 'I am in receipt of your favour'), *your good self*

(A) UNTOUCHED

for you of even date for of today for instance your favour of even date your letter of today for i beg or hereby beg to remind you that . . . write i remind you that or more politely may i remind you that . . . . . . avoid per for by as in per messenger and have nothing to do with same for it or that as in thank you for the specimen copy we received same on the 31st ult and by the way avoid also ult for of last month inst for of this month and prox for of next month such examples of what not to do are called commercial english or commercial jargon officese too easily confused with officialese or commercialese you begin a business letter with dear sir or dear madam if the plural is required note that the masculine is dear sirs employable also when you are in doubt but that the feminine is mesdames gentlemen is an occasional variant of dear sirs you end a business letter with yours faithfully which if you know the firm slightly you may if you wish vary to yours truly americans however are much less formal than britons and often fluster them with yours cordially or even yours sincerely a letter to a newspaper usually begins rather with sir than with dear sir and usually ends with yours etc the more polite of us preferring yours faithfully in a business letter or in any other you put your own address in the top right hand corner and the date immediately under it nowadays the address of the person or firm to whom or which you are writing is usually put at the end of the letter to the left hand side and slightly lower than ones signature if for convenience you prefer to place the recipients address at the beginning of the letter it comes under your own but on the left hand side to avoid confusion preface the addressees name etc with

(B) SEMI-LITERATE; OR CARELESS

good self' or 'selves' for 'you,' 'of even date' for 'of today,' for instance 'Your favour of even date' your letter of to-day. For 'I beg' or 'hereby beg to remind you that' . . . write 'I remind you that' or more politely 'May I remind you that' . . . . . . Avoid 'per' for 'by' as in 'per messenger.' And have nothing to do with 'same' for 'it' or 'that' as in 'Thank you for the specimen copy, we received same on the 31st ult.' And by the way avoid ult. for 'of last month,' inst. for 'of this month,' and 'prox.' for 'of next month.' Such examples of what not to do are called commercial English or commercial jargon, officese, too easily confused with officialese, or commercialese.

You begin a business letter with 'Dear sir' or 'Dear madam.' If the plural is required, note that the masculine is 'Dear Sirs', employable also when you are in doubt, but that the feminine is 'Mesdames.' 'Gentlemen' is an occasional variant of 'Dear Sirs.' You end a business letter with 'Yours faithfully,' which if you know the firm slightly you may if you wish, vary to 'Yours truly.' Americans however are much less formal than Britons and often fluster them with 'Yours cordially' or even 'Yours sincerely.'

A letter to a newspaper usually begins rather with 'Sir', than with 'Dear Sir' and usually ends with 'Yours, etc.', the more polite of us preferring 'Yours faithfully.'

In a business letter or in any other you put your own address in the top right hand corner and the date immediately under it. Nowadays the address of the person or firm to whom or which you are writing is usually put at the end of the letter to the left hand side and slightly lower than one's sig-

(c) AVERAGE; OR MERELY COMPETENT

or *selves* for 'you' – *of even date* for 'of to-day', for instance 'your favour of even date', your letter of to-day; for *I beg*, or *hereby beg, to remind you that* . . ., write 'I remind you that . . .' or, more politely, 'may I remind you that . . .'. Avoid *per* for 'by', as in 'per messenger', and have nothing to do with *same* for 'it' or 'that', as in 'Thank you for the specimen copy. We received same on the 31st ult.'; and, by the way, avoid also *ult.* for 'of last month' – *inst.* for 'of this month' – and *prox.* for 'of next month'. Such examples of what not to do are called 'commercial English' or 'commercial jargon' – 'officese', too easily confused with 'officialese', or 'commercialese'.

You begin a business letter with 'Dear Sir' or 'Dear Madam'; if the plural is required, note that the masculine is 'Dear Sirs', employable also when you are in doubt, but that the feminine is 'Mesdames'. 'Gentlemen' is an occasional variant of 'Dear Sirs'.

You end a business letter with 'Yours faithfully', which, if you know the firm slightly, you may vary to 'Yours truly'; Americans, however, are much less formal than Britons and often fluster them with 'Yours cordially' or even 'Yours sincerely'.

A letter to a newspaper usually begins rather with 'Sir' than with 'Dear Sir' and usually ends with 'Yours, etc.', the more polite of us preferring 'Yours faithfully'.

In a business letter – or in any other – you put your own address in the top right-hand corner and the date immediately under it. Nowadays, the address of the person or firm to whom or which you are writing is usually put at the end of the letter, to the left-hand side and slightly lower than one's signature. If, for convenience, you prefer

(d) PUNCTUATION AN ART

or *selves* for 'you'; *of even date* for 'of today' (for instance, 'your favour of even date' – your letter of today); for *I beg* – or *hereby beg* – *to remind you that* . . ., write 'I remind you that . . .' or, more politely, 'May I remind you that . . .'; avoid *per* for 'by', as in 'per messenger'; and have nothing to do with *same* for 'it' or 'that', as in 'Thank you for the specimen copy. We received same on the 31st ult.' And, by the way, avoid also *ult.* for '(of) last month', *inst.* for '(of) this month' and *prox.* for '(of) next month'. Such examples of what *not* to do are called 'commercial English' or 'commercial jargon', 'officese' – too easily confused with 'officialese' – or 'commercialese'.

You begin a business letter with 'Dear Sir' or 'Dear Madam'. If the plural is required, note that the masculine is 'Dear Sirs' (employable also when you are in doubt), but that the feminine is 'Mesdames'; 'Gentlemen' is an occasional variant of 'Dear Sirs'.

You end a business letter with 'Yours faithfully', which – if you know the firm slightly – you may, if you wish, vary to 'Yours truly'. Americans, however, are much less formal than Britons and often fluster them with 'Yours cordially' or even 'Yours sincerely'.

A letter to a newspaper usually begins rather with 'Sir' than with 'Dear Sir' and usually ends with 'Yours, etc.'; the more polite of us preferring 'Yours faithfully'.

In a business letter (or in any other) you put your own address in the top right hand corner and the date immediately under it. Nowadays the address of the person or firm to whom or which you are writing is usually put at the end of the letter – to the left-hand side and slightly lower than one's signature. If, for convenience, you prefer

(A) UNTOUCHED

to or to preferably in the line next above the address a business letter should be to the point never wander from that point and make it as brief as possible without falling either into obscurity or into discourtesy be polite but never obsequious if it is a long letter paragraph it adequately try to avoid bad grammar and illegible hand or type writing above all be as clear as you can in what you have to say an ungrammatical or rambling or badly typed letter is hardly complimentary

(B) SEMI-LITERATE; OR CARELESS

nature; if for convenience you prefer to place the recipient's address at th beginning of the letter, it comes unde your own, but on the left hand side To avoid confusion preface the addressee's name, etc., with 'to:' or *to*, preferably in the line next above the address. A business letter should be to the point, never wander from that point, and make it as brief as possible without falling either into obscurity or into discourtesy. Be polite – but never obsequious.

If it is a long letter, paragraph it adequately. Try to avoid bad grammar and illegible hand and typewriting. Above all be as clear as you can in what you have to say, an ungrammatical or rambling or badly typed letter is hardly complimentary.

II (6) there arose a lively discussion begun by the chairman and shared by most of the members present on the matter of the following passage a learned professor objected to a e housemans the bells they sound on bredon that the they is superfluous and the line ungrammatical and went so far as to say that a man who cannot write better english than that has no business to write at all such a rash judgement would condemn most of our greatest writers for they have all made such mistakes indeed as flaubert remarked in a letter to turgenev it is not to the greatest but to lesser masters that we look for models of style the pedant critic overlooked the fact that

II (6) There arose a lively discussion, begun by the chairman and shared by most of the members present on the matter of the following passage: –

'A learned professor objected to A. E. Housman's "The bells they sound on Bredon" that the *they* is superfluous and the line ungrammatical and went so far as to say that "a man who cannot write better English than that has no business to write at all." '

'Such a rash judgement would condemn most of our greatest writers, for they have all made such mistakes. Indeed, as Flaubert remarked in a letter to Turgenev, it is not to the greatest but to lesser masters that we look for

(c) AVERAGE; OR MERELY COMPETENT

to place the recipient's address at the beginning of the letter, it comes under your own, but on the left-hand side. To avoid confusion, preface the addressee's name, etc., with 'To:' or To, preferably in the line next above the address.

A business letter should be to the point. Never wander from that point, and make it as brief as possible without falling either into obscurity or into discourtesy. Be polite – but never obsequious. If it is a long letter, paragraph it adequately. Try to avoid bad grammar and illegible hand or typewriting. Above all, be as clear as you possibly can, in what you have to say. An ungrammatical or rambling or badly typed letter is hardly complimentary.

Note. Some persons will prefer this version to the one that follows: and I quite see why they would.

II (6) There arose a lively discussion, begun by the chairman and shared by most of the members present, on the matter of the following passage:

'A learned professor objected to A. E. Housman's "The bells, they sound on Bredon," that the "they" is superfluous and the line ungrammatical, and went so far as to say that, "a man who cannot write better English than that has no business to write at all." Such a rash judgement would condemn most of our greatest writers, for they have all made such "mistakes". Indeed, as Flaubert remarked in a letter to Turgenev, it is not to the greatest but to lesser masters that we look for models of style. The pedant

(d) PUNCTUATION AN ART

to place the recipient's address at the beginning of the letter, it comes under your own, but on the left-hand side. To avoid confusion, preface the addressee's name, etc., with 'To:' or To, preferably in the line next above the address.

A business letter should be to the point: never wander from that point, and make it as brief as possible without falling either into obscurity or into discourtesy. Be polite, but never obsequious. If it is a long letter, paragraph it adequately. Try to avoid bad grammar and illegible hand- or typewriting. Above all, be as clear as you possibly can in what you have to say. An ungrammatical or rambling or badly typed letter is hardly complimentary.

Note. This version constitutes a slight adaptation of a passage taken from the chapter 'How to Write a Letter' in Book I of *English: A Course for Human Beings.*

II (6) There arose a lively discussion, begun by the chairman and shared by most of the members present, on the matter of the following passage.

'A learned professor objected to A. E. Housman's "The bells, they sound on Bredon", that the "they" is superfluous and the line ungrammatical, and went so far as to say that "a man who cannot write better English than that has no business to write at all". Such a rash judgement would condemn most of our greatest writers, for they have all made such "mistakes". Indeed, as Flaubert remarked in a letter to Turgenev, it is not to the greatest, but to lesser masters, that we look for models of style. The pedant

| (A) UNTOUCHED | (B) SEMI-LITERATE; OR CARELESS |

this ungrammatical construction is an idiom so characteristic of english ballad poetry that modern poets writing in that style have adopted it as a matter of course.

he rendered tunstall all his right
knowing his valiant blood unstained
the king he caused this trusty knight
undefiled tunstall to be named
    an elizabethan ballad of
        the battle of flodden

last night the moon had a golden ring
and tonight no ring we see
the skipper he blew a whiff from his
                                pipe
and a scornful laugh laughed he

mrs jones gave a musical party
her friends she invited them all
there was old mr jenkins so hearty
and young mr jenkins so tall
        mid victorian comic song

this idiom is particularly common in rustic speech to which ballad poetry always tends and sometimes as in the line of housman quoted above serves to suggest the homely character of the person speaking it also falls naturally from the lips of a shakespearean character of the utmost beauty and dignity viola twelfth night when on learning that the coast on which she has been shipwrecked is that of illyria she says meditatively my brother he is in elysium it is a matter of emphasis and of the subtle process of thought . . . . . . within an hour or two of writing the above I had occasion to buy some flowers in holborn from a man who complained the growers and the dealers they fix the price between em an error of a different and more serious kind is that of shakespeare in the song

---

models of style. The pedant critic overlooked the fact that this ungrammatical construction is an idiom so characteristic of English ballad poetry that modern poets writing in that style have adopted it as a matter of course.

He rendered Tunstall all his right
Knowing his valiant blood unstained,
The king he caused this trusty knight
Undefiled Tunstall to be named.
    An Elizabethan ballad of
        the Battle of Flodden.

Last night the moon had a golden ring
And to-night no ring we see,
The skipper he blew a whiff from his
                                pipe
And a scornful laugh laughed he.

Mrs. Jones gave a musical party,
Her friends she invited them all,
There was old Mr. Jenkins so hearty,
And young Mr. Jenkins so tall.
        Mid-Victorian comic song.

'This idiom is particularly common in rustic speech, to which ballad poetry always tends, and sometimes as in the line of Housman quoted above, serves to suggest the homely character of the person speaking. It also falls naturally from the lips of a Shakespearean character of the utmost beauty and dignity, Viola (*Twelfth Night*), when on learning that the coast on which she has been shipwrecked is that of Illyria, she says meditatively, "My brother he is in Elysium." '
'It is a matter of emphasis and of the subtle process of thought. . . . .'
'Within an hour or so of writing the above I had occasion to buy some flowers in Holborn from a man who complained, "The growers and the dealers they fix the price between 'em." '

(C) AVERAGE; OR MERELY COMPETENT

critic overlooked the fact that this grammatical construction is an idiom so characteristic of English ballad poetry that modern poets writing in that style have adopted it as a matter of course.

He rendered Tunstall all his right,
Knowing his valiant blood un-
    stained,
The king he caused this trusty knight
Undefiled Tunstall to be named.
    An Elizabethan ballad of
        the Battle of Flodden.

'Last night the moon had a golden ring
And tonight no ring we see.'
The skipper he blew a whiff from his
    pipe
And a scornful laugh laughed he.

Mrs. Jones gave a musical party,
Her friends she invited them all.
There was old Mr. Jenkins so hearty
And young Mr. Jenkins so tall.
    Mid-Victorian comic song.

'This idiom is particularly common in rustic speech, to which ballad poetry always tends, and sometimes, as in the line of Housman quoted above, serves to suggest the homely character of the person speaking. It also falls natur-ally from the lips of a Shakespearean character of the utmost beauty and dignity – Viola (*Twelfth Night*), when, on learning that the coast on which she has been shipwrecked is that of Illyria, she says meditatively, "My brother, he is in Elysium." It is a matter of em-phasis and of the subtle process of thought . . . . . .'
    'Within an hour or two of writing the above, I had occasion to buy some flowers in Holborn from a man who complained: "The growers and the

(D) PUNCTUATION AN ART

critic overlooked the fact that this grammatical construction is an idiom so characteristic of English ballad poetry that modern poets writing in that style have adopted it as a matter of course.

He rendered Tunstall all his right,
Knowing his valiant blood un-
    stained,
.The king he caused this trusty knight
Undefiled Tunstall to be named.
    An Elizabethan ballad of
        the Battle of Flodden

'Last night the moon had a golden ring
And tonight no ring we see.'
The skipper he blew a whiff from his
    pipe
And a scornful laugh laughed he.

Mrs Jones gave a musical party,
Her friends she invited them all;
There was old Mr Jenkins so hearty
And young Mr Jenkins so tall.
    Mid-Victorian comic song.

'This idiom is particularly common in rustic speech, to which ballad poetry always tends; and sometimes, as in the line of Housman quoted above, serves to suggest the homely character of the person speaking. It also falls natur-ally from the lips of a Shakespearean character of the utmost beauty and dignity: Viola (*Twelfth Night*), when, on learning that the coast on which she has been shipwrecked is that of Illyria, she says meditatively, "My brother, he is in Elysium". It is a matter of em-phasis and of the subtle process of thought . . . . . .
    'Within an hour or two of writing the above I had occasion to buy some flowers in Holborn from a man who complained, "The growers and the

(A) UNTOUCHED

hark the lark at heavens gate sings
and phoebus gins arise
his steeds to water at those springs
on chaliced flowers that lies

but shakespeare wanted his rhyme and the words were to be sung to the accompaniment of music the error would pass unnoticed scholars suggest that lies is here a plural form borrowed from the northern dialects

(B) SEMI-LITERATE; OR CARELESS

An error of a different and more serious kind is that of Shakespeare in the song

Hark the lark at heaven's gate sings
And Phoebus gins arise,
His steeds to water at those springs
On chaliced flowers that lies

'But Shakespeare wanted his rhyme and the words were to be sung to the accompaniment of music. The error would pass unnoticed. Scholars suggest that *lies* is here a plural form borrowed from the Northern dialects.'

(C) AVERAGE; OR MERELY COMPETENT

dealers, they fix the price between 'em." '

'An error of a different and more serious kind is that of Shakespeare in the song –

Hark, the lark at heaven's gate sings,
And Phoebus 'gins arise
His steeds to water at those springs
On chaliced flowers that lies.'

'But Shakespeare wanted his rhyme, and the words were to be sung to the accompaniment of music. The error would pass unnoticed. Scholars suggest that *lies* is here a plural form borrowed from the Northern dialects.'

(D) PUNCTUATION AN ART

dealers, they fix the price between 'em".

'An error of a different and more serious kind is that of Shakespeare in the song:

Hark, the lark at heaven's gate sings,
And Phoebus 'gins arise
His steeds to water at those springs
On chaliced flowers that lies.

But Shakespeare wanted his rhyme, and the words were to be sung to the accompaniment of music; the error would pass unnoticed. Scholars suggest that *lies* is here a plural form borrowed from the Northern dialects.'

WILSON BENINGTON, in a paper entitled 'Poets' Licence'.

Book IV
AMERICAN PRACTICE
by
JOHN W. CLARK
University of Minnesota

A CHAPTER ON
AMERICAN PRACTICE *

by

JOHN W. CLARK

WITH MANY of the particulars of difference between British and American practice in punctuation and its allies Mr. Partridge has already dealt, incidentally but sufficiently, in the main part of this book, so that I need not deal with them in this chapter in much detail. And yet some things remain to be said.

The principal impression that grew on me as I read Mr. Partridge's chapters was one that confirmed Mr. Partridge's several-times-repeated statement – and my previous general impression – that American punctuation tends to be more rigid than British, and more uniform, more systematic, and – I hope I shall be forgiven for adding – easier to teach and, once learnt, easier to use. (But note that I do not mean that in my opinion it is in all respects *better*.) This difference, for weal or woe, is owing, I think, to two facts: (1) Individualism or independence is less esteemed and less tolerated in the United States today than in Great Britain, especially that of the educated by the uneducated and (even more) by the half-educated. (2) Cultivated Americans more commonly and predominantly than cultivated Britons depend on reading and formal instruction rather than on oral (or aural) tradition. Both these facts, especially the latter, are in part results of the greater fluidity of American social classes, of the greater frequency and success of social climbing, of the often wider social breaches between generations of the same family, and of the insecurity and sequacity of social climbers. The secondary-school or college handbook of English usage (including punctuation and its allies) is more important and influential in the United States than in Great

* Note that in this chapter, in my use of "punctuation and its allies," I follow what I believe to be the standard (or at least generally acceptable) contemporary usage of the most reputable American printers (and of the most reliable American handbooks) of the present time. I do so not because I always think it ideally best (or even always use it), and certainly not in any spirit of intransigently chauvinistic nationalism, but because I think it will provide illuminating examples (in "orchestration," to boot) of some of the principles and practices discussed. For the same reason, incidentally, I use American spelling.

Britain for the same reason as the handbook of etiquette is more important and influential: it is more widely felt, and to a large extent rightly felt, to be necessary. American punctuation in general is probably as various as British; but in the United States the departures from the national norm are probably to be found in greater number among the uneducated. A well-educated American almost always tries, at least, to adhere as a rule to (his conception of) the national standard; a well-educated Englishman is more likely, I think, to regard the practice he prefers, however idiosyncratic, as one that ought to be standard or at least permissible, whether the dons or the printers like it or not.* In short, an American is likely to punctuate unconventionally only because he doesn't know any better; a Briton, at least the typical British writer, because he is jolly well sure he does. And yet there is one way in which American punctuation may perhaps be called no more rigid than British, viz., that American is at least as liberal as British in countenancing either "close" or "open" styles – but perhaps insists more commonly on a consistent adherence to one or the other in a single piece of writing.

This conventionality and this rigidity – working sometimes together and sometimes separately – explain most of the prominent differences of American practice from British. The main ones, I should say, are as follows: (1) The very common American preference (especially among more or less academic people) of some punctuation between the clauses of almost every sentence of the sort usually called in the United States (see below) compound. (2) The very common American preference (very common in the handbooks if not among printers, especially of newspapers) of a comma before the conjunction preceding the last member of a series of three or more ("a, b, and c" rather than "a, b and c"). (3) The placement of commas and (punctuational, not only abbreviational) periods (but not other points) before quotation marks rather than after them, regardless of logic. (4) Beginning the alternation (in quotations within quotations) of single and double quotation marks with double ones instead of single ("He said 'yes,' not 'no.' " *rather than* 'He said "yes", not "no".'

---

* I am reminded of an English friend of mine who told me that when, in her childhood, she used to call in "the" dictionary to support her in a disagreement with her stepfather (a country clergyman and an Oxford man) concerning pronunciation, the old gentleman would say, with a sort of mild testiness, "But my dear, dictionaries are made to *record* the pronunciations of people like me, not to *determine* them." He would doubtless have said the same, *mutatis mutandis*, of punctuation.

And note that this illustrates not only Point 4 but also Point 3.). (5) A comparatively infrequent use of what I will call the fancy uses of semicolons and colons as substitutes for parentheses, dashes, and parenthetical commas.

I propose to deal with these five matters in order and in some detail, and then to subjoin a series of subordinate and incidental comments "keyed" to Mr. Partridge's table of contents.

(1) Some of Mr. Partridge's statements about the uses of commas and semicolons in what he usually calls compound sentences would puzzle most conventionally educated Americans because those statements use certain grammatical terms otherwise than almost all American handbooks – and hence almost all conventionally educated Americans – use them. I refer especially to the terms simple, compound, and complex sentences. In the United States, very generally, the use of these and certain other terms is illustrated by the following table:

(1) Simple sentence (one subject, one verb):
  John left.
(2) Compound sentence (two or more simple sentences combined as two or more principal clauses):
  John left, but Mary stayed.
  John left, but he left late.
  John left, and he left early.
  (Note that no distinction is made here between sentences shifting the subject and those not shifting it, or between sentences connected by *and* and *but*.)
(3) Complex sentence (one principal clause and one [or more] subordinate):
  John left when I arrived [, though he wanted to stay].
(4) Simple sentence with compound subject (two or more subjects, one verb):
  John and Mary left.
(5) Simple sentence with compound verb (one subject, two or more verbs):
  John stayed late but left at last.
(6) Simple sentence with compound subject and compound verb (two or more conjoined subjects, two or more conjoined verbs):
  John and Mary stayed late but put on their coats and left at last.

(7) Compound-complex sentence – combination of (3) with (2): John left when I arrived, but Mary stayed [, though she wanted to leave].

Combinations of (3) with (4), (5), and (6) are of course also possible. E.g., (3) plus (4) would be "John and Mary left when I arrived."

Generally speaking, American handbooks, though by no means always American printers (especially of newspapers), call for a comma between any two principal clauses, as in (2) and (7), joined by a simple co-ordinating conjunction (*and*, *but*, *for*, *or*, and a few others); they call for a semicolon otherwise – i.e., if there is no conjunction ("John left; Mary stayed") or if there is only what is usually called in the United States a conjunctive adverb ("John left; nevertheless Mary stayed"). American printers have long been (harmlessly enough, especially in very short sentences) less fussy about the medial comma in such sentences than they used to be or than the handbooks usually prescribe; they are becoming less fussy (unfortunately, I think) about the semicolon. [See further my note, below, on Chapter 5, § 2 (4).]

(2) Last comma in "a, b [,] and c." Mr. Partridge, in agreement with general British prescription and practice, recommends, "a, b and c"; American handbooks generally recommend "a, b, and c"; American printers, especially of newspapers, usually prefer the British practice but can often be got to use that recommended by most American handbooks. I prefer it, and on the same grounds as it is usually recommended on, viz., that "a, b and c" may momentarily lead the reader to expect "a, b and c, and d," or rather "a, b-1 and b-2, and c." In other words, "a, b and c" does not provide so conveniently and systematically for the occasional occurrence of a series within a series; the American "a, b, and c" forewarns the reader that there is no closer connection between *b* and *c* than there is between *a* and *c*.

(3) The placement of commas and (punctuational, not only abbreviational) periods (but not other points) before quotation marks rather than after them, regardless of logic. Here there can be no doubt, to my mind, of the logical superiority of the British practice: it is more sensible to be guided, in this matter, entirely and consistently by logic, as British practice is and American is not. But the difference in practice remains, and is likely to remain – commonly, though not universally – for a long time. American handbooks usually apologize for it but accept it, and I use it in this chapter.

(4) Beginning the alternation (in quotations within quotations) of single and double quotation marks with double ones instead of single. Here again the British practice is more sensible than the American; but also here again the American practice is what it is, it is likely to remain so for quite a long time, and I follow it in this chapter. I will point out that, if a reform is to be effected, it may at least as well go the whole length and use single quotation marks for primary quotations, double for secondary, *triple for tertiary*, and so on. The American printer's excuse (and there is something to be said for it) for holding out for double quotation marks for primary quotations is probably that doubles are more conspicuous and inescapable than singles, that primary quotations are much the most frequent, and that as much use as possible should be made of conspicuousness.

(5) The (mainly archaic but recently more or less revived) substitution (especially in decidedly "literary" use) of semicolons and colons for parentheses, dashes, and parenthetical commas. (See above, Chapter 5, § 2, (11), and Chapter 6, § 9.) This is almost certainly rarer among American writers than among British, and quite certainly rarer among American printers and proofreaders: they just won't have it. On the whole I am disposed to sympathize with them, on the grounds that, in my opinion, the reader is less likely to be confused if semicolons and colons are pretty much reserved for employment in what have come to be regarded as their more normal functions – as points proper, i.e., of usually a more forcible separative or balancing import than commas – instead of being extended to parenthetical uses. I admire Laurence Sterne, but I had just as soon his punctuation were left to lie with him in St. George's burial-ground, and I think most Americans, at least, agree with me.

Now for the more incidental comments keyed to Mr. Partridge's table of contents.

Title page: The title of this book is, I agree, witty (it is, I hardly need say, Mr. Partridge's, not mine), but, interestingly enough, it will not be apprehended so readily as witty in the United States as in Great Britain, for the reason that in the United States, with a perhaps characteristic verbosity and formality, "point" and "pointing" are today little used for "punctuation mark" and "punctuation."

Chapter 2, paragraph 3: "Full stop," however common in Great Britain, is very seldom used (nowadays) for "period" in the United States. By many Americans, in fact, it would not even be understood. I remember being puzzled the first time I heard my grandfather (born in 1857) use it.

Chapter 3, § 11: Note that the comma between house numbers and street names disappeared in the United States long before it began to do so in Great Britain. And note also, incidentally, that in some American cities it is usual to put a hyphen before the last two digits of a house number containing more than three (sometimes two): "31-42 Upton Drive" instead of "3142." In either case, the number would be pronounced "thirty-one-forty-two."

Chapter 3, § 12: Note that in the United States spaces are never substituted for commas in figures of a thousand or more.

Chapter 3, § 21, "Fourthly": " 'My cousin John Smith died in 1952 [.]'. . . . If I write – 'My cousin, John Smith, died in 1952 [.]' – I am implying that I have only one cousin [, which] . . . is unlikely. . . ." This is certainly true as a rule, but I think there are certain exceptions that would be taken account of in the best American usage. In introducing John to a friend, might not one say, "This is my cousin, John Smith," even though he were not one's only cousin, if one's purpose were, as it probably would be, not to distinguish him from other cousins, but to convey his name to the friend?

Chapter 4, paragraph 1: A more common distinction in the United States is between abbreviations (curtailments, including initials as an extreme and perhaps special case) and contractions (forms not omitting the last letter). This distinction is certainly made only sometimes and by some people; but a distinction that I should say is never made by anyone in the United States is that between abbreviations (or, if you like, contractions) that consist of initials only, and those that don't. I don't, really, see much utility in the latter distinction, and though the former might be useful, it is in fact only occasional. Note incidentally that in the United States, *percent* is nowadays almost always so written – always without the period and usually "solid." "Esq.," on the rare occasions of its use in the United States, always has the period; "Esqre," with or without a period, is never used. "Jr." and "Sr.," like "Mr.," "Dr.," etc., seldom omit the period. Again, in the United States "sha'n't" is almost never written (or at least printed), but almost always "shan't." The form "sha'nt" is conceivable, I suppose, in either country, but, so far as I know, never written; and I think that "shant" has been written by hardly anyone but George Bernard Shaw, who had a "thing" about this. Something is to be said for every form but "sha'nt."

Chapter 5, § 2 (4): (Cf. generally my main point (1) above.) American usage, at least in handbooks, and to a considerable extent among printers, even of newspapers, is very fussy in distinguishing (in the connective between two principal clauses) between what it regards as simple co-ordinating conjunctions and what it calls conjunctive adverbs. With the former, it usually prefers a comma to no punctuation, and sometimes a semicolon (if the two or more principal clauses have internal punctuation, or if they are long, or if they express sharply contrasting ideas); with the latter it usually insists on a semicolon. According to this system, *and, but, for, or, nor,* and (sometimes) *neither* are pretty nearly the only words universally accounted simple co-ordinating conjunctions. They may for the most part be distinguished from what are thought of as conjunctive adverbs by the fact that the latter may usually be preceded by a simple coordinating conjunction – "and so," "and yet," "and then," "and therefore," "but nevertheless," but never, e.g., "and but." It is true that this distinction appears to break down with *however*, which is never (in good contemporary American usage) preceded by *but*; but note that in *bad* American usage it often is – and is so, I suspect, as a relic of once-good usage, which has first discarded the *but* as redundant (as it is, owing to to its virtual identity in meaning with *however*), and then proscribed it. I am a little troubled by the fact that *but* is still often used with *nevertheless, on the other hand*, etc., which seem no less adversative than *however*; it may be that the precise kind of "adversation" they convey is felt to be a little less close to that conveyed by *but*. I should add that three general relaxations of this principle have crept in: (1) A comma is permitted and even customary when there are more than two clauses – e.g., "He bought it, I cooked it, and we both ate it" as against "He bought it; I cooked it." (2) A comma may be tolerated with any conjunctive adverb in very short sentences lacking other internal punctuation. (3) A few of the conjunctive adverbs have come by common consent to be treated (punctuationally) very generally like simple co-ordinating conjunctions – i.e., are usually, not just occasionally, preceded by commas (though seldom by no punctuation) rather than by semicolons. The commonest instances are *so* and *yet*, and some people feel the same way about *then* (temporal) and even *still*. Any further relaxation is usually felt by the judicious (in the United States) to be illiterate, or at least careless or idiosyncratic or wilful or perverse. This "rule" I take to have arisen in the days of very full punctuation, when most conjunctive adverbs, being felt as parenthetical, almost always had a *comma after* them and hence seemed to demand a *semicolon before* them in order to make it clear that they began the first, rather than ended the second, of the two principal clauses. The frequent American requirement of at least a comma before a simple co-ordinating conjunction between two principal clauses I suspect arose from a somewhat similar cause: when a principal clause is followed by *and*, *but*, *for*, or the like, the fact that the conjunction is meant to connect the two principal clauses as entities rather than the last word of the first clause and the first word of the second clause is made clearer by the use of the comma.

I perhaps ought not to leave this subject without saying that I realize both that the practice set forth in the foregoing paragraph is not essentially different from normal British practice and that, where it differs, it differs in the expected direction of rigidity and uniformity.

Chapter 6, § 2 (end): In the United States, after "Dear Sir" and the like at the beginning of a letter, the comma is often used – perhaps as often as in Great Britain – in social letters, but hardly ever in business letters.

Chapter 6, § 14 (5): In the United States also often (and increasingly) "*Quarterly* 20.96."

Chapter 7, paragraph 2: Parentheses are sometimes called "curves" by American printers (but hardly by anyone else).

Chapter 7, § 5: Some American printers, objecting to marking a parenthetical element within a parenthetical element by parentheses, mechanically substitute square brackets for the internal parentheses, especially if the final internal one happens to precede immediately the final external one: they print, i.e., not "))," but "])," regardless of whether or not the internal parenthetical element is of the sort normally marked by square brackets (i.e., editorial matter and the like).

Chapter 7, § 5, paragraph 2: "[ ]" are practically always called simply "brackets" or "square brackets" in the United States; practically never "square parentheses," which would puzzle most Americans.

Chapter 7, § 5, last paragraph: The third sort of parenthesis is almost never used in the United States, even in MS or typescript; such matter as is enclosed here is ordinarily put into marginal notes directed to the printer.

Chapter 8, paragraph 1: In the United States the dash is practically always single in print and almost always so in MS, though the latter occasionally shows a double dash - - in imitation of typewriting, where the standard keyboard necessitates the use of the double "hyphen" to do duty for the dash. (But some American typists use a spaced single hyphen for a dash.)

Chapter 8, § 12: This use of the dash is perhaps less commonly substituted in the United States than in Great Britain (and in any event, very uncommonly) for the full and normal use of quotation marks.

Chapter 9, paragraph 1: "Question mark" is certainly much the commonest term in the United States, except perhaps among some printers and proofreaders and bibliographers.

Chapter 9, examples 5 and 6: Most American printers and practically all American handbooks would call for a period rather than a question mark after "I wonder" as well as after "I wondered." For better or worse, this is another reflection, I suppose, of American rigidity and (in general) adherence to logic.

Chapter 10, § 1: In philological works an asterisk is printed before a hypothetical (i.e., unrecorded or non-existent but probable) word or form; e.g., "The Modern English word *day* is traced back to a hypothetical Primitive Germanic *dags*," and, "If the Modern English word *gate* had descended regularly from the Old English, it would probably be *yeat*."

Chapter 10, I, § 3, paragraphs 4, 5, and 6: American printers do not consistently or even usually observe these distinctions between three, six, or more dots. Their official or formal American name is "ellipsis (or, when used as in Chapter 10, II, § 1, *suspension*) dots (or periods)," and sometimes, by extension, "leaders," a term transferred from the proper use, dealt with in Chapter 10, II, § 2. Some American printing offices use invariably three such dots elsewhere than at the end of a sentence, where they will use four; others as invariably use four and five respectively; and in either case a wider space is usually left between the last dot at the end of a sentence and the first word of the following sentence, on the principle, apparently, that the last "dot" is a genuine punctuational period. On the other hand, the practice, followed by many British printers, of always leaving a wider space both before and after a set of ellipsis periods, whether between sentences or not, is very uncommon in the United States. Finally, American printers usually indicate the omission of a line of verse by *spaced* ellipsis periods extending to about the length of the average line, or sometimes to about that of the preceding or following line.

Chapter 10, II, § 4, paragraph 4: Webster is right about the general American avoidance of such compound points.

Chapter 13, paragraph 1: The verb "capital" in this sense is almost never heard in the United States. Perhaps a characteristic case of what Fowler would call "love of the long word"?

Chapter 13, VII (1): In a few decidedly reputable publications (notably the *Cambridge History of English Literature*) the somewhat Gallic practice is followed of leaving most such words uncapitalized, but it is certainly not commoner in the United States than in Great Britain.

Chapter 13, VIII, paragraph 1: Many writers in the United States do not capitalize pronouns referring to God or Christ; contrariwise, some others do capitalize pronouns referring to the Blessed Virgin.

Chapter 13, XI, last paragraph: In many American newspapers and street-directories, *street*, etc., are not capitalized, though they always are in the addresses of letters.

Chapter 17, I, 1.: (*a*) *Syllabification* is at least as common in the United States as *syllabication*. (*b*) American printing offices and handbooks (which generally follow them in such purely typographical matters) are very fussy and uniform and unbending about syllabification (both in dividing words at the end of a line and in indicating the pronunciation of words in dictionaries and the like). Generally, they would never allow *div-i-sion* or *di-vis-ion*, but would insist on *di-vi-sion;* never *sy-llabification*, but *syl-labification*. And in dividing words at the end of a line, American printers frequently will not break before the third letter, though American typists will: the printer, i.e., if he were breaking for the end of a line and not in order to indicate pronunciation, would avoid *di-vision* and would try for *divi-sion*.

Chapter 17, II, § 2, i, 2., paragraph 2: In the United States, *King Mark-like*, however much less desirable than *King-Mark-like*, is a good deal commoner. The succession of capital initials is taken, so to speak, as unifying the capitalized words.

Chapter 17, II, § 2, i, 6.: In the United States, this job is sometimes done by a diaeresis – "coöperative" instead of "co-operative." (And note that the diaeresis – or umlaut sign – can be and often is satisfactorily simulated on the typewriter by the double quotation mark.)

Chapter 17, II, § 2, iv, 1.: *Dark* and *light* as modifiers of the names of colors are usually not hyphenated in the United States.

Chapter 17, "The Virgil (or Virgule) or the Oblique," paragraph 3: The forms *u/m* and *i/c* are certainly rare in the United States, though *c/o* and *a/c* and military abbreviations like *A/C.*2 (or rather *A/C*2) are common enough. Incidentally, American typists commonly substitute % for *c/o*, and the usage has to some extent worked its way over into handwriting.

Chapter 17, "The Virgil," etc., paragraph 4: The oblique is never used in expressing amounts of U. S. money (as doubtless most Britons know); only the period, between dollars and cents (and the comma when the number of dollars is a thousand or more). And note that this period is never raised or "centered" as it sometimes is in Great Britain in expressing these and other decimal fractions. In expressing amounts of British money, knowledgeable American writers sometimes follow British practice, but in newspapers and the like the amount is usually written out – "9 pounds (or £9, if the typecasting machine has "£" – as, incidentally, the standard American typewriter never has), 6 shillings [,] and 3 pence," or more rarely, "£9, 6s., 3d." The use of "l." after instead of "£" before the number of pounds is practically unknown in the United States. Also note that in the United States fractions are usually written, e.g., "$\frac{2}{7}$" rather than "2/7," though they are printed and typewritten "2/7" when no separate fraction-type is provided.

Chapter 18, § 3, second (1), (3), and (4): In the United States (I am uneasily aware of having begun several earlier sentences with that phrase) *Lewis's* would probably be as often written as *Lewises* (there is a kind of jealous restriction of the -*es* plural to *common* nouns ending in a sibilant); *grandpas* is probably commoner than *grandpa's* (for a related same reason); and *thine*s (no apostrophe, but *s* in roman instead of in italic) would be generally preferred.

Chapter 18, § 4, v: There is some tendency in America to add the possessive *s* to monosyllables but not to longer names: "Keats's poems," but "Roberts' Rules of Order."

Chapter 19: Note that most American handbooks recommend italicizing the non-geographical part of the name of a newspaper but leaving the geographical part in roman, without regard to whether or not the complete official – or at least the "running head" – name of the paper includes the geographical part. E.g., "the New York *Times.*" But also "*The Times* of London" more commonly than any form inserting "London" between "The" and "Times." A very special typographical distinction observed by many newspapers and some magazines is to italicize or quote (or sometimes merely to capitalize the initials in) the names of all other periodicals but to put their own into small (in the predictably egregious case of T I M E, large) capitals.

Chapter 20, paragraph 1, f.n.: For better or worse, *indentation* is probably oftener heard in the United States than *indention*.

Appendix I

A FEW NOTES ON OTHER WORKS

EVERY SCHOOL and college textbook on English grammar and composition contains sections on punctuation and its accessories. Those sections mislead either by excessive brevity or by sheer perfunctoriness or by an inhuman rigidity.

If I appear to ignore the University of Chicago's *A Manual of Style*, anonymous but important, and the excellent work done by such scholars as Canby, Krapp, Leonard, Hulbert, Marckwardt, Perrin, and others, it is because American practice is virtually the same as British and because Professor John W. Clark has ably dealt with the differences. The greatest difference of all is that American punctuation tends to become rather monotonous: see, for instance, T. L. de Vinne's *Correct Composition*, 1901, and the aforementioned *Manual of Style*, which, sound and thorough, to at least one student seem almost Procrustean.

Of the British works rising above the level of schoolbooks, we may note : –

1863: HENRY ALFORD, *The Queen's English*; 7th edition, 1888. The spiritual father of the Fowler brothers.

1872: ALEXANDER BAIN, *A Higher English Grammar*; revised edition, 1879.

1880: HENRY BEADNELL, *Spelling and Punctuation*. Good; but very much from the printer's standpoint and, like Bain, out of date.

1884: PAUL ALLARDYCE (*i.e.* GEORGE PAUL MACDONELL), *"Stops": or, How to Punctuate*. A small, practical handbook.

1893: HORACE HART, *Rules for Compositors and Readers at the University Press*; 36th edition, 1952. Tersely admirable.

1905: T. F. & M. F. A. HUSBAND, *Punctuation, Its Principles and Practice*. Valuable for the history – dependable (and un- imaginative) for the practice – of punctuation.

1905: F. HOWARD COLLINS, *Authors' and Printers' Dictionary*; latest revised edition (the 9th edition), 1946. Briefly excellent.

1906: H. W. & F. G. FOWLER, *The King's English*; 3rd edition, 1930. Very good indeed; still better, perhaps, is the more compact treatment in –

1926: H. W. FOWLER, *A Dictionary of Modern English Usage*; many, many reprints, but no new edition. Excellent, although perhaps a shade too academic.

1933: REGINALD SKELTON, *Modern English Punctuation*; the 2nd edition, much enlarged, 1949, contains some brief notes on the history and theory of the subject. Workmanlike and useful.

1936: WILFRED WHITTEN & FRANK WHITAKER, *Good and Bad English*; 4th edition, 1950. Brief section; eminently sensible and practical.

1939: G. V. CAREY, *Mind the Stop*. The best short guide to the subject.

1947: ERIC PARTRIDGE, *Usage and Abusage*; 4th edition, 1948. A brief section. More systematic is –

1949: ERIC PARTRIDGE, *English: A Course for Human Beings*; 3rd edition, 1950. In Book I: Punctuation; in Book II: Advanced Punctuation.

1951: G. H. VALLINS, *Good English: How to Write It*; Library edition, revised and notably enlarged, 1952. Has a dependable and attractive chapter on punctuation. – In *Better English*, Library edition, 1954, Vallins treats of several further points.

Appendix II

A BRIEF LIST OF ACCENTS

‾ over a vowel indicates that it is long. Technically known as *macron*.
◡ over a vowel indicates that it is short. Technically known as *breve*.
(As *macron* = *makron*, neuter of the Greek adjective *makros*, long,
so *breve* = *breve*, neuter of the Latin adjective *brevis*, short.)
◡̄ indicates that the vowel is sometimes long, sometimes short.
╱ indicates an acute accent, as in *blasé*⎫
╲ indicates a grave* accent, as in *brève*⎬French accents.
‸ indicates a circumflex accent, as in *fête;* in a French word an omitted *s*
is implied. But this accent is also used by phoneticians to indicate
certain sounds. In Ancient Greek, the accent ‸ or ⌢ or, later, ~,
placed over long vowels, indicated a compound tone – a rising-
falling tone.
’ the cedilla, under *c*, before *a* or *o* or *u*, indicates in French that it is
pronounced as *s*, as in *façade*.
‥, the umlaut or the umlaut sign, as in German *ä, ö, ü*, denotes a vowel
resulting from umlaut, assimilation of one vowel by a succeeding
vowel (*Müller* = *Mueller*, *Göring* = *Goering*). In English and
French, ‥ shows that the second of two sequent vowels is to be
pronounced, as in *Boötes* and *coöperative*, and it is then named
the diaeresis or, by some Americans, dieresis.
~, the tilde, belongs to Spanish and Portuguese; in the former it indicates
a palatal nasal sound, as in *cañon*, anglicized as *canyon*, and in the
latter that a tilde-surmounted vowel is pronounced nasally, as in
João.
◡ over *c* especially, but also over *s* and *r*, shows that *č* is pronounced *tch*,
as in *Čapek* (*tchapek*). This Slavic, especially Czech, accent
aspirates the consonant. It is sometimes called 'a wing'.
╱ through a vowel, or ° over one, indicates, in Scandinavian languages,
a sort of umlaut (compare the already mentioned ‥); the former
accent occurs, for instance, in the Danish place-names *Birkerød*
and *København* (Copenhagen), and at least one printer calls it
'a bar-*o*'. The accent in *å* is, in colloquial reference by Danes,
called 'a volle', literally a little round cake; *å* is also known as
'a Swedish – *or*, a Norwegian – *a*'.†
In prosody, a stressed syllable is indicated by either an acute accent,

---

* In Italian a grave accent, as in *facoltà*, denotes that the syllable (*-tà*) is
stressed.
† I owe much of the information about *č*, *ø* and *å* to Professor Clark.

as in *Mánchester*, or, less frequently, a grave, as in *Mànchester*. A secondary stress is usually shown by a smaller accent, as in *Húngárian*. Recommended: *Hùngárian*.

ODDMENTS. The sign §, as in '§ 3: Asteroids', indicates a section within a chapter or within an essay or study or article.

¶ or ℙ: paragraph.

&, the ampersand (a slurring of *and per se and*, '& by itself [*sc.* makes] *and*'): a convenient symbol for *and*. It has been formed by a combination of the letters *e* and *t* of the Latin *et*, and.

* and †, asterisk and dagger (or obelus or obelisk), are used for footnotes where 1 and 2 are not used. For more footnotes than two, numerals are recommended; but if not, the following are often used: * (1), † (2), ** (3), ‡ or †† (4), *** or *₊* or ₊*₊ (5), ††† (6); for three footnotes, however, some use successively *, **, ***.

In philological works, * indicates a hypothetical form, and † an obsolete form, as in '*Brood* († *brod*) derives from a stem *bro- or *bru-'.

POSTSCRIPT. The following remarks by Professor John W. Clark are too valuable to be omitted:

I have several times remarked on the influence of the typewriter on recent MS practice. A little more may perhaps profitably be added. The limitations of both the typewriter and such type-setting or -casting machines as the Linotype and the Monotype have affected MS practice in a number of ways, and the whole thing is bemusingly typical of the way in which old habits are often modified by technology. E.g.: (1) Most typewriters and Linotypes and the like have no square brackets: consequently, parentheses are often substituted, by imitation, even in MS. (2) All standard English typewriters and many English Linotypes, etc., lack italics, and extensive underlining is troublesome on the typewriter (and normally impossible on the Linotype). By consequence, even in MS, book titles and the like are often quoted instead of being italicized. (3) Many Linotypes, etc., (at least those used by most American newspapers) lack diacritic types (*à, ê, ü, å, č*, etc.), and as a natural result (again, especially in most American newspapers) foreign words properly requiring such symbols are usually printed with ordinary English letters, without any effort to compensate for the missing diacritics, even when some recognized method of doing so exists. E.g., most American newspapers will render *Conzertstück* as *Conzertstuck* rather than as *Conzertstueck:* and such practices have a way of getting imitated in MS, and are probably (however deplorably) likely to become yet more commonly so. The practice certainly to be recommended to all but merely popular and ephemeral writers – especially to all scholarly ones – is to be as fussy as they can, both with themselves and with their printers and typists.

SUBJECT INDEX

ABBREVIATIONS, 42–3, 152, 159, 216
abruptness, 69, 70
accents, 225–6
acute accent, 225
addresses, 25–6, 61; American: 216
adjectives, 17–19, 143–6 (hyphens)
adverbial clauses, 38
— phrases, 38
adverbs, 20–1, 142, 147
—, connective, 100–1
all in all, 101
also, 46
ambiguity, 137, 183, 184
American characteristics, 6; 211–13; 223
— punctuation, x, 181, 211–21
ampersand, 226
and, 101
annunciatory, 53–4, 72
anomaly, an, 13
antithesis, 45–6, 57, 119, 123
apostrophe, the, 155–61; 221
apparently, 100
apposition, 37, 41, 47, 55, 69; American: 216
assent, 38
asterisk, 82–3, 219, 226
at least, 47–8

BECAUSE, 101
besides, 98
best, better, 144
bibliography, punctuation in, 47, 218
brace, the, 153–4
brackets, 65–6; 218
breve, the, 225
business aspects, 11–12, 111, 183–4
but, 217
but nevertheless, 217
by the way, 99

CALENDAR, the, 113
capitals, 107–17, 127–9, 151 (hy-

phens), 171 (quotation); American: 219–20
capitals, small, 107, 129
catalogues, 47, 108
causal clauses, 38
cedilla, 225
centred headings, 169
circumflex, 225
clarity, 8, 103, 183
clauses, 29–36, 45–6, 50
close punctuation, 94–103
co-, 137, 151
colon, 52–62; 77, 92, 131, 172–3; American: 213, 215
— dash, 87, 92, 172–3
comma, 14–41; 77, 92, 94–103 (passim), 173–4 (quotations); American: 14, 216, 217–18
— dash, 87, 92
commonsense, and good sense, 7, 160–1
compound points, 86–9, 219
— words, 136–51
conclusions, conclusives, 60, 72–3
conditional, the, 38
conjunctions, 21–2; American: 217–18
contractions, 42–3, 216
conventions, 211–12
cumulatives, 45, 59–60
curtailments, 216
curves = parentheses, 218

DAGGER, the, 226
dash, compound, 83, 86–8, 92
—, simple, 68–78; 83, 92, 131; American: 218–19
dates and times, 61–2
definitions, 108
diacritics, 225–6
diaeresis, 220, 225
dialect, 120, 124
dialogue, 7, 73–4
differentiation, 39–40

227

disruptive matter, 68–78
dissent, 38
distinction, 39–40
division of words, 134–6
dots as leaders, 85
— in interruptions, 77, 78
— — omissions, 84
— — suspense, 84, 219

EARLY opinions and practices, 3–5,
    6
ellipsis, 219
elocutionary stops, 6–7; 109 (capi-
    tals)
emphasis, 71, 118–19, 123
—, modes of, 127–33
enumeration, 47
epigrammatic, 74–5
equipoise, 55–6
Esq. and *Esqre*, 216
exclamation mark, 79–81, 88
— question, 80
explanatory, 54–5, 64

FIGURES, arithmetical, 27, 61–2,
    156; American: 216
footnotes, 226
for, 217
— *example, for instance*, 47–8
foreign words, 120–1, 124
fractions, 152, 221
full stop. *See* period
full point, 9
further, 98–9

GENITIVE. *See* possessive
geographical, 23, 114, 221
grammar and punctuation, 6–8
grave accent, 225
Greek elements, 150, 225
group genitive, 159–60

HANDWRITING, punctuation in,
    169–75
hanging indention, 166
haphazardry, 182–4
headings, 169
hence, 46
hesitation, 74, 84–5, 135

history of punctuation, 6–7, 113–14
however, 46, 98, 217
humdrum punctuation, 7–8, 102, 103
hyphens, 130–1, but esp. 134–51;
    American: 220

ILL. 145–6
incidentally, 99
incoherence, 74
indeed, 100
indention, 165–9; 221
initials, 42–3, 139
interjections, 79–80
internal quotation, 108, 179–82, 215
    (American)
interpolation and interruption, 58,
    71–2, 76–8
in the main, 101
inverted commas. *See* quotation
    marks
italics, 118–21; 164, 171

LATIN elements, 149–50
leaders, 85; 219
legal punctuation, 102, 111
letter-ends, 26–7
— headings, 25–6
linotype, influence of, 226
literary colon, 58, 77; American: 213,
    215
— semicolon, 49, 77; American: 213,
    215
logic, influence of, 7, 181, 214

MACRON, the, 225
manuals, influence of, 211–12, 219
marks, x, 79
method of teaching punctuation, ix–
    x, 182–3
moreover, 46, 98
multiple dots and punctuation, 82–9;
    cf. 131–3

NAMELY. 47–8
negatives, 151
nevertheless, 46, 101, 217
newspapers, 216–17, 226
no (dissent), 38
non, 138

non-punctuational stops, 61–2, 67, 75–6
— restrictive clauses, 35
no one, 143
nouns, 15–17, 138–42 (hyphens)
now, 100
numbers. *See* figures

O, 109
obelus, 226
oblique, the, 151–3; American: 220–1
official, strictly, 111–12, 116
oh, 109
omissions, 82–5, 155–6
on the other hand, 217
— — *whole*, 101
open punctuation, 94–103
opposition, 57
orchestration, 179–207
over-punctuation, 94–103

PARAGRAPH, the, 165–9
parallelism, 56–7
parentheses, 63–7; 88, 92; American: 218
—, varieties of, 65–6
parenthetical colons, 58, 77
— commas, 37, 77
— dashes, 68–9, 71–2, 77
— semicolons, 49, 77
participles, 28–9, 37, 145
particles in book titles, 162–3
particularization, 120, 124
pause, 3–5 (passim), 6–7
perfunctoriness, 182–4
perhaps, 107
period, the, 9–13; 42–3 (abbreviations); 87, 92 (period dash); 94–103 (passim); American: 216
personification, 109
philology, punctuation in, 71, 219, 226
phrases, hyphenated, 136, 146
—, punctuation of, 24–5, 28
point, 9, 215
possessive, the, 157–61; 221
power, 139
predecessors in field, ix, 3–5, 223–4

prefixes with sequent hyphens, 137, 148–51
prepositions, 21, 147
prices, 152, 221
printers, printing, 109–10, 125–6, 169, 175; American: 215, 216–17, 218, 219, 226
promotion of stops, 51, 60–1
pronouns, 15–17, 143
Proper Names, 107, 116–17, 158, 162–4 (book titles)
propriety, 84
prosody, 225–6
psychology, 7, 102
punctuation, an art, 12, 94, 102–3, 182–4
—, competent, 94–103 (passim), 102–3, 186–207 (examples)
—, deficiency of, 94–103, 186–206 (examples)
—, definition of, 94
—, excess of, 94–103
—, illiterate, 102, 186–206 (examples), 217
—, relation to accessories, 185–207
—, role of, 94, 102–3, 182–4

QUESTION mark, 79–81; 88; American: 219
— — in exclamations, 80
— —, origin of, 79
quotation, modes of, 121, 170–5
— marks, 122–6, 129–30, 170, 179–82 (in punctuation), 214–15 (American)

RE-, 138
relative values of the stops, 91–3
religion, 112–13, 220
restrictive clauses, 35
resumptive, 73
rhetorical. *See* elocutionary

SCIENCE, punctuation in, 115
second thoughts, punctuation of, 58, 64–5, 73
self-, 137
semicolon, 44–51, 131; American: 213, 215, 217–18

semicolon dash, 77, 92
— value, 44
sentence, nature of the, 167
sentences, adversative, 37–8
—, complex, 10, 31–5, 213–14
—, compound, 10, 29–31, 213–14
—, co-ordinated, 48, 213
—, incomplete, 74
—, simple, 9–10, 213
separation, separatives, 38–9, 71, 77
side headings, 169
slang, 120, 124
so, conjunctive, 48, 217
spaces, 172
square brackets or parentheses, 65–6;
     218
stating and stated, 36
still, conjunctive, 217
street names, 25–6; American: 220
stress. See accent and emphasis
stylistic aspects, 11, 182–4
suspense, 84, 135, 219
syllabification, 134–6, 220
symbols, 28, 156
syntactical aspects, 6–8, 92–3, 133,
     175, 213

TECHNICAL terms, 115, 120, 124,
     139
temporal clauses, 38
that, relative, 35–6
— is (i.e.), 47–8
then, 46, 101
thence, 46
therefore, 46, 100

thought, 8
thus, 100
tilde, 225
titles of books, newspapers, etc., 121,
     125, 162–4; American: 221
— — persons, 116
to wit (viz.), 47–8
trade names, 111
tradition, 211–12
triple s, 138
typewriting, punctuation in, 169,
     171, 226
typography. See printers

UMLAUT, 225
underlining, 169
under-punctuation, 94–103
uniformity, 218

VARIETY, 183
verbs, 19–20, 146–7 (hyphens)
verse, 110, 165
vinculum, 153–4
virgil or virgule, 151–3; American:
     220–1
vocative, the, 109
volle, 225

WELL, 146
'wing, the', 225
word-groups, 23–4, 70
worse, worst, 144

YES, 38
yet, 217